LITHICS AFTER THE STONE AGE

FOR ARLENE, YANIV, AND BOAZ

sine qua non

Lithics After the Stone Age

A Handbook of Stone Tools from the Levant

STEVEN A. ROSEN

ALTAMIRA
PRESS

A Division of Sage Publications, Inc.

WALNUT CREEK • LONDON • NEW DELHI

For information address:

AltaMira Press
A Division of Sage Publications, Inc.
1630 North Main Street, Suite 367
Walnut Creek, CA 94596

SAGE Publications, Ltd.
6 Bonhill Street
London EC2A 4PU
United Kingdom

SAGE Publications India Pvt. Ltd.
M-32 Market
Greater Kailash I
New Delhi 110 048 India

LIBRARY OF CONGRESS CATALOGING-IN-PUBLICATION DATA

Rosen, Steven A.
    Lithics after the Stone Age : a handbook of stone tools from the
        Levant / author, Steven A. Rosen.
        p. cm.
    Includes bibliographical references and index.
    ISBN 0-7619-9123-9 (alk. paper). — ISBN 0-7619-9124-7
        (pbk. : alk. paper)
    1. Tools, Prehistoric—Middle East. 2. Stone implements—
        Middle East—Analysis. 3. Stone implements—Middle East—
        Classification. 4. Middle East—Antiquities. I. Title.
    GN857.R67 1997
    939'.4—dc21   96-51250
                                                         CIP

97 98 99 00 01 02 10 9 8 7 6 5 4 3 2 1

Printed in the United States of America

Design and production:
Gordon Chun Design, Berkeley, California

The author and publisher gratefully acknowledge permission to reprint the following copyrighted materials. Specific references are provided in the text.

The Israel Antiquities Authority (Figs. 3.9:2, 3.12:1, 3.30:4, 3.31:1, 3.33:2, 3.34:4–5, 3.40:2, 5.1, 5.4, 5.6)

The Israel Prehistoric Society (Figs. 3.26:10, 14, 3.27:1, 7–12, 3.31:3, 3.33:1, 4, 3.49:1)

I. Gilead (Fig. 6.5)

Tel Aviv (Figs. 3.22:11, 3.24:6–7, 3.38:3, 3.52:3)

Ann Roshwalb (Figs. 3.4:4–6, 3.24:1–2, 3.27:13, 3.31:4, 3.48:2–3, 3.49:3, 3.50:3)

Israel Exploration Journal (Figs. 3.2:7–8, 14–19, 3.3:3–4, 3.26:11, 3.32:3, 3.41:1–2)

Ofer Bar-Yosef (Fig. 6.2)

Eisenbrauns (Figs. 3.31:5–7)

Ben-Gurion University Press (Figs. 3.4:1–3, 3.10:11–12, 3.11:3, 3.24:3–5, 3.25:1–4, 3.43:2, 3.44:6, 3.45:2, 3.48:6, 3.49:2, 3.52:1)

Pontifical Biblical Institute (Figs. 3.10:3–4)

Association Paléorient and CNRS (Figs. 3.42, 6.2, 6.3)

Contents

About the Author

STEVEN A. ROSEN was raised in the San Francisco Bay Area, and received his bachelor's degree in mathematics and anthroplogy from the University of California at Berkeley. He completed his Ph.D. at the University of Chicago in 1983 after which he worked for the Archaeological Survey of Israel—Negev Emergency Survey. He began teaching at Ben-Gurion University in Beersheva in 1988.

Aside from lithic analysis, other professional interests include Levantine prehistory, the archaeology of the Negev, and the archaeological study of pastoral nomadism. Major publications include *Archaeological Survey of Israel Map of Machtesh Ramon.* (Israel Antiquities Authority, 1994); *The Oded Sites, Investigations at Two Nomadic Encampments in the Southern Negev Highlands* (with G. Avni, Ben-Gurion University Press, 1996); *The Decline and Fall of Flint*, in *Stone Tools*, edited by G. Odell (Plenum, 1995); Notes on the Origins of Pastoral Nomadism: A Case Study from the Negev and Sinai, *Current Anthropology* 29:498–506 (1988); and papers in *Bulletin of the American Schools of Oriental Research, Journal of Field Archaeology, Palestine Exploration Quarterly, Paléorient, Israel Exploration Journal, American Antiquity*, other journals and books. He has participated in excavations in North America, Europe, and the Levant, and has directed excavations ranging in date from Middle Paleolithic through Early Islamic Periods. Recent projects have included excavations at the Camel Site, an Early Bronze Age pastoral encampment in the Central Negev, and the epipaleolithic sites at Givat Hayil, in the western Negev. Non-professional interests include Raymond Chandler, Billie Holiday, and Bob Dylan. He is currently serving as chair of the Department of Bible and Ancient Near East and the Archaeological Division at Ben-Gurion University of the Negev. He lives with his wife, Arlene Miller Rosen, and two sons, Yaniv and Boaz, in Beersheva, in the northern Negev, Israel.

Acknowledgments

The number of people to whom I owe gratitude for help in completing this work seems endless. There is a very long list of people who over the course of more than a decade have granted me access to their materials and collections. Without mentioning each by name, I hope that they have been pleased with what I have done with their materials, both in the individual reports I have written and in this larger synthesis.

This research began as my doctoral thesis, many years ago, under the tutelage of Karl W. Butzer. Although he is not a lithic specialist, without his encouragement and support and his professional approach to archaeology, my research would not have near whatever merits it may have.

Officially the research for this book began in 1986, while I was a National Endowment for the Humanities Fellow at the Albright Institute of Archaeology in Jerusalem. Much of the research was conducted while I was working for the Archaeological Survey of Israel, the Negev Emergency Survey, and indeed the Uvda Valley materials result directly from my connections with the Survey. I am grateful to the Israel Antiquities Authority for granting me access to so many collections and to Rudolph Cohen for his constant support when I worked for the Survey. Other support has been provided by the Faculty of the Humanities and Social Sciences at Ben-Gurion University of the Negev.

The first draft of this book was completed while I was a Canada-Israel Academic Exchange Fellow at the Department of Archaeology at the University of Calgary, 1994–95. This is a fellowship endowed by Mr. and Mrs. H. Belzberg, to whom many scholars owe a debt of gratitude. My friends at Calgary, both faculty and students, provided a stimulus to writing that I do not believe I could have found elsewhere. I am also grateful to Nic David for reading and commenting on that first draft and for encouraging me to actually finish it.

Tom Levy and Yorke Rowan provided access to unpublished materials from Shiqmim, which will appear in final form in Yorke's Ph.D. and other work. I thank them. Tamar Noy was kind enough to provide me access to her work in progress on discoid tools and patiently explained her ideas to me.

My participation in the Second Tulsa Lithics Conference served as a kind of breakthrough for me psychologically. The excitement of that conference and the interaction between the participants pushed me toward trying to summarize more of my ideas. Ornit and David Ilan convinced me finally that it was time to synthesize—they were tired of searching through seemingly endless reports on individual lithic assemblages.

Patrice Kaminsky and Helena Sokolskaya, both from Ben-Gurion University, prepared the illustrations for publication and indeed drew many of them. Their talents are much appreciated.

The many students from Ben-Gurion University who have suffered through my courses on stone tool analysis have provided me with insights by forcing me to look at stone tools from their perspectives and not only from the perspective of the specialist.

Ben Saidel has provided the enthusiasm of a student to my aging cynicism, and it has been my pleasure to work with him and hear his comments on my ideas.

Mitch Allen, my editor, publisher, and good friend, gave this book whatever stylistic merits it may have. If it is at all readable to a public wider than lithic specialists, credit should be given Mitch.

I would also like to thank Gordon Chun Design for the extra efforts taken in designing this book.

My friends in the Prehistory Section at Hebrew University, Ann Belfer-Cohen, Naama Goren, Nigel Goring-Morris, and Erella Hovers, put up with me for many years. Their friendship and help are appreciated.

Ofer Bar-Yosef seems to have seen in me a reasonable archaeologist and has helped and encouraged me in my career and in this research. I hope he sees in the present work some justification for his efforts.

Itzik Gilead has proven an invaluable friend and colleague here at Ben-Gurion University. He has never failed to offer critical evaluation and reading of everything I have given him, including a draft of this book, as well as to offer constant encouragement in my research.

Avi Gopher has discussed with me virtually every idea I have expressed in this book. His feedback and friendship have been critical in my growth as an archaeologist.

My wife Arlene, the superior scholar in the family, has always encouraged and supported me. My children, Yaniv and Boaz, have been digging with me from a young age.

STEVEN A. ROSEN

Beersheva
July 1996

Illustrations

1 Lithic Analysis in the Levantine Metal Ages: A Preview

Introduction

And Joshua made knives of flint and circumcised the children of Israel at Gibeath-ha-Araloth.

–JOSHUA 5:3

The Interpreter's Bible commentary (Buttrick 1952, 882; also see Allen 1969, 34) on this passage (and others, e.g., Exodus 4:25) suggests that since Joshua and other biblical events are well situated in the Bronze Age (and according to some sources in the Iron Age), the use of flint knives must be a reflection of inherent conservatism in religious ritual, or a historical or literary anachronism. This misapprehension, based on simplistic perspectives toward technological change and periodization in the Near East, pervades popular perceptions on technological progress. It has also affected archaeological research, in spite of early recognition that chipped stone tools were an important component of material culture, even into the Iron Age.

"The [Megiddo] tomb deposits have shown that flints, far from being an attribute of only the earliest periods, were of considerable importance well into historic times. In fact, the present day use of flint implements argues for uninterrupted continuity. Specimens as late as the Early Iron Age have come from the tomb deposits, while excavation on the tell has shown that all Iron Age strata contained flints in abundance" (Guy and Engberg 1938, 70).

The "present day use" of chipped stone tools in the eastern Mediterranean region includes flint and basalt threshing teeth (e.g., Bordaz 1969, Whallon 1978), presumably gun flints in the eighteenth and nineteenth centuries (cf. Oakley 1975, 26–28, for English example), and strike-a-lights, known ethnographically (e.g., Runnels 1994; Murray 1935, 70). Flint knives have also been documented in other rituals and even bloodletting ceremonies in other regions (e.g., Schele and Friedel 1990, 202, 233, 275; Stevens 1870, 87–91, 110–12), inviting comparison to the lead quotation from the Bible. Disregarding Guy and Engberg's assumptions concerning uninterrupted continuity, the combination of the early archaeological documentation and recent use is justification for the analysis of chipped stone artifacts in the Metal Ages. However, the rationale can be extended far beyond the somewhat esoteric analysis of stone tools, and indeed beyond the confines of the Near East.

Analyses of chipped stone tools provide insights into processes and events that cannot be documented by other means, at least not nearly as easily. They also complement other studies, in some cases lending additional weight to conclusions drawn from other components of the archaeological record, and in others, by contrast, demonstrating greater complexity than previously assumed. At the risk of later repetitiveness, a brief review of some of these potentials is worthwhile.

First, perhaps even foremost, the documentation of a previously virtually unrecognized technology is of great importance. The ubiquitous use of stone tools well into the "civilized" Metal Ages is not merely a matter of adding another technology to the repertoire of those available to ancient peoples. Rather, it implies a full range of activities and skills for which there is no counterpart in our own society. Understanding the uses, functions, and roles of stone tools in these ancient cultures is not merely a case of simply replacing them with modern metal equivalents, but involves entirely distinct socioeconomic frameworks. Just as the production of stone tools is entirely different from other elements of material culture, so is their use, both in a utilitarian sense and in a more "symbolic" sense. For example, cutting wood using stone tools is fundamentally different from cutting wood using metal tools, and therefore woodworking itself must be understood differently.

The fact that metallurgy and chipped stone technology overlap for more than three millennia is sufficient reason to reexamine the assumed roles of metal tools in ancient societies. The claim, in hindsight, of "superiority" of early metallurgy over flint tools is simply untenable, and the long process of metal-stone replacement is neither obvious, preordained, nor simple. The factors effecting this replacement cannot be directly linked to the greater utility of metal tools. In short, one cannot understand the rise of metallurgy without understanding its complement, the decline of stone.

The issue of utilitarian function is, of course, directly related to these questions of technological change. Even beyond establishing the function of specific tools and tool kits, stone tools provide an important means of examining function on the site or regional level. Differing proportions of arrowheads, sickles, celts, drills, scrapers, etc., on either the subsite or the site level, can reflect differing configurations of activities or discard. These, in turn, can be compared to other elements of the archaeology, such as architecture, ceramics, or site distributions, to provide more overarching explanations of assemblage and site variability.

Beyond the implications of the integration of an old-new technology into our understanding of Metal Age societies, lithic analysis holds great potential for other sorts of investigations. The most obvious among these are those associated with various economic functions, such as the organization of production and exchange. The fact that lithic production leaves in its wake great masses of diagnostic waste can serve as a key element in the demonstration of on-site/off-site production, the distinction between different stages of production, the different degrees of manufacturing specialization, and, associated with all of these, the organization of exchange of different lithic implements. Thus, using stone tools, the origins of craft specialization can be explored quantitatively, in ways rarely accomplished using other elements of material culture. Of especial interest here is the time depth achievable using lithic analysis. Unlike other realms of material culture, like ceramics or metallurgy, specialization in lithic production can be examined from the most simple levels of individual domestic production in the late Paleolithic, through the rise of incipient specialization in the Neolithic, and on into periods of greater socioeconomic complexity and more specialized production. This long span is unique to lithic analysis.

In the desert regions, the general scarcity of material culture remains renders the lithic component all the more important. Aside from establishing the

"functions" of desert sites, and of loci within these sites, the stone tools provide a primary means for establishing cultural and chronological affinities. Desert Bronze Age sites are more akin to their Neolithic cousins than to the tells of northern Israel, in terms of material culture as well as architecture. Ignoring the stone tools from these sites is to reject their most significant component of material culture, both functionally and numerically.

Finally, the analysis of stone tools from the historic periods can feed back into our comprehension of the roles they played in earlier prehistoric societies. The rich historical and archaeological framework available for the Metal Ages, including the texts, provides a control against which lithic schema can be compared. Such issues as the roles of style, defining ethnicity, and the meaning of geographic and chronological variability can be examined using the lithic data, and then tested against frameworks established from the entire range of archaeological and historical materials from the "post-prehistoric" periods. In a sense, the lithic materials from the early historic periods can be used as a kind of ethnohistorical database, in much the same way that ethnoarchaeological materials are used. Unlike ethnoarchaeological materials in the Near East, these lithic materials are a closer analogue to prehistoric times, in terms of both chronology and the roles that stone tools played in these periods.

Thus, the potentials from the study of stone tools of the Metal Ages are great. The development of these studies, however, has been only a recent phenomenon. The work presented here cannot possibly be definitive since the materials available are still limited and often problematic. However, there is clearly enough to begin.

The primary purpose of this study is to provide a first approximation framework for the interpretation of protohistoric and early historic lithic assemblages in the southern Levant. In doing so, three goals can be achieved. On the simplest level, an illustrated guide to lithic types, with general reviews of their chronologies, distributions, and functions, is a necessity for basic reference. Amiran's (1969) classic work on ceramics and for that matter Bordes' (1961) typology for the Lower and Middle Paleolithic in some ways serve as models for the first half of this book (Chapters 2 and 3).

Beyond such a guide, the integration of lithic assemblages into their historic and cultural contexts requires more than a typological framework. The essays following the methodological and typological reviews (Chapters 4–7) are an attempt to provide more overarching syntheses. It is on such syntheses that the value of any archaeological method ultimately rests. In this context, it is worth noting that lithic analysis does provide information on social and economic systems unavailable from other sources. This is especially so in desert areas, where ceramics are rare, but is true of the Mediterranean zone as well. For example, underlying economic continuities are well reflected in lithic technological systems, where they may be masked by typological variability in ceramics, as in the case of the Early Bronze to Middle Bronze I transition (see Chapter 4). The lithic perspective may also shed light on other phenomena, such as the rise of metallurgy. Although archaeometallurgy is usually seen as an independent subdiscipline, the rise of metallurgy should also be examined in the context of apparently competing technologies (Rosen 1984a, 1996, Chapter 7). Examined in this light, the specific patterns in the adoption of metallurgy are comprehensible beyond the simplistic assumptions of greater utility and efficiency of metal tools.

In these essays a third goal is also hopefully achieved, that of the more theoretical perspective. Lithic analysis is a subdiscipline that spans the entire archaeological world. Although typologies and even technologies vary from region to region, the approaches to their analysis do not. If the essays here are not intended as specifically theoretical statements, the general processes and models nevertheless can have implications beyond the southern Levant in the protohistoric and early historic periods. The rich archaeological and historical records for these periods provide controls for these models that are not usually available to prehistoric archaeologists, enhancing their reliability and, hopefully, therefore, their appeal.

Time

The Chalcolithic, Bronze, and Iron Ages, the primary periods covered in this work, extend from around the middle of the fifth millennium B.C.E., in calendar years, through the middle of the first millennium B.C.E. This long span, which can collectively be referred to as the Metal Ages, encompassed the rise of social and political complexity. In particular, in the Levant, the period is marked by the rise of urbanism and city-states in the Early Bronze Age and by the rise of state-level society in the Iron Age. These political developments are accompanied by increasing social complexity (read stratification), economic specialization, and technological achievement. Historically, numerous "ethnic" groups, without belaboring the definition of the term, can be identified and historical events examined.

It is beyond the scope of this work to review in detail the culture history of the region, and several recent syntheses are available (e.g., Ben-Tor 1992; Mazar 1990; Kenyon 1980 [rev. ed.]). Nevertheless, table 1.1 presents a summary chronology and periodization of the time span covered in this work, intended primarily for readers unacquainted with the basic chrono-cultural framework of the region. Absolute chronologies are based on calibrated radiocarbon years for the Chalcolithic and early stages of the Early Bronze Age, calibrated radiocarbon years and historical dates fixed by Egyptian chronologies and parallels for the Early Bronze Age and, to a lesser extent, the Middle Bronze I, and primarily texts and established historical frameworks and parallels for later periods (cf. Ben-Tor 1992; Mazar 1990; Stager 1992).

Periodization is a historiographical construct, based on a variety of inconsistent criteria, but entrenched in the literature of the discipline. Thus, the primary period distinctions of Neolithic, Chalcolithic, Bronze Age, and Iron Age are made on the basis of ostensibly technological criteria, even though the true importance of those criteria is often doubtful. Even the reality of the technological change is sometimes questionable. Thus, the Late Pottery Neolithic (Pottery Neolithic B) is separated from the Chalcolithic primarily on the basis of the introduction of smelted copper, even though there is good evidence for cultural continuity between the periods. The Bronze Age is separated from the Chalcolithic, if we are to believe the terminology, on the basis of the introduction of bronze, even though it is not available at all in the

Date B.C.E.	Period	Notes
	Late Pottery Neolithic (Qatifian, Wadi Raba, En el Jarba, etc.)	village farming and pastoral societies
ca. 4500 –	Chalcolithic (Beersheva, Ghassul, Golan, etc.)	village farming and pastoral societies, copper smelting
ca. 34/500	Early Bronze Age	
	I	village system, Egyptian infiltration in south
2900	II	early urbanism
2700	III	urbanism, city states
ca. 2200	Middle Bronze I (Intermediate, etc.)	urban collapse, village and pastoral societies
ca. 1950	Middle Bronze II	urban resurgence
		common use of bronze
1550	Late Bronze	Hyksos expulsion from Egypt
	I	urban decline
1400	II	urban resurgence, Sea Peoples
1200	Iron Age	
	I	Philistines, Israelite settlement
1000	II	Israelite kingdom
	III	(later, Judah, Israel)
586		destruction of Judah

TABLE 1.1. Annotated periodization of Israeli archaeology from the end of the Neolithic through the Iron Age.

early part of the period and does not become common until the Middle Bronze II, fifteen hundred years into the Bronze Age. The Iron Age, ostensibly defined by the introduction of iron, is in fact defined by a socio-political event, the arrival of the Israelites, an event notably difficult to define archaeologically. Lower level within-period divisions are also inconsistent. Thus, Early Bronze I, II, and III are distinguished primarily on ceramic criteria, whereas Iron I, II, and III are historical-political divisions. Distinction between Middle and Late Bronze is based on an external event, the expulsion of the Hyksos from Egypt. The problems of periodization are perhaps epitomized in the debates over the Middle Bronze I (MBI), also called by different scholars Early Bronze IV (EBIV), Intermediate Bronze (IB), and Early Bronze–Middle Bronze (EB-MB) (see Richard 1980 for general review), in spite of substantive agreement on the basic nature of the actual culture period!

One other point regarding this periodization should be addressed—its applicability, or inapplicability, as the case may be, beyond the borders of modern and ancient Israel. For example, the end of the Iron Age has been defined by Israeli archaeologists to coincide with the destruction of the Judean Kingdom. The utility of this within Israeli and biblical archaeology is clear. However, the value of this event for defining periods beyond the confines of the ancient Israelite state is questionable. Similarly, the beginning of Israelite settlement defines the beginning of the Iron Age and is obviously not identifiable in areas beyond that settlement. The terminology is retained for the sake of convention, but its limitations must be recognized.

The above is not intended as a critique, but rather an explanation. In any dynamic, organically developing system, such inconsistencies are bound to develop. Rewriting the periodization to establish "consistency" results in confusion between the earlier and later literature, especially since as new knowledge accrues, new inconsistencies are bound to arise as well.

Place

The geographic and cultural differences in the Levant are crucial for comprehension of the lithic industries. Although often regarded as a near independent subdiscipline of archaeology, lithic industries and complexes cannot be understood without reference to larger region and culture. It is only by placing these industries in that larger context that we can begin to understand their role in those cultures and, perhaps even more important, their role in culture in general.

The focus of this work is the region encompassed by the modern state of Israel and parts of adjacent countries, including Lebanon, Syria, Jordan, Egypt (especially the Sinai Peninsula), and areas of transitional political status, the Gaza Strip and the West Bank (fig. 1.1). Excluding the Sinai, the entire region covers an area only between 30,000 and 60,000 sq km, depending on where one draws the borders. Although such terms as Palestine, the Southern Levant, the Land of Israel, the Holy Land, and Canaan have been used in attempts to characterize the region, in reality none are satisfactory.

Areal research foci too often have been dictated by political exigencies, with little direct relevance to the archaeology, and anyone working in the Near East today can testify to the problems that obtain. Unfortunately, publications, even when they are available, can rarely substitute for hands-on experience in archaeology, especially when dealing with material culture. Thus, the primary focus of this work has been Israel proper, for the simple reason of access to materials. This has been augmented by invaluable studies conducted by colleagues and friends working in neighboring countries, whose publications allow extension of the ideas suggested here beyond the confines of modern political boundaries.

The Mediterranean region of the Southern Levant is the core study area. Located on the southeast shore of the Mediterranean, the region can be characterized as a transition zone from a classic Mediterranean climate and environment along the coast and in the hills, through a steppe zone, and into true desert in the south and east. Climatically, it is characterized by hot dry summers and mild wet winters, becoming progressively drier as one moves into the desert zones (Orni and Efrat 1971, 135–90). Vegetation patterns follow suit, from typical Mediterranean oak forests and chaparral, to garrigue and steppe, and finally desert vegetation (fig. 1.2).

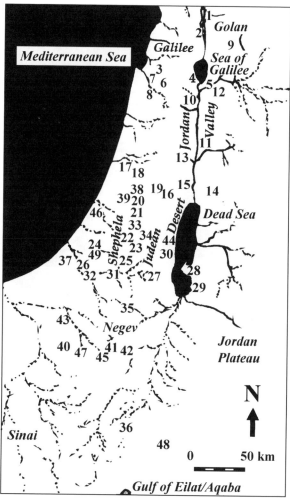

FIG. 1.1. *Geographic map of the Southern Levant with sites mentioned in the text: 1. Dan; 2. Teo; 3. Yiftahel; 4. Beit Yerah; 5. Shaar Hagolan; 6. En Shadud; 7. Qasis, Har Haruvim; 8. Megiddo; 9. Rasm Harbush; 10. Neve Ur; 11. Abu Hamid; 12. Shuneh; 13. Fasael; 14. Ghassul; 15. Jericho; 16. Jerusalem (Ir David; Sataf; Malha); 17. Azor; 18. Gezer; 19. Motza Ilit; 20. Hartuv; 21. Yarmouth; 22. Erani; Gat Guvrin; 23.Beit Mirsim; 24. Hesi; 25. Lahav (Halif); 26. Gaza sites (Besor sites); 27. Arad; 28. Bab edh Dhra; 29. Numeira; 30. Nahal Mishmar; 31. Beersheva sites (Abu Matar; Bir es Safadi; Horvat Beter); 32. Shiqmim; 33. Lachish; 34. Djebel Qaaqir; 35. Har Yeruham; 36. Uvda Valley sites (including Nahal Issaron); 37. Deir el Balah; 38. Beth Shemesh (Lower Horvat Illin); 39. Batashi; 40. Qadesh Barnea; 41. Kvish Harif; 42. Camel Site; 43. Nahal Nizzana sites; 44. Mitzpe Shalem; 45. Har Horsha; 46. Nizzanim; 47. Nahal Mitnan; 48. Djebel Jill; 49. Gilat.*

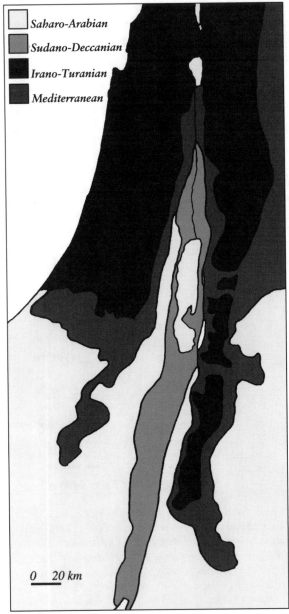

Legend (in map):

- Saharo-Arabian
- Sudano-Deccanian
- Irano-Turanian
- Mediterranean

0   20 km

FIG. 1.2. *Map of Southern Levantine phytogeographic zones (modified after Feinbrun-Dothan 1978; map 1, and Zohary 1956).*

Detailed discussion of the geography and environment of this region is not necessary for this study (but, for example, see Orni and Efrat 1971; Amiran et al. 1985), but several environmental and geographic factors nevertheless require review.

Topographically, the region is complex. The evolution of the Jordan Valley, and its associated features, an extension of the African Rift System, has resulted in a landscape that can be divided into a series of longitudinal strips. From west to east, these are the coastal plain, the central mountains, the Jordan Rift Valley, and the Jordanian Plateau, with subdivisions based on transitional zones (e.g., foothills), local variations (e.g., specific ranges), and north-south location (e.g., the southern coastal plain, 40 km wide, versus the northern coastal plain, only a few km wide). Although in absolute terms altitudinal variation is not great, distances between zones are small, and gradients are steep. Thus, for example, the drop from Jerusalem to the Dead Sea is on the order of 1,400 m, in the space of around 20 km. This topographical variability affects geomorphic processes, soils, vegetation patterns, and climatic patterns, such that they, too, tend to conform to a longitudinal patterning, albeit significantly affected by microscale variability.

Geologically, the region is dominated by late Mesozoic and early Cenozoic limestones, providing abundant sources of different kinds of flint. Exposure of these sources is dictated by both the local bedrock sequence and erosion resulting from topographical variation. Pliocene and Pleistocene basalt outcrops are found in the north, in the Galilee and the Golan; in the east, on the Jordanian Plateau; and in the south, both in the southern Negev and Sinai; and as exposures in the erosional cirques of the Central Negev. Other igneous bedrocks, such as granites (but not obsidian), are found only in the far south, in Sinai and the Aqaba-Eilat region.

In addition to the topographical and geological variability, the region is marked by a major north-south rainfall gradient, such that whereas parts of the Galilee may receive 800–1,000 mm of rainfall per year, Jerusalem receives only ca. 500 mm, Beersheva only ca. 200 mm, and Eilat only 25 mm of rainfall yearly on the average. Obviously, topographic variation affects this gradient, such that from west to east one can trace an increase in rainfall into the central mountains, a marked decline into the Jordan Valley, another increase onto the Jordanian Plateau, and a decrease into the eastern desert.

The only "natural" boundary to this region is the Mediterranean Sea in the west. The desert regions of Sinai, the Negev, and southern Jordan are part of the Levantine culture-geographic landscape. Important lithic data are available from these areas and can be incorporated into the larger picture. Similarly, the steppes and deserts of eastern Jordan, Syria, and the higher mountains of Lebanon constitute frontiers, but "true" cultural borders are difficult to draw (although the amount of data deriving from these areas is minimal).

16 • STEVEN A. ROSEN

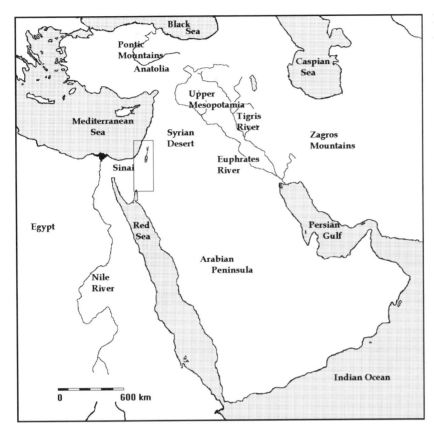

FIG. 1.3. *Southern Levant in the Near East.*

These rainfall patterns varied in the past, both in absolute terms and in affecting the boundaries between the desert and the Mediterranean zone (e.g., Bar-Yosef and Vandermeersch 1972; Goodfriend 1990; Magaritz and Goodfriend 1987). Although in the macroscale, it is clear that the region could always be characterized climatically and environmentally as Mediterranean, even during the Pleistocene (e.g., Farrand 1971), it is also clear that great variability exists within this climatic regime. Climatic fluctuations within the general Mediterranean range could, and did, have significant effect on human settlement and adaptations in the region during the Holocene (e.g., A. M. Rosen 1989, 1995).

Data for climatic reconstruction are now available from a wide range of sources, including palynology, alluvial terrace sequences, deep sea core oxygen isotope studies, Dead Sea sediment and shoreline analyses, and land snail isotope studies (see A. M. Rosen 1989 for review and references). Summarizing in simplistic terms, the Chalcolithic and early part of the Early Bronze Age both show wet episodes, with the possibility of a drier episode between them (e.g., Issar et al. 1992). The remainder of the Early Bronze Age is

marked by apparent gradual desiccation, terminating in a period of climatic instability in the Middle Bronze I. The Middle Bronze II through Iron Age is a generally dry period, reflected in an erosional water flow regime, and possibly interrupted by short wet fluctuations (A. M. Rosen 1986a).

These physical gradients are paralleled by cultural gradients. Traditionally the Levant has been characterized as lying at the crossroads of three primary centers of civilization, Mesopotamia, Anatolia, and Egypt (Aharoni 1979, 3–20), as well as lying on the eastern end of the Mediterranean world (fig. 1.3). The influences of the centers vary spatially such that northern sites are more prone to show affinities to Anatolia and Mesopotamia, and southern sites to Egypt. Clearly, influences vary in different periods as well.

Cultural gradients are also evident between the Mediterranean zone and the desert zones, especially in the varying degrees of integration exhibited between desert cultures and the heartland. These desert-sown relationships also vary diachronically.

The Rise of Lithic Analysis

Lithic analysis in the historic periods in the Levant can be traced back to the earliest scientific investigations of tells, at Tell Hesi, excavated by W. Flinders Petrie and his coworkers in the late nineteenth century (Bliss 1898; Spurrel 1898; Petrie 1891, 49–51). Although of little value today beyond the initial typological descriptions, the recognition that lithic artifacts played a significant role in early historical societies was in itself an achievement, probably deriving from Petrie's long experience working on the Egyptian Predynastic with its elaborate lithic assemblages. The importance of lithic artifacts was also recognized by Randall Macalister (1912, 32–34, 121–28), the early-twentieth-century excavator especially noted for his investigation of the large tell Gezer in the center of the country, who devoted a chapter in his Gezer monographs to flint knapping and included additional descriptions of flint tools in his chapter on agriculture. Macalister was the first to recognize "ribbon knives," later called Canaanean blades, as a discrete type. Although his methods and systematics left much to be desired (e.g., Dever et al. 1970, 2), Macalister attempted to provide an integrated view of ancient lifeways, which included the analysis of a wide spectrum of material culture.

However, even given the laudable recognition that stone tools did play a role in early societies, the methods of investigation employed by these early scholars were haphazard at best. The use of *baksheesh* to encourage workers to turn over valuable objects (e.g., Woolley 1954, 31) might well have been a valuable aid in the recovery of those objects, but it probably also served to discourage recovery of more mundane objects. Of course, the analytic value of lithic waste had not yet even been recognized by prehistorians, let alone those archaeologists working in later periods. At most sites, the stone tools were ignored altogether, but then, so were most artifacts, including potsherds.

The first attempts at systematization of historic period lithics were undertaken by Rene Neuville, the French consul and prehistorian (1930, 1934a), working at sites in and around the Judean desert, and slightly later by Joan Crowfoot (1935, 1937), who analyzed the lithic materials from Garstang's (1932, etc.) excavations at Jericho and continued on to a long career in Near Eastern lithic studies. At roughly the same time, Dorothy Garrod (1934), while digging the prehistoric caves at Mount Carmel, also worked on

materials from the huge University of Chicago project at Tell Megiddo. Like much of the rest of the archaeological work of the period, scholarship focused on establishing typological sequences that could be used to characterize periods or cultures. While perhaps easily dismissed in hindsight, it is important to note that in this period even such seemingly simple chronological and stratigraphic sequences as the sequence Pre-Pottery Neolithic A, Pre-Pottery Neolithic B, Pottery Neolithic (A to B, or early to late), Chalcolithic, and Early Bronze Age had not yet been worked out. Thus, Garrod (1934) suggested that the Early Bronze Age Canaanean industry could not be far removed from the Natufian!

This second period, from the late 1930s through the early 1970s, saw the recognition and definition of the primary formal or standardized types and the slow accumulation of descriptive reports on assemblages from different sites. However, the limited success of lithic analysis for chronological and cultural definitions, especially when compared with the truly impressive successes obtained from ceramic analysis, resulted in ever decreasing interest in the stone tools. After Neuville's (1930, 1934a) initial attempts at synthesis, incorporated in general reviews of Levantine prehistory, no further attempts at general synthesis were made until the late 1970s and early 1980s (e.g., McConaughy 1979; Rosen 1983a, 1983b, 1989a).

Even though chipped stone tools continued to be recognized as components of the material record (e.g., Albright 1936–37, 13, 23, 27; Waechter 1958), few projects included lithic analysts. Few archaeological reports included much more than an occasional drawing or mention of flint tools, and minimal descriptions were often based on misidentifications. Unlike the study of ceramics, which became a much demanded archaeological expertise, lithic analysis was often relegated to interested amateurs with little formal training in the study of stone tools (e.g., Swauger 1968). The major exception to this rule was, of course, the work of Crowfoot (Crowfoot 1935, 1937, 1948a, 1948b; Crowfoot Payne 1960; Payne 1978, 1980, 1983), who continued to refine her pioneering work during this period.

The neglect of lithic analysis is not merely the result of limitations of the stone tools in establishing chrono-stratigraphy. Bronze and Iron Age archaeology in the Near East was developing on a scholarly trajectory removed from that of similar societies of Europe and North America (cf. Glock 1985). Near

Eastern texts (and, for that matter, classical texts as well), most especially the Bible, provided both a scholarly and a public stimulus to archaeological work. Archaeology was perceived very much as a servant of history (e.g., Forrest 1963, xxiii). W. F. Albright, undoubtedly the leading scholar of Levantine archaeology during this period, exemplified the approach in his integration of textual expertise, field archaeology, and ceramic analysis. Remains not of direct relevance to historical questions as suggested by the texts were neglected. In many cases, of course, the historical issues addressed were dictated by the strong ideological underpinnings of Near Eastern and Levantine historical archaeology (e.g., Silberman 1982). Scholars working on these periods often seem to have been simply unaware of other realms of archaeological evidence, their training often primarily in texts with little background in material culture analysis. Thus, not only lithics but many subfields such as faunal analysis, environmental analysis, and archaeobotany are virtually absent from the archaeology of the early historical Near East prior to the 1970s.

In contrast, European Bronze and Iron Age archaeology, and North American archaeology of postarchaic societies, had no texts to provide any prior scholarly framework (but see Coe 1992, 271–74 for the fragmentation of Maya studies with the decipherment of Maya glyphs). Scholarship drew its inspiration from other disciplines, most notably anthropology. The specific historical frameworks applicable in the Near East were replaced by the culture-evolutionary framework (with its own set of ideological underpinnings). The apparently coarser grain of the record allowed scholars to view a larger picture, stretching from the Paleolithic through complex societies. Thus, in Europe and North America, the discipline drew on a wider range of other fields. In particular, the closer association with Paleolithic archaeology encouraged multidisciplinary approaches at an earlier stage than in Near Eastern archaeology.

Thus, the different academic trajectories, dictated by differences both in data and in underlying ideologies (beyond the scope of this work), resulted in markedly different research objectives. One consequence of this process was the relative neglect of chipped stone assemblages in the post-Neolithic assemblages of the Levant.

Recent interest in historic period lithic assemblages, beginning in the 1970s, can be attributed to two factors. The first is the rise of Levantine pre-

history, with connections to anthropology and evolution, as an independent subdiscipline with a large cadre of professional practitioners, and its integration both into Levantine archaeology and into a wider world of prehistoric archaeology. By the later 1970s, trained lithic analysts were available to study collections using the now more refined methods of recent prehistoric research (e.g., Betts 1991, 1992a; Cauvin 1968; Coqueugniot 1991, 1993; Gilead 1973; Hammond 1977; Hours 1979; Kozloff 1972–73; McConaughy 1979, 1980a,b; Ronen 1970; Milstein and Ronen 1985; Rosen 1989a; Schick 1978; Valla 1978; and continuing, Payne 1983). Prehistorians also expanded the traditional realms of prehistoric research beyond the Paleolithic, encompassing the Neolithic and Chalcolithic periods (e.g., Gilead 1988; Gopher and Orelle 1989; Levy 1986), and in some cases addressing problems of the origins of urbanism and the Early Bronze Age (e.g., Gilead 1988; Levy 1986, 1992; Rosen 1993a).

The second factor is an ever greater integration between Near Eastern archaeology and archaeologies of other periods and places. This is partially a consequence of connections with Levantine prehistory, but in general one can trace a general widening of research questions, perhaps exemplified in the debates over the nature of biblical archaeology in late 1970s and early 1980s (e.g., Dever 1982).

The end result of these trends is a clear broadening of the spectrum of questions addressed and data collected in Levantine archaeology. Lithic analysis is only one of these fields and has been accompanied by a full complement of other subfields of archaeology.

Aside from the increase in number of descriptive reports on lithic assemblages, the recent years have seen a broadening in the range of questions addressed from the lithic perspective and a greater range of methods used in posing them. Thus, beyond type fossils and chrono-stratigraphy, lithic analysts have dealt with issues of tool and assemblage function (e.g., Rowan and Levy 1991; McConaughy 1979, 1980a,b), ethnicity (e.g., Rosen 1988a) and regional variation (e.g., Gilead 1988), subsistence and farming (e.g., Gilead 1988; Rosen 1987), technology and raw material exploitation (e.g., Gilead 1989; Hammond 1977; Hours 1979), craft specialization (e.g., Cauvin 1968; Hours 1979; Rosen 1987, 1989b), and trade and exchange (e.g., Betts 1991, 1992a; Cauvin 1968; Rosen 1983a, 1983b). In accordance with these questions, typology was extended to include nonformal types and lithic waste, and quantitative analysis at varying levels became a standard tool in lithic studies. Additionally, attribute analyses on both the macroscopic and the microscopic (microwear) levels (e.g., Rowan and Levy 1991; McConaughy 1979, 1980a,b) were added to the repertoire of available analytic tools.

The situation as of writing is still not what one could call ideal. Numerous archaeologists, especially those working under the pressure of salvage projects, are not yet cognizant of the value of proper collection and analysis of lithic assemblages. In other cases, scholars assume that lithic analysis is a general expertise, transferable from one region to another, from New World to Old, with little need for background research, although such an assumption would be anathema to those same scholars with respect to ceramics. And finally, for many archaeologists, lithic analysis is still seen as a kind of scientific appendix, with little "true" importance, and therefore often little attempt has been made at integrating the results of these analyses into a larger synthetic perspective. Nonetheless, enough has been accomplished to begin the work of synthesis.

2 Analytic Approaches

Introduction

The analytic treatment of lithic assemblages is a subject suitable for numerous theses. Some of the more theoretical issues, such as the question of stylistic versus functional variation, will be dealt with on the case study level later in this book. In general this work is not intended as a theoretical treatise, but rather as a substantive case study, which will hopefully have its theoretical and methodological implications. Nevertheless, some statement of methods and methodological problems is a necessity to any work with pretensions of rigor. That is, this section is a statement of how and why, and not intended as a programmatic ideal.

Lithic industries from the protohistoric and historic periods in the Levant constitute a data set with unusual and occasionally unique problems, and with great potentials for a contribution to general archaeology. The following discussion is divided into three sections: a brief review of the principles of lithic analysis for the unacquainted reader, an explication of the general analytic methods used in this study of the stones, and a review of the nature of the artifact assemblages from the Metal Ages with emphasis on how they differ from Stone Age industries and how these differences have been accounted for in the analyses.

A Brief Introduction to Stone Tools

The manufacture of stone tools is a subtractive process wherein a block of stone, a core, is chipped and/or ground either to a desired shape or for the exploitation of the chipped pieces, flakes, which are further modified, retouched, to the desired shape. The key point to be emphasized in the analysis of lithic assemblages is that the production process is ordered, and that the different products resulting from this process reflect that order. This reduction sequence provides a natural analytic motif for lithic studies. The French *chaîne d'opératoire* (e.g., Sellet 1993) takes the concept a step further, incorporating the various physical and mental actions accompanying the actual flint reduction. Artifacts can indeed be classified according to the level or stage of reduction at which they were produced, from the initial splitting of the cobble and the first primary (decortication) flakes, through the different flake types, and on to tools at different stages of completion. A more detailed scheme is presented in the next section. The techniques utilized in this reduction range from the simplest crude splitting of cobbles to sophisticated shaping involving the delicate removal of hundreds of flakes and trimming flakes to produce fine finished pieces.

In fact, the actual techniques used vary in important particulars, involving such factors as the type of hammer used in flake removal, the nature of the blow struck on the original block (core), the location, direction, and force of the blow, and the raw materials selected or available, with all of these contingent on the general technological plan, that is, the specific reduction sequence used by the knapper to achieve the final product. For example, on a simple level, the production of crude Lower Paleolithic choppers and chopping tools involves the breaking (or smashing) open of pebbles and the removal of a few flakes to leave a sharp edge. In contrast, more sophisticated core reduction techniques require elaborate preliminary preparation (flaking) of the core such that the shape of the final flake or flakes is predetermined to produce, for example, points, blades, bladelets, or other special flakes.

In more detail, flake removal can be accomplished in the following ways (fig. 2.1):

1. **Direct percussion** consists of the delivery of a blow from the hammer directly on the core. The hammer can be either hard (stone) or soft (antler, bone, hardwood). The hammer does not need to be harder than the material being worked, the key issue being the delivery of a shock wave on the core. Detailed analyses of the morphology of flakes have sometimes been used to statistically separate the products of hard versus soft hammers. As a

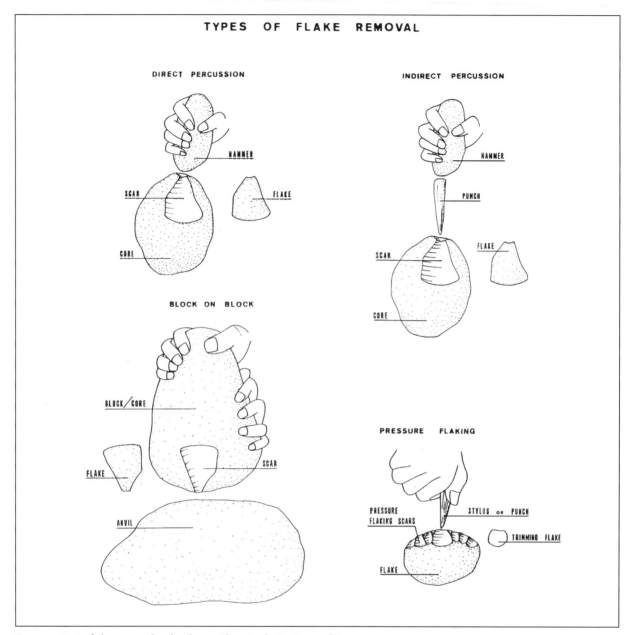

FIG. 2.1. *Basic flake removal technologies (drawing by P. Kaminski).*

general rule, soft hammers tend to produce finer, more delicate flakes, with less striking platform shattering. Direct percussion can also be used to modify and shape flakes already struck from a core, that is, to retouch them.

2. **Indirect percussion** requires the use of a punch intermediate between the hammer and the core. The punch is placed with the working end on the core where the flake removal is desired, and the other end is struck by a hammer. Punches in early periods were probably of antler. Metal punches are known from later periods, as, for example, in the production of gun flints. The primary advantage in the use of a punch is in the accuracy of the blow. In addition, the use of a punch probably results in less shattering of the striking platform and perhaps finer flakes than direct percussion.

3. **Block-on-block** and **anvil technique** are actually forms of direct percussion, but instead of the use of a hammer, cores or large chunks of raw material are struck against each other or against large blocks specifically selected to serve as anvils.

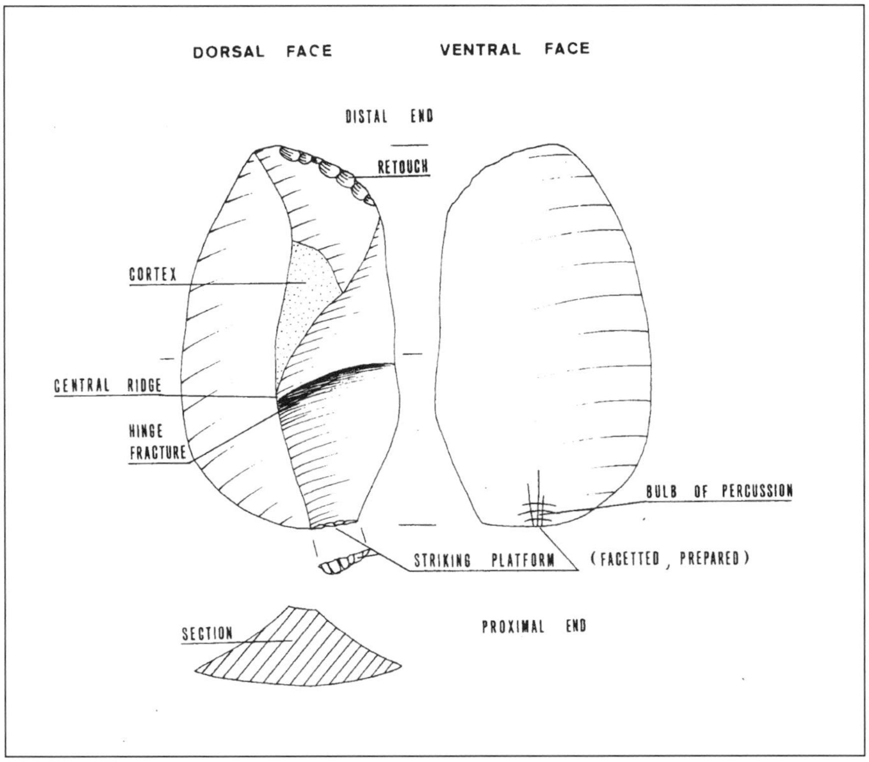

DORSAL FACE   VENTRAL FACE

DISTAL END

RETOUCH

CORTEX

CENTRAL RIDGE

HINGE
FRACTURE

BULB OF PERCUSSION

STRIKING PLATFORM   (FACETTED, PREPARED)

SECTION

PROXIMAL END

FIG. 2.2. *Basic features of a flake (drawing by P. Kaminski).*

These techniques are obviously crude and inaccurate, used primarily to split large blocks or to produce massive flakes.

4. **Pressure flaking techniques** involve application of pressure on the edge (striking platform) of the core or the flake using a punch or a stylus, in lieu of a blow. These result in small, fine trimming flakes. The technique allows great precision in retouch and was often used in the final stages of production of fine tools, like arrowheads and bifacial knives. Pressure flaking, using a chest punch (e.g., Crabtree 1967), can also be used to remove large flakes and especially blades from a prepared core.

These different techniques, collectively referred to as **knapping** or **flaking,** produce artifacts with generally diagnostic attributes. The family of knapped or flaked products, flakes, including more specific items such as simple flakes, blades, bladelets, and core trimming flakes, all share the following basic features (fig. 2.2):

1. **A bulb of percussion.** This is the protuberance on the ventral (inside) face of the flake, the side detached from the core.

2. **A striking platform.** This is the edge from which the flake was struck. The bulb of percussion is located adjacent to the striking platform.

3. **A ventral (internal)** or **bulbar surface.** This is the smooth plane from which the flake separated from the core.

4. **A dorsal surface.** This is the external surface of the flake, showing either the scars from previous flake removals or the cortex (skin) of the original flint block.

In most cases, these characteristics suffice to define an **assemblage** (as opposed to an individual piece) as human-made, since taken together they are indeed rare occurrences naturally. The actual mechanics of flake removal have also been studied (e.g., Speth 1972; Luedtke 1992, 79–98), and more detailed characteristics can also be enumerated, but are not necessary in a brief review.

Of course, in addition to the flakes themselves, there are two other by-products of knapping, cores and debris. As mentioned before, **cores** are the original blanks from which flakes are removed. These, too,

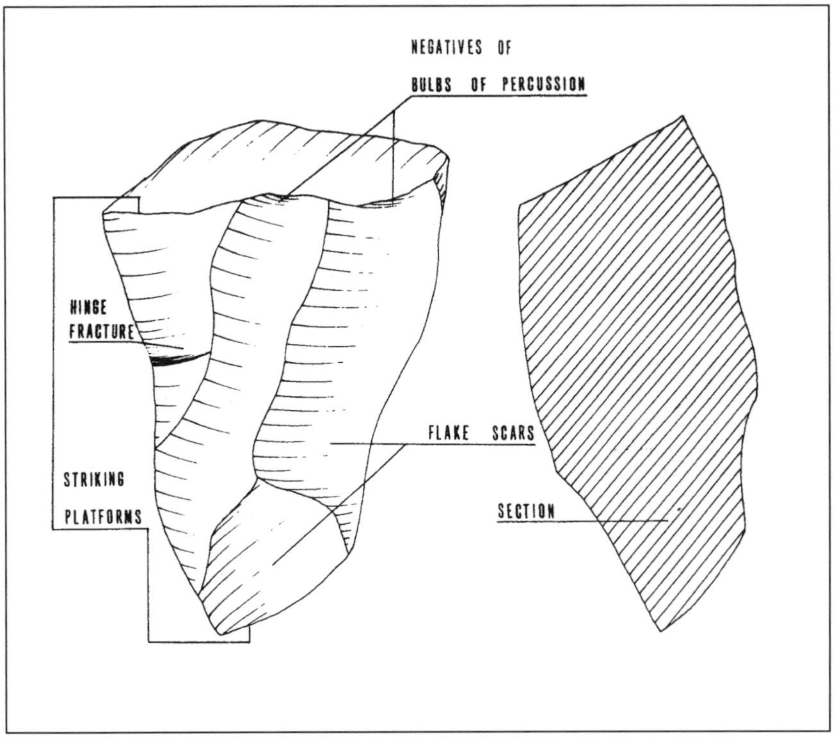

NEGATIVES OF
BULBS OF PERCUSSION

HINGE
FRACTURE

STRIKING
PLATFORMS

FLAKE SCARS

SECTION

FIG. 2.3. *Basic features of a core
(drawing by P. Kaminski).*

retain diagnostic characteristics allowing them to be identified as the products of human manufacture as opposed to natural agency. Thus, the following are the distinctive features of cores (fig. 2.3):

1. Scars or flake removals, the negatives remaining from earlier flaking.

2. Negatives of bulbs of percussion are also often evident at the head of flake scars, adjacent to the striking platform.

3. Striking platforms are the edges of the cores, from which flakes were removed. They often show battering or shattering.

The **debris** category is more problematic. By definition, these are the amorphous pieces that cannot be classified as either flakes or cores, the result of non-controlled shatter and breakage accompanying flint knapping (or heating and burning of stone). In association with flakes and cores, debris is clearly part of the general lithic assemblage. However, in the absence of cores and flakes, the identification of debris as human produced can indeed be problematic.

The different techniques used to produce flakes of different kinds are dependent to a degree on the differ-

ent raw materials available to, or selected by, the knapper. Essentially, the finer grained the material, the more easily the material is worked. Minerals with crystalline structures, like quartz, tend to break geometrically along the lines of that structure, along the **planes of cleavage**. Breakage of such materials is thus determined to a great extent by the specific molecular or crystalline geometry of the mineral. Other materials, best exemplified by obsidian, a natural volcanic glass, are structurally amorphous. They have no internal crystalline geometry. A shock wave passing through such material, as caused by a flaking blow, behaves much as a wave through water, controlled primarily by the location, direction, and force of the blow, and not by internal structure. This type of controlled breakage is called **conchoidal fracture,** since, as mentioned earlier, it results in the formation of a bulb of percussion that resembles a seashell (using one's imagination!).

Obsidian is relatively rare in the Levant, the nearest sources being located in Anatolia. Cherts (see Luedtke 1992 for discussion of the terminologies), or in the traditional Near Eastern terminology retained here, flints, are common and behave in a similar way. Although technically not amorphous since on the molecular level flint is crystalline in structure, these structures are small enough as to be virtually irrelevant to the knapping process. Such materials are collectively referred to as **crypto-crystalline** because the crystalline structures are effectively masked by their small size. Notably, for crypto-crystalline materials, conchoidal fracture can be enhanced through heat treatment, the slow baking of the material, resulting in a chemical breakdown of some of the crystalline bonds in these materials.

In addition to conchoidal fracture, amorphous and crypto-crystalline materials are generally harder and sharper than other materials. Nevertheless, hard limestones, dolomites, basalt, schist, and even quartz were often chipped for specific tools, either when better materials were unavailable or when the specific properties associated with crypto-crystalline materials were not important.

Analytic Methods

For our purposes, three types of analysis can be distinguished: typological analysis (the tools themselves), technological analysis (the waste products), and materials analysis (the different raw materials). The classic dichotomy in lithic analysis is that distinguishing between technology and typology, effectively waste and formal tools (cf. Marks 1992). In reality, as reflected in the idea of the reduction sequence, the separation between these two classes is difficult, the tools representing only the end product on a production spectrum. Raw material analysis, a distinct analytic class because of the different data collected and different methods exploited, constitutes a third approach (e.g., Hammond 1977; Schiffer 1976, 158–78; Rolland and Dibble 1990; Andrefsky 1994).

TOOL ANALYSIS

Tool assemblages can be studied on three levels: (1) the morphological classification of the artifacts into types and the analysis of type frequency variability; (2) within type, macroscopic analysis of different attributes or features of the artifacts; and (3) microscopic analysis of damage and polish patterns on selected artifacts within selected categories (microwear analysis). Each level has its own specific methods, advantages, and drawbacks.

Types

The construction and interpretation of archaeological typology constitute one of the complex methodological issues facing analysts of material culture. The approach adopted here is a pragmatic one. Types are viewed as recurring sets of correlated attributes (e.g., Hill and Evans 1972), which are intuitively recognizable and, hopefully, objectively reproducible. The legitimacy of a type or type list is to be found in (1) its reproducibility and (2) its analytic utility. Types need not represent the original producer's paradigm, although they may, depending on the purpose of the typology. Types may be viewed as modes, with attached variation. Thus an overlap between types does not negate typological distinction (see e.g., Whallon and Brown 1982; Dunnell 1986; Beck and Jones 1989; Clarke 1978, 205–9 for general discussions of typology and classification).

Analytic function or purpose must be considered in the formal construction of a typology, although it plays less role in the intuitive recognition of different types. For example, it is widely recognized that the classic Bordesian system for the French Lower and Middle Paleolithic (Bordes 1961) conflates functional, stylistic, and technological factors affecting the morphology of tools to the extent that interpretation of typological variability is difficult if not impossible (e.g., Dibble 1987; Rolland and Dibble 1990). That is, the types we recognize intuitively or informally result from a set of interacting factors that need not be intuitively obvious. These factors may crosscut typological criteria, but do so in different combinations and frequencies. Furthermore, types may exist only within specific contexts. That is, a distinct type in a particular area or period, with archaeological implications of one kind or another, need not be defined or identified as a distinct type in another. For example, the bitruncated blades found at Early Bronze Age Erani clearly constitute a distinct type, identified with the Egyptian presence at the site. In other chronological contexts, they fall into the general spectrum of variation in backed truncated blades and lack both the discreteness and the archaeological implications of those associated with the Erani assemblage. A type list must clearly be applicable beyond the confines of a specific site, but the archaeologist must be aware that the archaeological meaning of types may change in different contexts.

Recognizing this allows the construction of different typologies for different purposes (cf. Clark 1989). Alternatively, a single typology based on hierarchically

General Technology	Specific Technology	Function	Subtype
Blade Tools	**Canaanean**	sickles	reaping knives segments
		knives	retouched
	Large Geometric (blade-flake)	sickles	rectangles parallelogram trapezoids triangles other incomplete
	Prismatic Blades	sickles	truncated-backed truncated-unbacked incomplete
		knives (ret. blades)	bitruncated bitruncated-backed other
	Simple Blades	sickles	backed arched backed unbacked other incomplete
		knives (ret. blades)	arched backed straight backed unbacked
		awls on blades	

TABLE 2.1. Hierarchical organization of blade tools.

organized types and subtypes may operate in a similar fashion (e.g., Brezillon 1968, 27). An example for blade tools is given in table 2.1. Indeed, one of the primary problems of typology seems to be the confusion of different levels of typological analysis. Although the types themselves may be identified intuitively, where they are placed in a typological framework should be consistent and guided by the goals of the analysis. For example, in the case of the blade tools (table 2.1), it is possible to shift the different levels of the hierarchy to suggest different orders of analytic importance. Thus, function and specific technology can be reversed, and in some analytic contexts probably should be.

Unlike the Paleolithic, for which well-defined type lists set a comparative standard for lithic analysis (e.g., Tixier 1963; Bordes 1961; de Sonneville-Bordes and Perrot 1954–56; Brezillon 1968, Goring-Morris 1987, 454–59; Hours 1974), there is no well-established type list for the post-Neolithic periods in the Near East. Scholars have drawn on a variety of sources for describing tool assemblages from these periods, ranging from the Near Eastern and European Paleolithic and Neolithic (e.g., McConaughy 1979) to New

World lithic types (e.g., Warburton 1980; Bennett et al. 1989). Probably the most significant problem in generating a reasonable type list has been the fact that few scholars have examined more than one or two lithic assemblages from post-Neolithic sites, let alone a suite of them (excepting Neuville and Crowfoot, working on early collections that were badly selected). Thus, up to the 1980s, comparative work had been limited to literature reviews of individual reports, most of them quite dated. Even more recent lists, sometimes quite detailed and rigorous (e.g., McConaughy 1979, 42, table 1) were not deemed appropriate to the analytic goals of this work (and were, in any case, developed more or less concurrently).

Analytic comparison of typologies constructed by different scholars seems rarely to present any significant problem. Most investigators provide detailed descriptive typologies that can be more or less adjusted to different levels of analysis. Thus, for example, McConaughy's (1979, 42, table 1) typology from Bab edh Dhra can be matched easily to that used here, with only minor ambiguities (table 2.2).

In short, the type list and definitions presented in the next chapter were developed organically over the course of more than ten years of examining assemblages for which no previous framework had been firmly established. As a consequence, there is inevitable play in the system. Even given reexamination of a few assemblages (e.g., Hesi, Shadud), new types and subtypes, recognized only after cumulative experience, may be missing for the earlier reports. Furthermore, some types and attributes recognized in earlier studies (e.g., backed flakes) may be missing from later reports when they proved analytically of little use.

Attributes

Beyond the definition of types, based on recurring attributes, the attributes themselves can be examined for intratype variability (e.g., Sackett 1966, 1968; Clarke 1978, 152–62; Isaac 1977, 118–19, fig. 39; 155, fig. 46; Marks and Kaufman 1983). In a sense, attribute analysis can be a kind of single-variable typology, although in the case of metric attributes, variables are continuous and not discrete. The assumption is that some attributes will crosscut more coarse-grained typologies to provide additional information on specific types of variation. The added level of modification that defines tools suggests that intent, whether functional (including greater reduction) or stylistic, can be examined better on the tools than on the waste products.

The amount of information coded in the "attributes" of an artifact is infinite. Attributes are no more objective than types since they are selected by the investigator as having potential value for archaeological analysis. However, this "bias" is a necessity since we cannot physically measure or record the infinity of attributes. As noted earlier for waste, attributes can be either metric or nominal. Here attributes were recorded for specific types judged to have the greatest potentials for producing archaeological conclusions given current states of knowledge, methods, and analytic frameworks, and limited time and resources. For example, analysis was restricted to more formal or standardized types based on the assumption that they incorporate more cultural information than less standardized, less modified pieces. With the exception of some sets of Canaanean blades, attributes were not recorded for waste types. The specific attributes recorded are typical lithic analytic traits, the initial justification for which derives from a general tradition in lithic analysis as to what is worth recording. The

McConaughy 1979, 42	Typology used here
Notches/spokeshaves	J.1.a. flat notches
Utilized blades	C.4. simple retouched blades (or waste)
Side denticulates	J.1.b. flat denticulates
Flake cores	Flake cores (waste)
Sickle blades	B. Sickle Blades and segments
Unifaces	K. Retouched flakes and pieces
Backed blades	C.2.a. straight backed blades
End denticulates	J.1.b. flat denticulates
Chiseloids	E.4. miscellaneous points (Borers)
Denticulates	J.1.b. flat denticulates
Beaked denticulates— large var.	E.1. awls
Microtools	K. Retouched flakes and pieces
Gravers/Beaked denticulates—small var.	E.1. awls
Ghassulian form fan-scrapers	F. Tabular Scrapers
Steep edged endscrapers	I.3. steep scrapers
Bifaces	M.2. other choppers
Backed utilized flakes	K. Retouched flakes and pieces
Cobble bifaces	M.1. cobble choppers
Flakes with sickle sheen	B.5. other (Sickle Blades and Segments)
Hammerstones	O. Hammerstones
Scrapers	I. Scrapers
Endscrapers	I.1.a. simple endscrapers
Sidescrapers	I.2. sidescrapers
Burins	N.1. burins
Blade (?) cores	Blade cores
Awl/drill	E.2. drills
Serrated flake	J.1.b. flat denticulate
Thumbnail endscraper/ rt. flake	K. Retouched Flakes and Pieces
Convergent denticulate/ flake knife	J.1.b. flat denticulate

TABLE 2.2. Comparative typologies: McConaughy 1979, 42, from Bab edh Dhra versus the typology developed for use here (see Type List, Chapter 3).

Sickle and Blade Tool Attributes

TECHNOLOGY	METRICS	BACKING	TRUNCATIONS	BULB	GLOSS	BROKEN	RETOUCH	SHAPE
Canaanean	length	dorsal	o	+	absent	yes	none	rectangle
blade/flake	width	ventral	1	-	1 edge	no	edge	triangle
blade	thick	partial	2	thin	2 edge		damage	parallelogram
prismatic		natural	dorsal				nibbled	trapezoid
		alternate	ventral				serrated	quadrilateral
		absent					denticulate	

Microlithic Drill Attributes

SYMMETRY	FINISHED	GENERAL METRICS	BIT METRICS	BASE	BIT RETOUCH	BROKEN
good	yes	length	length	retouch	abrupt	yes
medium	no	width	width	shape	semi-abrupt	no
poor		thick	thick		bipolar	

Tabular Scraper Attributes

SHAPE	BROKEN	METRICS	RETOUCH	RETOUCH LOCATION	BULB	PLATFORM	CORTEX
round	yes	length	flat	right	+	present	total
fan	no	width	semi-abrupt	left	-	absent	partial
elongate		thick	abrupt	distal	thin	facetted	absent
oval			ventral	proximal		point	ground
irregular						flat	incisions
							coarse
							fine

TABLE 2.3. Attribute lists for selected tools.

ultimate justification can only derive from conclusions drawn. The selected types and attributes are presented in table 2.3. Actual data are presented only when relevant.

Microscopic Analysis

Microscopic wear analysis constitutes the third level of tool analysis. With the exception of informal microscopic examination of microlithic drills from the Camel site (Rosen 1995), no microwear analyses were conducted for this work, although several studies of materials from Jericho (Keeley 1983; Unger-Hamilton 1991), Bab edh Dhra (McConaughy 1979), and Shiqmim (Rowan 1990; Rowan and Levy 1991) provide important information on tool functions used here (Chapter 3). It is beyond the scope of this work to provide an overview of the methods of microscopic analysis (e.g., Keeley 1980; Cauvin 1983a; Hayden 1979; Odell and Odell-Vereecken 1980; Shea 1987,

for discussions). However, there are several points that may have bearing on this study. First, unlike other attributes whose general interpretations are often the subject of debate, the polishes, striations, microshatter, and general microscopic wear patterns found on the edges of stone tools are universally considered to be the result of either utilitarian artifact function or postdepositional processes, and the latter can usually be eliminated from consideration. Although there is some debate over the most appropriate means of identifying use wear patterns, specifically the use of high-power versus low-power magnification techniques and the identification of polishes and striations as opposed to shatter patterns (e.g., Odell and Odell-Vereecken 1980), ambiguity in interpretation seems to arise primarily in the identification of specific attributes as reflecting specific activities.

In addition to this, the time-consuming nature of most microwear analyses, and the need for a wide range of replicatory controls, virtually preclude the study of complete collections. That is, even were microwear studies absolutely reliable in their identification of function, the selection of artifacts for study reduces supposed objectivity. Thus, the assumption underlying much microwear analysis is that if function is identifiable on a specific example of a type, then that identification can be extended to the other representatives of that type in the rest of the assemblage. This is a difficult enough assumption in regard to relatively standardized tool types, such as those deriving from the Paleolithic. When applied to the *ad hoc* and expedient tools that dominate the post-Neolithic, it is problematic indeed. Nevertheless, accepting these problems, microwear analysis provides perhaps our best insights into specific tool functions.

WASTE ANALYSIS

The distinction between tools and waste is based on the presence of retouch, that is, deliberate secondary modification, on tools (e.g., Tixier et al. 1980, 59; Marks 1976, 378). The absence of retouch does not mean that a flake was not used, that it was not a tool in the common English usage of the term. Rather, retouch provides a convenient means for dividing assemblages into two sets: tools that generally encode a greater amount of cultural information by virtue of the greater effort invested in their manufacture (the added stage of retouch) and waste (the unmodified products of core reduction). Debates about the relevance of our own typological schemes for dividing lithic assemblages (e.g., White 1967; White et al. 1977; Hayden 1984) and whether our typological frameworks genuinely reflect ancient ones aside, the distinction is a useful one allowing reasonable reproducibility and satisfying conclusions to be tendered.

However, another problem in the distinction between tools and waste is the actual definition of retouch. Inherent in the definition is the assumption of deliberate modification. Tools not found in primary *in situ* context often exhibit abrasion, which in many cases cannot be distinguished from the low-level retouch found on many expedient tools. In these situations, such as at the Neolithic and Early Bronze Age site of Yiftahel where much of the material seems to have washed downslope into the excavated portion of the site (Rosen and Grinblatt n.d.), the type frequencies are presented in two forms, in one case including the artifacts that might have been tools, and in the other, excluding them. A similar problem exists for

distinguishing intensive use damage from retouch. In this case, at any rate, the conceptual problem seems less difficult, since the modification is the result of utilization, better fitting our common perception of what a tool is supposed to be.

Most archaeologists recognize the importance of "tool" collection and analysis. Intuitively, these are seen as functionally significant, perhaps incorporating chronological and cultural information as well. Although perhaps verging on the trivial to archaeologists working on Stone Age cultures, the absolute importance of waste assemblages needs to be reiterated for archaeologists who may relate to lithic waste as analogous to nondiagnostic body sherds in ceramics, worth little. Since waste products usually constitute between 60% and 90% of well-collected assemblages, archaeological discard of waste is a major loss of information. There are still not a few archaeologists digging sites with important lithic assemblages who regularly discard lithic waste instead of collecting and analyzing it.

The analysis of lithic waste, in fact, can provide information on craft specialization, trade (see especially Chapters 4 and 5), and production/technology, which cannot be obtained from any other source. Lithic manufacture produces diagnostic residues in large quantities that can signify on-site/off-site production, exchange of complete, partially complete, or component parts of tools, and degrees of craft specialization. They can provide information on activity areas, if appropriate provenience data are recorded (e.g., Ammerman and Andrefsky 1982; Mallory 1986; Odell 1989; Shafer and Hester 1983; Torrence 1986). The fact is that manufacture of specific tool classes leaves residues that can be associated exclusively with those tools (e.g., different sickle types, tabular scrapers, microlithic drills, blade tools of different types, and *ad hoc* tools as a general class [Rosen 1989a]). Identification and quantification of different waste types allows reasonable definition of production intensities and locales. These data can easily be incorporated into models of production and exchange, obviously of general significance for understanding the economies of these early complex societies.

There are several additional points worth noting with respect to waste analysis. Given that most archaeologists not trained in lithic analysis cannot distinguish between informal tools (retouched flakes and the like) and waste, in fact, noncollection of waste affects the recovery of reliable samples of tools as well. Finally,

DEBRIS	*chunks*	
	chips	
CORES	*blade cores*	Canaanean
		Chalcolithic
		simple
	bladelet cores	
	flake cores	simple
		tabular scraper
	mixed cores	blade-flake
		bladelet-flake
	other cores	
Waste		
DEBITAGE	*flakes*	simple flakes
		tabular scraper flakes
		sickle flakes
		other
	primary elements (decortication)	primary flakes
		primary blades
	blades	Canaanean blades
		Chalcolithic blades
		simple blades
		other
	bladelets	simple
		twisted
		other
	core trimming (CTE)	core tablets
		ridge blades
		other
Tools (retouched pieces)		

TABLE 2.4. Waste classification scheme. Incorporation of additional attributes, such as broken or unbroken, and raw materials, can achieve additional levels.

both general levels of reduction and specific technologies that may be sensitive to chronological and culture factors (e.g., Bar-Yosef 1987). Table 2.4 presents the general scheme. As mentioned above, the key element in this system is our ability to distinguish between the waste from the production of different tools and to define the stage of manufacture represented by the waste products (e.g., Ammerman and Andrefsky 1982; Moholy-Nagy et al. 1984; Sullivan and Rozen 1985).

Detailed definition of the different elements in the reduction sequence can be found in most introductions to lithic analysis (e.g., Brezillon 1968; Tixier et al. 1980; also see Goring-Morris 1987, 47–51). In brief, the following criteria for distinguishing the basic levels of reduction are noted in the order presented in table 2.4. More detailed discussion of specific debitage types (i.e., Canaanean blades, large geometric sickle flakes, etc.) are discussed in Chapter 3.

Waste Classes

Debris is amorphous, that is, without standardized features. The class consists of **chunks** and **chips**. Chips are less than 2 cm in maximal dimension, chunks greater. There is some inconsistency of usage such that all pieces under 2 cm are classified as chips (with some exceptions, such as broken blades or bladelets). The intent is the distinction between potential tool blanks and "true" waste, the assumption, more or less borne out in practice, being that most tools require flakes larger than the 2 cm in maximal dimension.

The conflation of true amorphous chips with small flakes, possibly trimming flakes, clearly results in loss of potentially important information. However, given the absence of sieving, the materials at this small end of the lithic spectrum do not constitute a good sample anyway, and the speed of sorting is considerably enhanced by simple size sorting at this level (cf. Ahler 1989 for other size sorting methods).

Debris is primarily the result of shatter during lithic manufacture or from heat breakage. An exception involves the classification of broken pieces. Although technically these should probably be incorporated into the debris category, blade and bladelet segments are classified with whole pieces when they incorporate attributes that can be used for other analyses (e.g., width of blades). Most broken flakes are counted as flakes as well. The problems of double counting are insignificant since it is virtually impossible

many waste products, such as twisted bladelets, Canaanean blades, tabular scraper blanks, large geometric sickle flakes, and various core types, can be culturally and/or chronologically diagnostic. Thus, they can be of significance even for traditional chronostratigraphic analyses.

Waste is usually analyzed at two levels: (1) a classificatory scheme based on the stage in the reduction sequence and (2) an analysis of attributes. The reduction sequence classification used here is that common to Israeli prehistory (e.g., Goring-Morris 1987, 48–49). It is organized hierarchically to incorporate

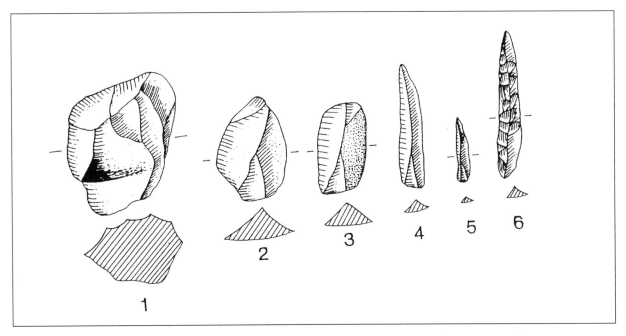

FIG. 2.4. *Basic debitage types (and core). 1, core (note flake scars, striking platform, nonflat section); 2, flake; 3, primary flake (note cortex); 4, blade (length more than twice width); 5, bladelet (small blade with length more than twice width); 6, core trimming element (ridge blade) (drawing by P. Kaminski).*

to refit pieces on the large sites studied here. This procedure can considerably augment the debitage categories and in the case of blades and bladelets is a virtual necessity in order to establish the classes.

Cores show striking platforms and multiple removals (fig. 2.3). Core fragments without striking platforms have usually been classified with debris. The core class can be divided into subtypes according to the kind of flake scars or removals: **blade cores, bladelet cores, flake cores,** and **mixed cores.** Mixed cores refer to cores with either flake and blade removals or flake and bladelet removals. The distinction between blade and bladelet cores is based on size. No set criterion was established; the differences are usually obvious and are often reflected in raw material as well as size. Regardless, when the distinction becomes difficult, the issue is usually irrelevant since the types clearly fall into a single continuum. Core sizes were recorded (see below for other attributes recorded). Other cores include special types, such as intrusive Levallois cores. Beyond this preliminary classificatory level, cores can be further divided according to specific technologies, as indicated in table 2.4 in such types as Canaanean blade cores.

The **debitage** (fig. 2.4) class consists of all unretouched pieces with bulbs of percussion, as well as those broken pieces that are obvious products of percussion and are large enough to preserve some of the other attributes of the piece, such as blade width. Debitage is assumed to be the result of intentional percussion. The distinction between various subclasses of debitage follows Paleolithic usage (e.g., Brezillon 1968; Bordes 1961; Tixier 1963; Marks 1976). **Flakes** are those pieces that do not incorporate special morphological attributes, but they may include a range of special technologies, as in tabular scraper flakes. **Blades** are minimally twice as long as wide, as measured along the striking axis at midpoint. **Bladelets** are small blades, maximally 14 mm in width (Tixier 1963; also see Kaufman 1986 for discussion). Primary, or decortication, flakes show minimally 30% dorsal cortex (e.g., Goring-Morris 1987, 49; Marks 1976, 376, uses a 50% cutoff; also see Sullivan and Rozen 1985). Although some systems recognize two levels of decortication (e.g., Sullivan and Rozen 1985), primary and secondary, initial analyses using two levels proved analytically ineffective and the distinction was dropped.

Core trimming elements (CTE) include ridge blades, core tablets (e.g., Goring-Morris 1987, 49; Payne 1983) and other trimming elements and mistakes, such as plunging blades, hinged flakes, etc. (e.g., Hayden 1979, 133). These reflect core preparation and renewal, and a range of by-products caused by poor execution, by impurities in the raw material, or simply through expedient production, i.e., mistakes. The simple *ad hoc* nature of much of the technology resulted in a near absence of the more formal trimming elements. The question of what constitutes a "mistake" in such an expedient technology is problematic, and the apparent numerical scarcity of these other core trimming elements is mostly a function of definition. Many, if not most, flakes from the Early Bronze Age would quality as CTE in one form or another, and many CTE were subsumed into the flake category as a consequence.

Waste Attributes

On the attribute level of analysis, metric and/or nominal attributes can be recorded for specific waste types or samples taken from the assemblage. Standard metric attributes, for example, are length, width, and thickness of various debitage classes (e.g., Hietala 1983c; Jelinek 1982). Scar patterns, striking platforms, and bulbs of percussion can also be counted or measured in various ways (e.g., Brezillon 1968, 70, fig.3). Nominal attributes can include presence/absence or classification of specific features found on the artifact.

Aside from recording some attributes of cores and Canaanean blades, little attribute analysis of waste products has been conducted on later lithic assemblages in the Near East. However, of special note here are recent studies of Canaanean blade striking platforms, which suggest different technological modes for different areas of the Near East (e.g., Betts 1991, 1992a; Edens 1995).

Cores were measured to maximal dimension. The number of striking platforms and the location of the platforms with respect to each other were recorded, along with the core type. The Canaanean blades were analyzed because of the unique specialized nature of the technology and the clear connection to Canaanean sickle blades, allowing direct inferences to be drawn concerning the reduction sequence. Specifically, length, width, thickness, presence/absence of bulb of percussion, cross-section shape, status as to broken or complete, and proximal, medial, or distal segments, and raw material were recorded.

Although the methods for analyzing general reduction sequences used in this work primarily involve classification of waste products, it is important to note that conjoinable piece analysis, that is, the refitting of cores, waste, and tools back together to the original block (cf. Volman 1983; Marks and Volman 1983; Morrow 1996) has been a primary stimulus to work on reduction sequences. A reconstructed core allows precise delineation of the exact sequence of flake removals and reduction decisions, whereas simple classification of artifacts into reduction stages, as outlined above, can only give an approximation of this process. Much of our detailed understanding of how reduction sequences work derives from core reconstruction, and for the sake of general completeness, it is necessary to indicate that this method is quite important in Stone Age studies. Unfortunately, given the postdepositional processes acting on virtually all later period sites, the opportunities for this of analysis are virtually absent, and none have been attempted in this work.

Raw Materials

The examination of raw materials is an important complement to technological and typological analysis. It is clear that ancient people were aware of the properties of different types of flint and other materials, and deliberately selected specific raw materials for specific tasks (e.g., Hammond 1977; Andrefsky 1994; Rolland and Dibble 1990).

Flint[1] in its various forms is ubiquitous in the Southern Levant, a direct consequence of the limestone substrate present in virtually the entire region. However, variability in sources (e.g., wadi cobbles, vein flint, and nodular flint, from different geological strata) results in a wide range of nodule sizes, colors, degrees of internal fracture, and graininess. Furthermore, some technologies and types may require specific flint types that may be found only in restricted locations. For example, Canaanean blades were manufactured, for the most part, from Eocene flints, probably a necessity due to the large size of Eocene nodules, their fine grain, and their general lack of internal fractures. Tabular scrapers also require very large nodules of good-quality flint, which seem to be most abundant, or accessible, in the southern regions.

One of the problems encountered in the analysis of raw materials is in the actual classification of the flint. Variability in color and grain may be quite high, even within single sources and even within single artifacts, and different sources, such as widely separated Eocene flint outcrops, may produce virtually identical flint types. Chemical and elemental analysis of flint also shows great variability, which makes reliable classification difficult, and virtually no analyses of this kind have been conducted anyway. Cortex classification according to microfossils may be more reliable, but in most cases is not possible since cortex is usually removed. As a result, data have not been systematically collected on raw materials, although in some cases cores and/or specific artifact types were classified according to raw material. General impressions were recorded regardless.

At least five types of raw material could be identified, although all show variation. These are the following:

1. Fine-grained brown Eocene and late Cretaceous flint is usually found in large nodules. This material is found in restricted exposures in the hills of Samaria, the northern Galilee, the Shephela, and parts of the Central Negev. It is significantly absent from the coastal plain, the central hills around Jerusalem, most of the northern Negev, and the southern Negev (fig. 2.5).

2. Very fine-grained, gray, glossy translucent flint or chalcedony is usually found in small nodules or conglomerates. It is especially common in the wadis of the Central and northern Negev.

3. Striped medium- to fine-grained flint, occurring in small to medium-sized cobbles, originated in Transjordan and was transported to wadi beds, especially of the Negev, prior to the development of the Jordan Rift Valley.

4. A wide range of mottled and variably grained flints, usually in browns and grays, often with many impurities and fractures, is found throughout the country in various Cretaceous and early Cenozoic limestone strata and in wadis.

5. Hard limestones (e.g., Gilead 1989) are found throughout the hilly regions of the country.

Essentially there is no shortage of raw materials, although the best-quality materials, those of the Eocene strata, are somewhat more restricted in their distribution.

Obsidian is extremely rare, although not totally unknown, in these periods. It derives exclusively from Anatolia (Perlman and Yellin 1980). Basalts, although used during Acheulean times, seem not to have been exploited in later periods for chipped stone tools, although basalt grinding stones and vessels were common.

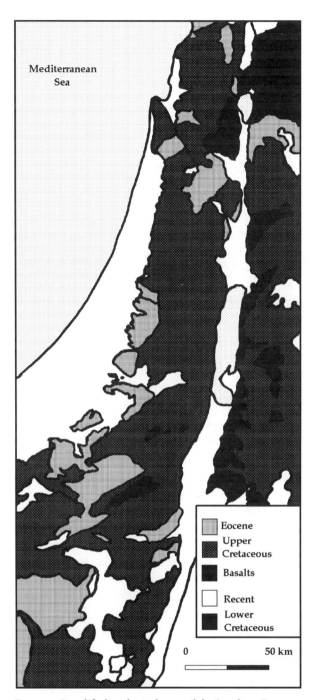

FIG. 2.5. *Simplified geological map of the Southern Levant showing especially Eocene and Upper Cretaceous bedrock as sources of flint.*

Geological and geomorphological maps (e.g., Amiran et al. 1985) are of some use in determining source areas for some of these flint types, such as the Eocene flints. However, even here, multiple sources prevent unequivocal identification of flint origins.

The Nature of the Lithic Assemblages from the Metal Ages

Lithic assemblages from the historic and proto-historic periods in the Levant differ from their Stone Age counterparts in three primary ways. First, modes of lithic manufacture, distribution, and discard in the societies of the post-Neolithic Levant are structurally more complex, an obvious concomitant of the greater socioeconomic complexities of the societies from which they derive. Second, the nature of the samples obtained from city and town sites can never approach the completeness nor general representativeness of those deriving from small Paleolithic campsites or even relatively small Neolithic villages. In direct relation to this, the site formation processes associated with large city and town sites create difficult problems of chronological and cultural association. Even village sites, when exposed beyond relatively small exposures, can present impossible stratigraphic problems. Finally, and not least significantly, collection techniques utilized for later period archaeology rarely achieve the exhaustiveness or provenience detail achieved by Paleolithic archaeology. This is due primarily to the need to open larger exposures to gain even minimal understanding of the site, and the immense time and effort required to do so using even the relatively "crude" methods of historical archaeology. In a word, the sieving of construction fills is hard to justify. Each of these contrasts with Paleolithic archaeology, or perhaps more appropriately, small-scale archaeology, and has its ramifications for the analysis of lithic industries in the later periods.

SOCIOECONOMIC COMPLEXITY

Beginning with the issue of socioeconomic complexity, Paleolithic and sometimes even Neolithic chipped stone tool assemblages deriving from a single site or site horizon are usually (implicitly or explicitly) viewed as integrated units, assemblages. In a real sense, these are often viewed as proxies for human groups, which are given cultural identity on the basis of the distinct characteristics of these assemblages. Of course, this is hardly avoidable given the scarcity of other artifactual remains. Analyses usually seek either

to compare these assemblages with others or to break them down into functional components, i.e., tool kits (e.g., S. R. Binford 1968; Freeman 1978), which integrate into a whole.

When examining lithic assemblages from complex societies in the Levant, factors such as craft specialization in both manufacture and use of chipped stone tools, a range of differing modes of distribution and exchange, and much regional, ethnic, and chronological variation render the idea of integrated assemblages almost useless. Historic period assemblages are the results of the physical convergence on the site of what can in essence be considered independent industries, each with distinct cultural trajectories (Rosen 1989a). Specifically, for example, a lithic assemblage from a typical northern Early Bronze Age site is comprised of Canaanean sickle blades, tabular (fan-) scrapers, and *ad hoc* tools, each with different modes of manufacture, distribution, and technology, sometimes exploiting different raw materials, being used for different functions, and with different historical origins. Each essentially constitutes a discrete lithic industry (see Parry 1987 for parallel Mesoamerican case; Gero 1991 for parallel South American case). Incorporating a somewhat larger area, on into the Negev, additional components are added to the lithic system, such as the Egyptian elements derived from the Egyptian presence in southern Shephela in the Early Bronze I, or the pastoral nomadic industries of the Negev and Sinai, incorporating a different range of functions, different organizational strategies, different economy, and indeed a different history.

It simply is not possible to talk about a unified Early Bronze Age industry. Instead, the chipped stone assemblages may be viewed as an array of industries, or subindustries, intersecting in time and space. Thus, in contrast to the Stone Age industries, there is a wider range of cultural processes and features that can be reconstructed through analysis and comparison of these different components. Recognition of the discreteness, or at least relative discreteness, of these industries is the key to comprehension of such processes. Indeed, a primary goal of the analysis of chipped stone assemblages in these periods should be the integration of this realm of material culture in all its complexity with other components of the archaeology (cf. Runnells 1985) precisely because the stones can add so much to our general comprehension of the larger cultures.

SAMPLING FROM COMPLEX SITES

The second point of contrast with Stone Age lithic analysis concerns the problem of sampling. The small size of Paleolithic encampments, the great density of lithic artifacts at many of these sites, and the implicitly assumed homogeneity of most assemblages, even given recognition of assemblage-level functional variability (e.g., Binford and Binford 1966; Freeman 1978), result in what appears to be a relative ease in obtaining a "representative sample" of an industry (but see Cahen et al. 1979 for problems of intra-assemblage and intrasite variability). Assemblages are defined on the basis of discrete stratigraphic units, or cultural horizons, and although there may be problems of context and degrees of *in situ* (cf. Schiffer 1987, 17–18, 199–200; Butzer 1982, 35–42), they are treated as representative of the cultural horizons from which they derive. There are two issues here: (1) the theoretical issue of what constitutes an industry, a horizon, a complex, etc. (e.g., Clarke 1978, 152–360; also see Brezillon 1968, 27) and how lithic assemblages reflect that (e.g., Bar-Yosef 1987, 1981), and (2) the issue of physical association. The first is a general theoretical question and beyond the scope of this work. The issue of samples and the assumption that lithic assemblages can somehow represent normative idealized cross-sections of culture have been dealt with by others (e.g., Binford 1972, 195–205).

The issue of physical association is of great importance. If stratigraphic mixture is occasionally a problem in rigorously defining Neolithic and Paleolithic assemblages (e.g., Gopher 1994, 23–29; Villa 1982; Goring-Morris 1987, 46–47), there are usually enough assemblages so that mixtures can at worst be ignored and at least be debated on their merits. The problem of stratigraphic mixture is of crucial importance in dealing with historic assemblages. Excluding the single horizon sites of the desert regions (indeed these are more akin in almost all ways to their Paleolithic counterparts), lithic assemblages derived from tells are almost always mixed.

The complexities of tell formation (A. M. Rosen 1986b) result in assemblages totally dominated by artifacts from mixed contexts. Fill layers of various types (destruction debris, construction fills, colluvia, etc.) constitute the bulk of any tell excavation, and sealed in situ floor deposits are a relative rarity. Even in floor deposits and the like, there may be serious problems of intrusions since the first collapses will be deposited on the floor, but need not be related to the cultural activi-ties associated with it. This is especially so in the case of lithic artifacts, whose small size allows them to shift vertically with relative ease (e.g., Villa 1982).

Thus, although precisely defining an assemblage as deriving physically from a specific stratum is rarely a problem, defining an assemblage as a whole as deriving from a specific *cultural* horizon as represented by that stratum is far more difficult. In cases where mixtures derive from the same general cultural horizon, for example, several phases of Early Bronze I, this may sometimes be less of an issue. However, when mixtures derive from several more disparate horizons, for example, Neolithic, Early Bronze Age, and Iron Age at Tell Hesi, or when no rationale can be made for accepting the mixed horizon as an analytic unit, then analysis is problematic.

There are two points here. First, if the investigator discounts lithic artifacts from these mixed contexts, i.e., various fill loci, the resulting assemblages will be too small to provide enough data from which to draw conclusions. Second, even were this feasible, in the case of individual lithic artifacts (as opposed to assemblages), there is no guarantee that physical associations indeed reflect original cultural associations. The difficulties are readily apparent when dealing with pits and pit fills, dug into earlier strata, which seem to reflect good context, but are notorious for the presence of intrusions.

There are several ways of approaching this dilemma, none of which are truly satisfactory, but which at least allow research to continue. Archaeological strata from tells can be dated in several ways. For most purposes, archaeologists are interested in the date of deposition, that is, when a building or floor was constructed, a structure collapsed, or a fill laid down. For such purposes, the date of the latest artifact in the stratum matrix defines the date of deposition (e.g., Walker 1978). For analysis of artifactual assemblages not of themselves chronologically or culturally diagnostic, that is, especially most lithic artifacts and bones (cf. Hesse 1986), the relevant date is when the stratum matrix was consolidated or integrated, not necessarily coinciding with when it was last laid down. Pottery readings, which provide information on dominant the ceramic types represented in a matrix, provide the key to determining the date of the matrix. Thus, if 5% of the ceramics from a locus date to Middle Bronze II, and 95% to the Early Bronze Age, it is clear that the stratum was deposited in the Middle Bronze II, but that the lithic assemblage deriving from it should be dated, for the most part, to the Early Bronze Age.

A significant point here is that "clean" strata are literally nonexistent, although individual loci may be unmixed. This means that establishing a precise chronology of type origins and type disappearances can be very difficult. Inevitable intrusions cannot be easily distinguished from low-frequency type continuity, and conclusions as to type life spans can be drawn only on the basis of close examination of specific contexts, preferably on the basis of single horizon occupations.

Obviously, the usefulness of assemblages declines with the degree of mixing in the strata from which they derive. It is possible to achieve a measure of that mixing by reference to artifacts that are chronologically diagnostic (cf. Hesse 1986; Rosen 1996; Rosen and Grinblatt n.d.). Ideally this should be done with ceramics since they provide most of the diagnostic artifacts on historic period sites, as well as the bulk of the material in general. Unfortunately, quantitative data on ceramics from tell excavations is rarely available, especially from fill strata, so that the lithic analyst (and faunal analyst for that matter) is often left with lithic diagnostics.

One method[2] used here is based on the assumption that intrusive artifacts in one stratum derive from donor strata beneath it. Thus, if one can establish a rate of loss, or intrusion index based on a diagnostic artifact, that index can be applied to the general assemblage as well and can provide insight into how intact that assemblage really is. For example, I have computed the intrusion index for the Early Bronze Stratum II at Yiftahel based on the occurrence of burins, a tool type absent from the Early Bronze Age and which disappeared in the Pottery Neolithic. Some nine burins were recovered from Stratum II (Early Bronze I) at Yiftahel, undoubtedly deriving from the lower Neolithic strata (III, III–IV, and IV). The burin assemblage from the Neolithic numbered 80, so according to the model, the original Neolithic stratum consisted of 89 burins, 9 (10.1%) of which were "lost" to the Early Bronze horizon. The proportion 10.1% (=0.101) can now be applied to the rest of the assemblage, such that the recovered Neolithic assemblage of 1,040 tools consisted originally of 1,156, of which 116 (10.1%) were lost to the Early Bronze horizon. Thus, of the 535 tools recovered from the Early Bronze stratum, we may assume that 116 (22%) are intrusive. The point here is, of course, that 78% of the assemblage can indeed be assumed to relate to the

Early Bronze Age. This is meaningful since, for example, there were very few sickle blades recovered from the Early Bronze Age stratum at Yiftahel. The scarcity of sickle blades is an important functional datum if it is reliable, and the intrusion index suggests that it is.

In a situation where several diagnostics are available, it is also possible to compute intrusion indices for each and perhaps establish some set of parameters for the reliability of the index. While it is clear that great variability between the different indices will render the specific numbers generated difficult to use, they nonetheless provide a good qualitative base for ascertaining the general reliability of an assemblage for different analytic purposes. As with all statistics, the final interpretation of reliability is a subjective judgment.

EXCAVATION AND COLLECTION TECHNIQUES

The lithic assemblages analyzed here were excavated and collected in a variety of ways. It is impossible to review retrieval methods for each site and assemblage, but this discussion is intended as a general review.

Excavation of tells cannot be conducted as painstakingly as that of small prehistoric encampments, nor should it be. For the purposes of this discussion, differences between the two can be classified according to provenience data and retrieval techniques.

The maximal standard provenience units used in recent excavation of Stone Age sites in Israel are meter grid squares with some vertical unit (rarely greater than 10 cm) (e.g., Bar-Yosef and Phillips 1977, 4–6; Goring-Morris 1987, 47). Some prehistoric excavations are conducted with considerably greater precision than this, including piece plotting and *in situ* drawing of nearly all remains (e.g., Goren 1990, figs. 24a, 24b.). The advantages with respect to lithic analysis are obvious, among other things allowing easy spatial comparison through the use of standardized units (e.g., Hietala 1983a, 1983b).

In contrast, standard grid sizes for historical period excavations are rarely less than 5x5 m squares. The standard system employed can be dubbed the locus/basket system. Although varying from excavation to excavation, a typical definition of a locus is "any stratigraphic unit which can be meaningfully isolated from those adjacent to it" (Lance 1978, 76). Loci thus include such features as walls, floors, hearths, ash lenses, pits, room fills, etc. The definition of a basket also varies between projects, but following Lance

(1978) and the Gezer excavations (Dever and Lance 1978; also see Aharoni 1973), which set a general model for much of the later American work in the Levant, a basket is an arbitrary subunit of a locus consisting of a bucketful of artifacts, often, but not always, restricted to one particular part of a locus. Baskets are changed when they are full of artifacts, or if a locus is changed, and in this sense they represent both the physical basket of artifacts and the more abstract subdivision of the locus.

The advantage to this system, which has developed organically with the field discipline, lies in its flexibility and in the immediate cultural or stratigraphic significance of the basic provenience units. That is, the locus-type provenience units are nonarbitrary and in a real sense can be seen as the building blocks of the site. The sections, or baulks, left between the grid squares are carefully recorded so as to provide exhaustive graphic record of the stratigraphic sequence (cf. Kenyon 1957, 76–80, 122–32; Dever and Lance 1978). Artifacts found together in a provenience unit are there due to the specific nature of the unit, assuming field control is sufficiently fine-tuned. Reconstruction of the loci and associated baskets can literally provide a site history (c.f. Harris 1989).

The disadvantage of the system is that provenience units are nonstandardized. It is difficult, in many cases impossible, to generate small-scale artifact density plots since the smallest standard unit is usually the 5 x 5 m square (or usually the 4 x 4 m square given the presence of meter-thick baulks). Sublocus provenience information, usually the basket, is often simply arbitrary. Even in the case when locus/basket information has been sufficiently detailed to allow standardized comparison between or within loci, the documentation may be nearly impossible to comprehend without a detailed key and complete plan. In short, spatial analyses using this method require at least intimate knowledge of the site, and the site can be easily overwhelming for the outside specialist. In fact, the general dearth of spatial analyses based on artifact frequencies from tell sites at least in part may stem directly from these methodological problems. Some recent excavations, as at Ashkelon, have adopted more detailed grid provenience systems in selected situations, such as on floors.

Collection of artifacts also presents its problems. Modern lithic analysis, especially as directed toward comprehension of different reduction sequences, is predicated on the assumption of either complete collection or nonbiased sampling. The collections analyzed must be understood in relation to how they were collected. Retrieval methods can be divided into four general classes of increasing rigor.

1. **The pretty piece syndrome:** This method consists of the collection of only the most obvious and usually the prettiest pieces. It reflects early approaches to archaeology that stressed selective collection of pieces a priori considered diagnostic. In the periods under discussion here, sickles and fan-scrapers might be the only flint artifacts collected. Waste is virtually always discarded (except when misidentified as a tool).

The analytic use of such assemblages is extremely limited, essentially restricted to paradigmatic studies of specific types and noting presence in general distributional studies. Microwear analysis also can be conducted on artifacts recovered. Most early reports (and several recent ones) suffer from this faulty method of retrieval.

2. **All pieces seen** (nonsieved): The rigorous collection of all pieces seen in the field is a tremendous improvement over the pretty piece syndrome. Although a proportion of artifacts, especially the small ones, will undoubtedly be lost without the use of sieves, excluding that problem (and perhaps a slight overrepresentation of larger pieces since they are less easily missed), assemblages based on the principle of complete collection in the field are quite reliable. Notably, they incorporate large waste assemblages, a critical element for all economic reconstructions. In fact, given the general absence of microliths from most post-Chalcolithic assemblages, especially those from central and northern Israel, it is unlikely that the tool assemblages would be significantly complemented by sieving. Sample sieving undertaken at some sites (e.g., Hesi, Yarmouth, Qasis) allows comparison of unsieved and sieved collections. The only difference (in the Early Bronze Age) seems to be the addition of a large quantity of small chipping debris to the assemblage, a general artifactual class less used in most analyses.

Numerous recent excavations have stressed the collection of all pieces, including waste. These provide the primary basis for much of the technological and economic analyses presented here.

3. **Sample sieving:** This method consists of the sieving and "total" collection of selected areas and the collection of all seen flints on others. It provides a check on the presence/absence of microliths and increases the small waste count. Sieving can be controlled either through proportional sieving of the site, e.g., every tenth basket, through selected sieving of specific loci types, such as floors, or both. Only a few sites, such as Hesi, Ashkelon, and Qasis, utilized this method.

4. **Total sieving:** The complete sieving and collection of all artifacts is obviously the preferred method from the lithic analyst's point of view. In essence this is feasible only at small sites with limited fill horizons. In fact, in the *desert* sites of the Early and Middle Bronze Ages, complete sieving is essential since microliths form a significant and diagnostic component of the lithic assemblages. Fill loci are of less import on these sites anyway. The size of the mesh is of some importance since too large a mesh is self-defeating. Standard mesh size for prehistoric excavation is 2–3 mm. Few sites have been completely sieved, but they include some of the Uvda Valley sites and those excavated by the author in the Negev.

Lest these remarks be misconstrued, even sample sieving is not always feasible given the heavy clay soils of many parts of the Levant. Wet sieving has only rarely been carried out and only on a sampling basis. It is a logistical impossibility in the desert.

Summary

The study of chipped stone assemblages from the Metal Ages in the Levant is analytically similar to that of early periods. The same essential principles defining stone tool reduction in the Stone Age can be applied to later periods as well. However, the complexities of the protohistoric and historic periods bring their own problems and potentials to lithic analysis. Thus, sampling problems from large urban sites with complex stratigraphies are difficult, and collection strategies must be modified from standard prehistoric techniques both to allow excavations to proceed and to provide a representative lithic sample. The use of earlier, less rigorously collected assemblages also poses challenges.

On the plus side, the social complexities of these early historical societies are well reflected in the assemblages. Beyond the inherently important documentation of a previously little-known technology, quantitative analysis of both waste and tool assemblages allows detailed economic reconstructions that are virtually unparalleled by other realms of material culture.

NOTES

1. The use of the term *flint,* as opposed to *chert,* is retained for the sake of literary consistency. Although Luedtke's recent (1992) synthesis attempts to instill some terminological order on the confusion of cherts, flints, chalcedonies, jaspers, etc., the use of a term other than the traditional *flint* in the Old World would seem only to add greater confusion.

2. This method was developed with Ilan Sharon while I was working on the materials from Ir David. The equation for this calculation is as follows:

$$Ec = Ea - \frac{I \times N}{1 - I}$$

Ec = the original, clean, unmixed, undisturbed (Early Bronze Age at Yiftahel) assemblage

Ea = the (Early Bronze Age at Yiftahel) assemblage as recovered from the excavation, including intrusions

N = the donor (Neolithic at Yiftahel) assemblage, as recovered in the field

I = the rate or index of intrusion, as calculated from known diagnostics (see text)

3 A Typology of Stone Tools

Type Descriptions and Contexts

A. Arrowheads and Projectile Points

(Figs. 3.1–3.3)
1. Transverse arrowheads
   a. concave triangles
   b. isosceles triangles
   c. rectangles/trapezoids
   d. microlithic lunates
2. Small points
   a. Nizzanim points (tanged)
   b. Haparsa points (winged)
   c. Herzliya points (leaf shaped)

TECHNOLOGY

The arrowheads found in Chalcolithic and Early Bronze Age assemblages were manufactured on bladelets (Bar-Yosef et al. 1971) and small elongate flakes. The truncated nature of most transverse arrowheads precludes precise definition of original blank morphology, but the presence of small blade/bladelet cores and mixed flake/bladelet cores on some sites (e.g., Rosen 1995; Henry and Turnbull 1985; Bar-Yosef et al. 1986), along with simple small blade/bladelets and flakes, suggests that the distinction is probably irrelevant. Retouch on the transverse arrowheads is usually semi-abrupt and abrupt, that is, blunt and approaching a 90° angle, and is rarely bipolar (worked using an anvil, from both top and bottom). Pressure retouch, often partially bifacial, is common on the small points, which were made on small blades and bladelets. There is no evidence for the use of the microburin technique, used commonly in the Epipaleolithic period for snapping bladelets to a desired size and shape.

TYPOLOGY

Transverse arrowheads (fig. 3.1) show a broad sharp edge. Within this group, concave triangles show lateral concavities forming almost a tang between them. They are somewhat smaller than the isosceles triangles, which show straight sides. Rectangles/trapezoids can be elongate or wide, and show lateral truncations. They may be backed or may show a sharp "back" edge. Microlithic lunates (fig. 3.1) are crescent shaped with backing. Notably, they are virtually indistinguishable from small Harifian and Late Natufian lunates, but never show Helwan backing and only rarely bipolar backing.

The small points (fig. 3.2) are divided according to basal characteristics (e.g., Gopher 1994, 30–42, for general typology; Burian and Friedman 1979). Nizzanim points and Haparsa points both show tangs, with pronounced shoulders or wings in the case of Haparsa points. Herzliya points are leaf shaped, occasionally even approaching oval. All three show pressure retouch covering much of the dorsal surface, and occasional bifacial retouch around the tang and point, and sometimes greater portions of the ventral surface. Symmetry is generally good.

FUNCTION

The assumption that the geometric microliths discussed here functioned as transverse arrowheads is based on (1) the discovery at (Old Kingdom) Sakkara, in Egypt, of transverse points still intact in shafts (e.g., Emery 1961, 113), (2) ethnographic parallels from Africa (e.g., Clark 1975–77; Wiessner 1983), and (3) roughly contemporary Old Kingdom Egyptian wall and palette reliefs showing the use of transverse points in arrowshafts (e.g., Clark et al. 1974; Emery 1961, 113, fig. 70). Additionally, in one case, transverse arrowheads have been recovered in association with a desert kite, an early animal drive-trap, at Wadi Mara in Sinai (A. Goren, pers. comm.). The case for microlithic lunates is somewhat less strong since they show no obvious tang for hafting, but they may well have been hafted obliquely. Ethnographically, transverse points have often been associated with the use of poison (Clark 1975–77).

The small points are identified as arrowheads by their morphology and size, rarely exceeding 4 cm in length. The size contrast with morphologically

Type List

A. ARROWHEADS AND PROJECTILE POINTS
    1. Transverse arrowheads
        a. concave triangles
        b. isosceles triangles
        c. rectangles/trapezoids
        d. microlithic lunates
    2. Small points
        a. Nizzanim points (tanged)
        b. Haparsa points (winged)
        c. Herzliya points (leaf-shaped)

B. SICKLE BLADES AND SEGMENTS
    1. Non-Canaanean prismatic blade technology
        a. backed, truncated segments
        b. simple truncated segments
    2. Canaanean technology
        a. truncated segments
        b. reaping knives
    3. Simple blade technology
        a. backed truncated segments
        b. arched backed blades
        c. simple blades and segments (unbacked)
    4. Flake-blades (Large Geometrics)
        a. parallelograms
        b. rectangles
        c. trapezoids
        d. triangles
        e. quadrilaterals
    5. Other

C. BACKED AND RETOUCHED BLADES
    1. retouched Canaanean blades and blade segments
    2. backed blades
        a. straight backed blades
        b. arched backed blades
    3. bitruncated blades (no backing)
    4. simple retouched blades

D. BLADELET TOOLS
    1. microendscrapers
    2. retouched twisted bladelets
    3. retouched bladelets

E. BORERS
    1. awls
    2. drills
    3. microlithic drills
        a. single shoulder
        b. double shoulder
        c. straight
        d. triangular
        e. narrow
    4. miscellaneous points

F. TABULAR SCRAPERS
    1. round
    2. oval
    3. elongate
    4. Fanscrapers
    5. knives
    6. irregular

G. BIFACIAL KNIVES AND INVASIVELY RETOUCHED PIECES
    1. roughouts
    2. bifacial knives
    3. unifacial knives

H. DISCS AND HOLED TOOLS
    1. discs
    2. holed discs
    3. stars

I. SCRAPERS
    1. endscrapers
        a. simple endscrapers
        b. tongue-shaped endscrapers
    2. sidescrapers
    3. steep scrapers
    4. small scrapers
    5. massive scrapers

J. NOTCHES AND DENTICULATES
    1. flat
        a. notches
        b. denticulates
    2. steep
        a. notches
        b. denticulates

K. RETOUCHED FLAKES AND PIECES

L. CELTS
    1. Axes
        a. straight edge
        b. rounded edge
    2. Adzes
    3. Chisels
    4. Picks
    5. Votive axes
    6. Miscellaneous
        a. roughouts
        b. other

M. CHOPPERS
    1. cobble choppers
    2. other choppers

N. EPHEMERAL TYPES
    1. Burins
    2. Threshing teeth

O. HAMMERSTONES
    1. spheroids
    2. pecked stones

TABLE 3.1.

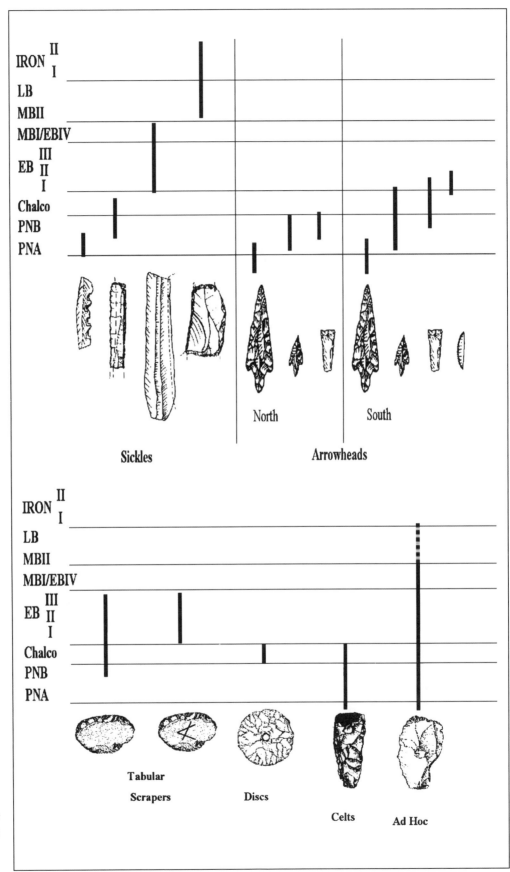

IRON II
     I
LB
MBII
MBI/EBIV
EB III
   II
   I
Chalco
PNB
PNA

Sickles

North   South

Arrowheads

IRON II
     I
LB
MBII
MBI/EBIV
EB III
   II
   I
Chalco
PNB
PNA

Tabular
Scrapers   Discs   Celts   Ad Hoc

FIG. 3.1. Chronological overview of selected major tool classes by general region.

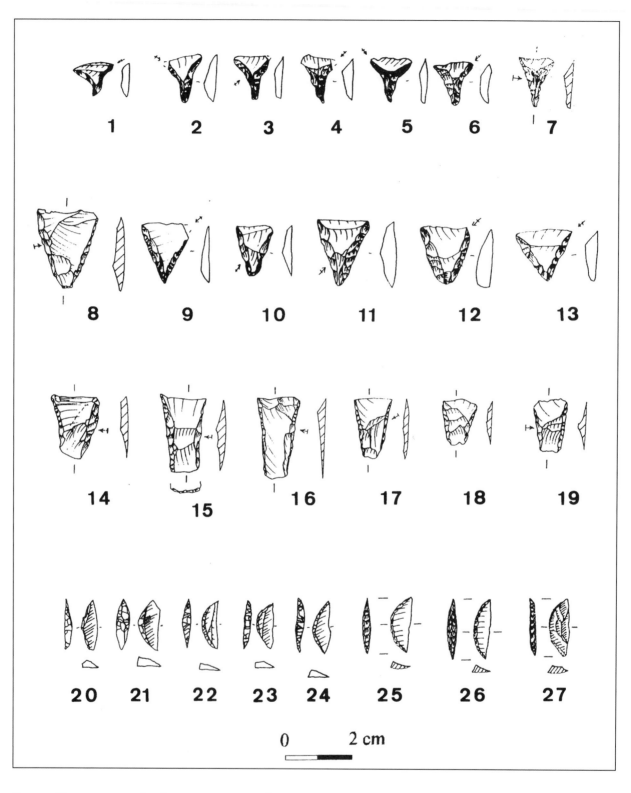

FIG. 3.2. *Transverse arrowheads. 1–7, concave triangles; 8–13, isosceles triangles; 14–19, rectangles/trapezoids; 20–27, microlithic lunates. (1–6, 9–13, Kvish Harif [Rosen 1984b, fig. 6]; 7–8, 14–19, Gebel Gunna [Bar-Yosef et al. 1986, figs. 7, 9, 11]; 20–24, Uvda Valley 9 [Rosen 1983c, fig.1])*

analogous but much larger Pre-Pottery Neolithic B types, and coincidence between the rise in the use of the small points and the general decline in the importance of hunting in Neolithic economies, suggests that this change is related somehow to hunting behavior, but a more detailed explanation cannot yet be tendered. It is tempting to see some parallel with the switch from dart points to arrowheads in the New World (e.g., Odell 1988), but exact analogy is difficult.

GEOGRAPHICAL DISTRIBUTION

For the periods under discussion, i.e., the post-Neolithic, these arrowheads are known almost exclusively from the desert regions, the Negev, Sinai (both north and south), and southern Jordan (see Gopher 1994, 221–25 for summary). They are notably totally absent from the Beersheva Chalcolithic horizon. In fact, with the exception of microlithic lunates found in Early Bronze I tombs at Azor, near Tel Aviv (Ben-Tor 1975; Rosen 1983c), and a few rare transverse arrowheads found at the Jordan Valley Chalcolithic site of Abu Hamid (Dollfus et al. 1988, fig. 14.3), chipped stone arrowheads in good contexts are unknown from the Mediterranean zone in the periods under discussion.

CHRONOLOGY

Arrowheads in the Levantine heartland disappear from the general material culture repertoire during the late Neolithic period, apparently in the transition from early to late Pottery Neolithic (figs. 3.3, 7.6). Within the Neolithic period, Gopher (1994, 226–43; also see Burian and Friedman 1979; Mortensen 1970; M. C. Cauvin 1974) has shown that typological changes can be traced and used as chronological indicators. The types described here appear first in the late Neolithic, the small points apparently somewhat earlier than the transverse arrowheads. Claims (Miller 1985) for the occurrence of these types in Early Bronze Age Syria, at Tell Hadidi, are most likely the result of mixture and

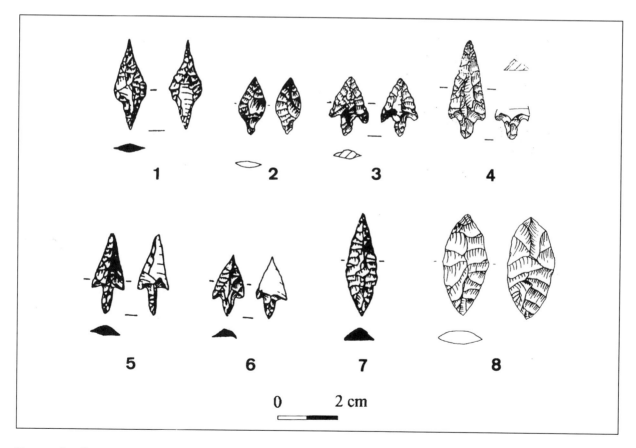

FIG. 3.3. *Small points. 1–2, Nizzanim points; 3–6, Harparsa points; 7–8, Herzliya points. (1, 5–7, Nahal Issaron [Gopher 1994, fig. 5.36a]; 2, 8, Kvish Harif [Rosen 1984b, fig. 7]; 3–4, Gebel Gunna [Bar-Yosef et al. 1986, fig. 11])*

disturbance in deeply stratified tell sites. It is interesting to note here that in the later publication of the materials from Jericho, Payne (1983) was explicit in attributing the arrowheads found in Early Bronze Age strata to the Neolithic occupation. In her earlier publication of the materials from Amuq, in Syria (Crowfoot Payne 1960), this is not clear, although in hindsight it may be considered in a similar light.

In the southern desert regions, the small points also predate the transverse arrowheads, appearing in the middle of the sixth millennium B.C.E. at sites such as Wadi Jibba, in western Sinai, and Qadesh Barnea 3, in eastern Sinai (Gopher 1994, 226–43). There is no clear chronological patterning to the small point subtypes, in contrast their Pre-Pottery Neolithic B analogues. It is difficult to precisely date their disappearance. They certainly occur in late fifth–early fourth millennium sites such as Kvish Harif, in the Central Negev (Rosen 1984b); Gunna 50, in south Sinai (Bar-Yosef et al. 1986, fig. 11); Nahal Issaron Stratum B, in the southern Negev (Goring-Morris and Gopher 1983); and Gebel Jill, in southern Jordan (Henry and Turnbull 1985); and may occur as late as the early–middle third millennium B.C.E., for example, the rare finds at Uvda Valley (Biqat Uvda) 9, in the southern Negev (Rosen 1983d, 214), and the Camel Site, in the Central Negev (Rosen 1995). However, with isolated finds, it is difficult to know if we are not dealing with collected pieces, as opposed to those actually a part of the material culture. Certainly, by the second half of the fourth millennium B.C.E., these points are very rare.

In the desert, transverse arrowheads seem to appear as a class in the late sixth to early fifth millennium B.C.E., as at Nahal Issaron (Goring-Morris and Gopher 1983) and other sites in the Uvda Valley. They seem to achieve a peak of popularity during the late fifth and fourth millennium B.C.E., and are present at least through Early Bronze II (in the form of microlithic lunates). They are absent from (unmixed) Middle Bronze I sites, although collection from these sites has not been as rigorous as might be desired.

The subtypes seem to follow a chronological pattern wherein the concave triangles are the earliest form, followed by isosceles triangles. Rectangles/trapezoids appear in the Chalcolithic and especially in the Early Bronze I, in the middle to late fourth millennium B.C.E., as in the Nawamis and associated sites in south Sinai (Bar-Yosef et al. 1977; Bar-Yosef et al. 1986), and in sites in north Sinai (Oren and Gilead 1981, fig.

11:9; I. Gilead pers. comm.). The microlithic lunates appear to be the final type, beginning perhaps as early as the Chalcolithic, but achieving their peak in the Early Bronze I and into the Early Bronze II (contradicting initial evaluations that viewed the chronological distribution as restricted to the Early Bronze I [Rosen 1984b]). Unfortunately, no reliable data are available from Egypt, which might provide a good control over some of the chronological ambiguities (cf. Baumgartel 1960, pl. 5:7).

B. Sickle Blades and Segments

(Figs. 3.4–3.19)

    1. Non-Canaanean prismatic blade technology
        a. backed, truncated segments
        b. simple truncated segments
    2. Canaanean technology
        a. truncated segments
        b. reaping knives
    3. Simple blade technology
        a. backed truncated segments
        b. arched backed blades
        c. simple blades and segments (unbacked)
    4. Flake-blades (Large Geometrics)
        a. parallelograms
        b. rectangles
        c. trapezoids
        d. triangles
        e. quadrilaterals

TECHNOLOGY

Four basic technologies were used for the manufacture of sickles in the post-Neolithic periods.

Non-Canaanean prismatic blade (called such because of the regular, prismlike scar patterns on the dorsal surface of the blades) production occurs primarily in the Chalcolithic period, although present in Early Bronze sites with Egyptian influence as well. Cores are usually single platform split cobbles (fig. 3.4), worked on a single face or two adjacent faces. Cortex is often retained on much of the core surface, although some examples show greater cortical removal, with lateral flake scars showing core trimming and preparation. Cores are not large, rarely exceeding 10 cm in length and usually averaging around 6–8 cm in length. Wadi cobbles, of striped flint originating geologically in Transjordan, are the most common raw materials for blade production in the

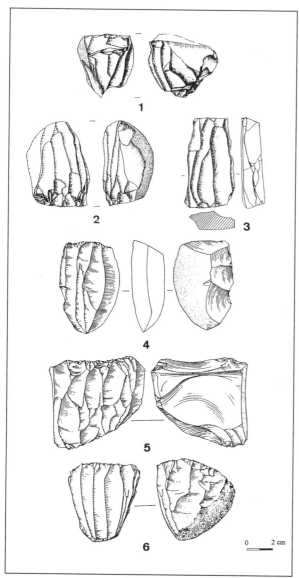

FIG. 3.4. *Non-Canaanean prismatic blade cores (Chalcolithic). (1–3, Grar [Gilead et al. 1995, fig. 5.7]; 4–6, Gaza A [Roshwalb 1981, fig. A.10])*

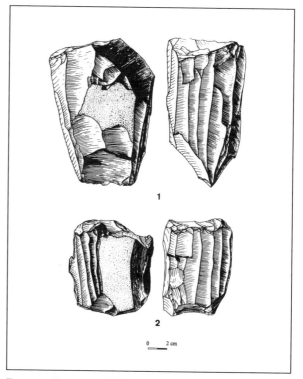

FIG. 3.5. *Canaanean blade cores. (Har Haruvim [Rosen 1983a, fig. 7])*

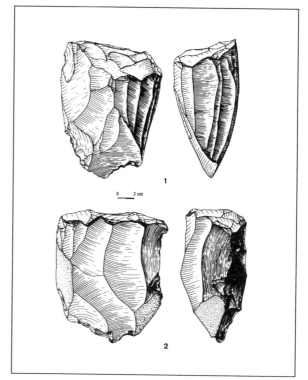

FIG. 3.6. *Canaanean blade cores. (Har Haruvim)*

Beersheva Basin from where most of our information derives. Other raw materials seem to have been utilized in other parts of the country, and it is likely that this would have affected blade production and proportions (cf. Kaufman 1987 for the Upper Paleolithic), but data are not available for reliable testing.

The blades themselves are relatively short. There is no evidence for platform preparation. Cross sections are variable, with trapezoid shapes typical, but lacking the regularity and long parallel ridges of Canaanean technology.

Backing and truncation retouch is usually dorsal abrupt (blunt) and semi-abrupt, although occasional pieces may show ventral truncations. Working edge retouch varies from nibbling to light serration, in the cases when retouch is present.

Canaanean technology is a specialized prismatic blade technology associated with the Early Bronze Age. Cores are large single platform blocks, worked on one to three faces, sometimes greater than 15 cm in length (figs. 3.5–3.6). The presence of decortication blades, that is, blades retaining external cortex, at many sites (e.g., fig. 3.7:1) indicates that cortical removal did not require elaborate lateral preparation, although ridge blades (core preparation blade removals) found at Saida Dakerman (Hours 1979) and En Shadud (Rosen 1985: figs. 41:1, 42:1; also Pelegrin and Otte 1991, fig. 43) indicate that preparation and/or rejuvenation did occur. Raw material is usually confined to brown, fine-grained Eocene nodules.

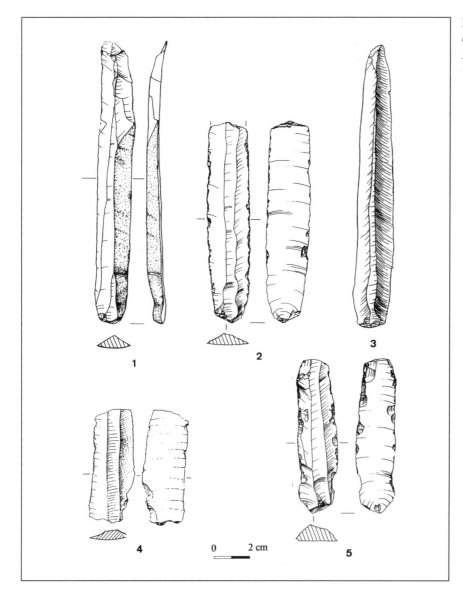

FIG. 3.7. *Canaanean blades and blade segments. (1–2, 5, Qasis; 3, Erani; 4, Yarmouth [Rosen 1988b, pl. 52])*

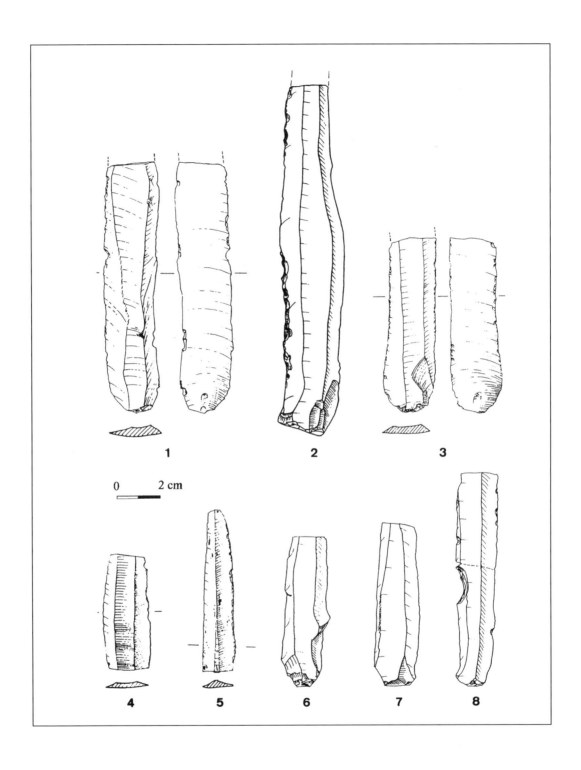

FIG. 3.8. *Canaanean blades and blade segments. (1, 3–5, Yarmouth [Rosen 1988b, pl. 52]; 2, 6–8, Beit Yerah)*

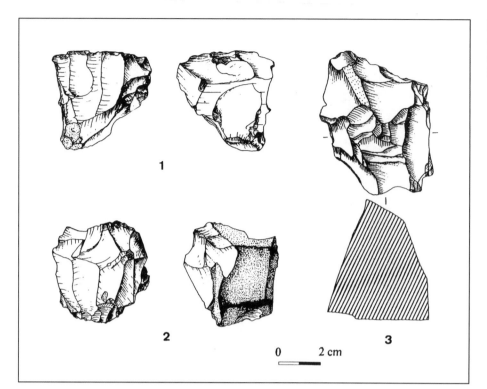

Fig. 3.9. *Mixed flake-blade cores. (1,3, Uvda Valley 16 [Rosen n.d.a]; 2, Mitnan [Rosen 1993b, fig. 1])*

0   2 cm

Blades are long and wide (figs. 3.7–3.8), usually averaging ca. 2 cm in width and sometimes achieving lengths of greater than 15 cm. Striking platforms are usually narrow relative to blade width (Crowfoot 1948) and often show facetting. Betts (1992a, 129) suggests a distinction between wide platforms in the Levant and punctiform platforms in Mesopotamia, implying different methods of blade removal. This is of importance, but remains to be studied in detail. Unlike the other sickle-producing technologies, for which a single blade could produce only a single sickle segment, the great length of Canaanean blades allows the snapping of the blades into several sections and use of each one as a sickle segment. One blade could conceivably have been used for as many as three segments, and the occasional use of proximal segments (the pieces retaining the bulb of percussion and the striking platform) for sickles supports the supposition that this indeed did occur. A deep negative bulb of percussion accompanied by lateral spurs from previous removals is often present adjacent to the striking platform (Crowfoot 1948). Distal ends are either feathered or hinged. The most striking feature of these blades, referred to as ribbon knives in early literature (e.g., Macalister 1912, 121–27; Petrie 1891, 49–50) is the pair of parallel ridges down the length of the dorsal surface, giving a trapezoidal cross section. Neuville

(1930, 1934a, 1934–35), who coined the term *Canaanean*, referred to them as *des couteaux à arêtes*, in regard to this feature.

Although it is clear that Canaanean technology produced other cross section shapes, for example, single ridge blades with triangular cross sections, the dominance of the parallel ridges and the great standardization in production indicate that the shape was deliberately sought. This conscious selection, along with the facetted platforms, suggests the use of indirect percussion (the use of a punch), which would provide considerably more accuracy in knapping. Indeed, the discovery of a pointed horn core in association with a Canaanean core at Lahav (Futato 1990; Forshey 1987) confirms this suggestion. Replication experiments (Otte et al 1990) suggest that indirect percussion using copper punches may have also been employed. Interestingly, the facetting of platforms, usually associated with creating a raised platform for direct percussion, would seem to render the use of a punch redundant. The rationale is unclear.

Backing on Canaanean sickles is virtually absent. Some rare pieces seem to show a kind of burin-blow backing (that is, a longitudinal blow along the length of the piece), but it is difficult to know if this is intentional or the result of longitudinal breakage. Truncation retouch is abrupt and semi-abrupt, almost always dorsal. Some pieces may be deliberately snapped. It is difficult to distinguish a deliberate snap from a broken end when the segment itself is of the appropriate length for hafting (ca. 5 cm). Edge retouch varies from nibbling to serration, on one or both edges. Up to 40% of the sickles from any particular assemblage may show ventral nibbling or serration on one or both edges. A similar percentage may show some kind of retouch on two edges, indicating blade reversal in the haft.

Simple blades were manufactured from mixed flake-blade cores (fig. 3.9), considerably less standardized in size and shape than the two technologies described above. In northern areas, these blades are probably by-products of *ad hoc* flake manufacture and are difficult to characterize. They constitute only a small percentage of any sickle assemblage. They are generally short, with little evidence for either core or platform preparation. Raw materials vary considerably. In the desert regions, these blades constitute the

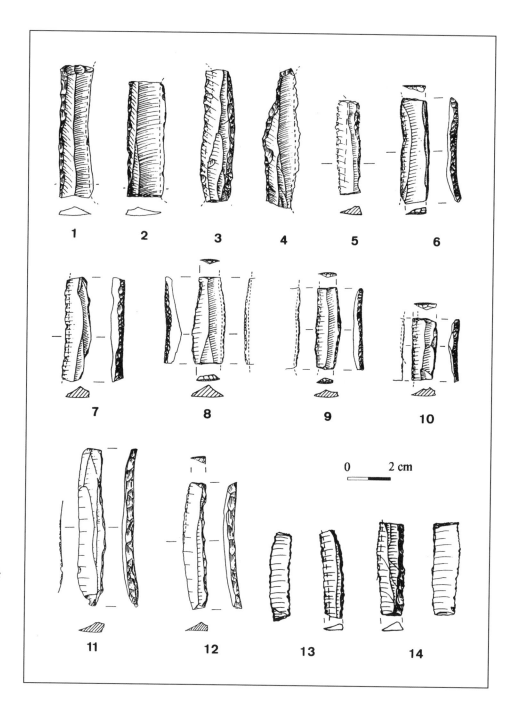

FIG. 3.10. *Backed blade sickles (Chalcolithic). (1–2, Tell Qitan; 3–4, Ghassul [Mahan 1940, pl. 110]; 5, Yarmouth [Rosen 1988b, pl. 51]; 6–10, Sataf; 11–12, Grar [Gilead et al. 1995, pl. 5.18]; 13–14, Shiqmim [Levy and Rosen 1987, fig.10.1])*

primary technology for the manufacture of sickles in those sites or areas where sickles do occur (e.g., the Uvda Valley, in the southern Negev). Cores are usually on the order of 5–10 cm in maximal length. There is little evidence for sophisticated preparation, although reduction tends to remove much of the cortex, suggesting greater than minimal exploitation.

Backing and truncation retouch is similar to that described for the non-Canaanean prismatic blades. Occasionally pieces were used without either backing or truncation. There is rarely retouch on the working edge beyond use damage.

Flake/blades, utilized in the manufacture of post–Early Bronze Age Large Geometric sickle segments, are fundamentally different in morphology from the above blade technologies. Although no cores related to the manufacture of these sickles have yet been recovered, caches of unworked flake/blades and incomplete sickles have been recovered at the large tell sites of Gezer, in Central Israel (Rosen 1986) and Dan, in the far north (pers. obs.). The unworked blanks are usually elongate flakes with pronounced bulbs of percussion and relatively narrow striking platforms relative to the width of the flakes. There is rarely evidence for facetting or other obvious forms of platform preparation, but there is high standardization in flake shape and size, averaging roughly 5–6 cm in length and 3–4 cm in width. Raw material is often, but not exclusively, the fine-grained brown Eocene flint utilized for Canaanean blade production.

Backing and truncation retouch is usually semi-abrupt, only rarely achieving truly abrupt angles. Naturally backed pieces, that is, retaining cortex along the back edge, are not uncommon. Ventral retouch occurs, especially on the bulbar end, where it was often apparently used for bulbar thinning, presumably to facilitate hafting. Occasionally, truncation totally removes the bulb. Working edge retouch spans nibbling through heavy serration. Some pieces, especially those lacking sickle gloss, may lack working edge retouch.

The four technologies described above are clearly discrete when examined as assemblages or as technologies. They utilized different techniques of core preparation, different raw materials, and perhaps different forms of percussion. These resulted in different products, varying in size and shape, and these blanks were modified using varying kinds of retouch. However, all these techniques produce a range of blades

and blanks that overlap with each other at their extremes. There will always be ambiguities at the level of classification of individual artifacts. "Obvious" Canaanean blades have been recovered from Pre-Pottery Neolithic B contexts, produced from classic PPNB bipolar naviform cores. The less standardized techniques are even more prone to overlap, accenting the need for assemblage level study and not the subjective comparison of individual artifacts.

TYPOLOGY

Sickle segments manufactured on non-Canaanean prismatic blades can be divided into two types, backed truncated segments (figs. 3.10, 3.12:7), and simple, unbacked truncated segments (figs. 3.11:3, 6–10). The backed truncated segments (Rosen 1982) are typical of most Ghassulian-Beersheva Chalcolithic sickle assemblages and are typical of the northern Chalcolithic as well. In addition, Early Bronze I Egyptian sickle segments, found at Erani (Rosen 1988a) and other sites (e.g., Gophna and Friedman 1993) fall into this category as well and indeed were initially assumed to be Chalcolithic. Morphologically, the sickles are elongate rectangles. The unbacked segments, showing only truncations, are also especially common in the Early Bronze I Egyptian horizon at Erani, but notably are also typical of the Qatifian Late Neolithic culture of the northern Negev (Gilead 1990).

Canaanean sickles can be divided into two types, sickle segments (figs 3.13, 3.14:4–7) and reaping knives (fig. 3.14:1–3), that is, complete blades utilized without truncation. Breakage is a major problem in identification of subtype. Unbroken segments usually show at least one truncated end. Retouch may be present on one or both lateral edges and may be dorsal or ventral, although dorsal retouch is more common. Reaping knives show little modification beyond working edge retouch.

Sickles based on simple blade technologies are divided into three types. Backed bitruncated segments (figs. 3.11:2, 4–5, 3.12:4–6), in fact, closely resemble Chalcolithic types based on prismatic blades. Typologically there is little to distinguish them, although examination of associated cores and debitage reveals the technological distinction outlined above. Arched backed blade sickles ("macrolunates") show crescent-shaped backing (fig. 3.12:1–2), obviating the need for truncations (also, atypically, fig. 3.12:3). Simple blade sickles show either truncations or no blade modification at all (fig. 3.11:1).

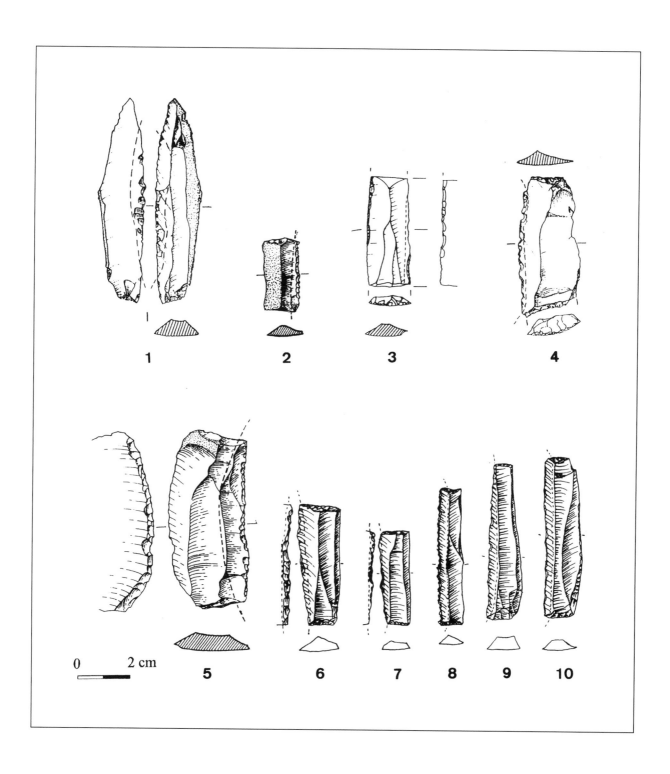

FIG. 3.11. 1–5, *sickles on simple blades (nonbacked); 6–10,*
sickles on non-Canaanean prismatic blades (nonbacked).
(1, 4–5, Uvda Valley 16 [Rosen n.d.a]; 2, Hartuv [Rosen
n.d.b]; 3, Grar [Gilead et al. 1995, fig. 5:18]; 6–10, Erani
[Rosen 1988a, fig. 6])

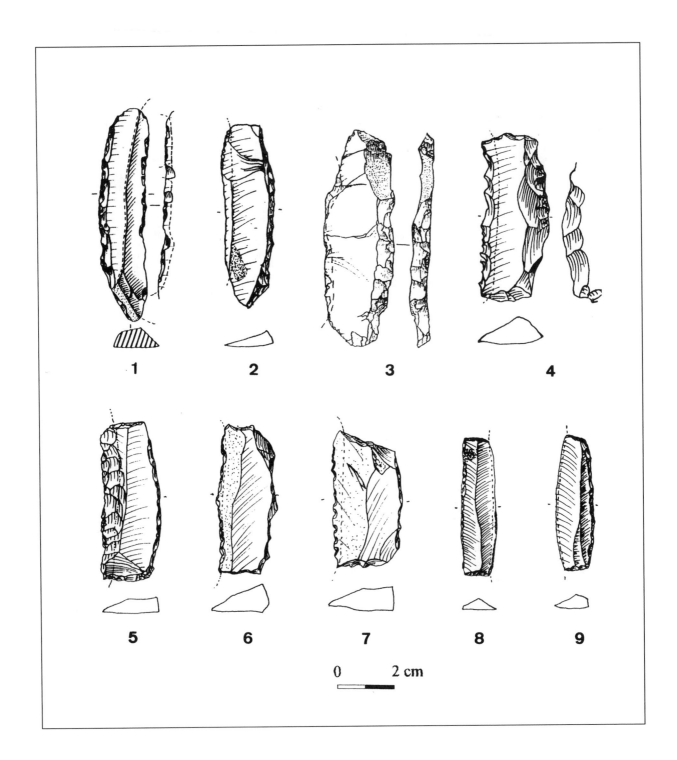

FIG. 3.12. *Backed sickle segments (non-Chalcolithic).
1–2, arched backed blade sickles; 3, backed blade sickle
without truncations; 4–9, backed truncated sickle
segments. (1, Mitnan [Rosen 1993b, fig. 1]; 2–3, Uvda
Valley 16 [Rosen n.d.a]; 4–7, selected Negev Iron Age sites
[Haiman 1988, fig. 55]; 8–9, Erani [Rosen 1988a, fig. 6])*

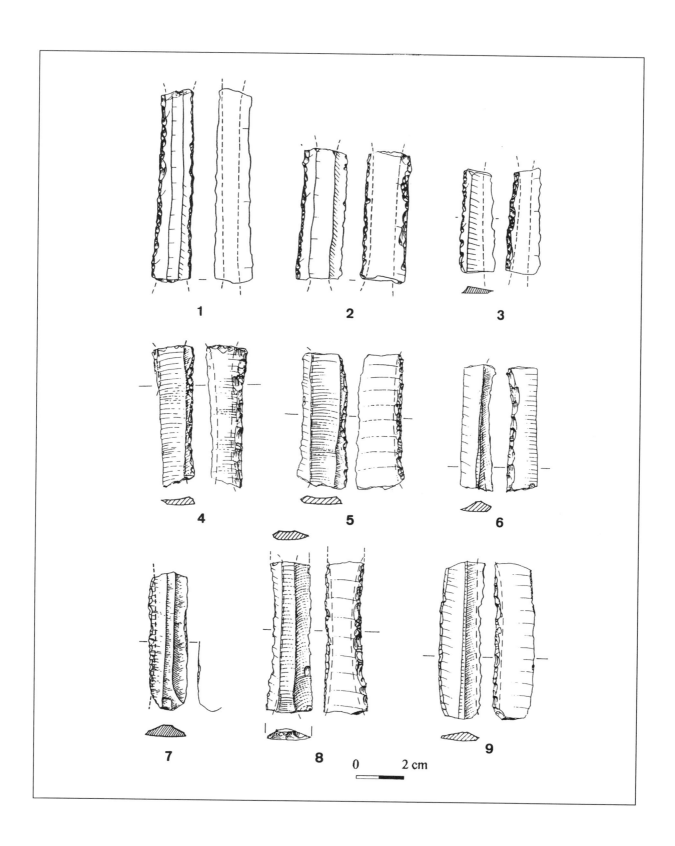

FIG. 3.13. *Canaanean sickle segments. (1–3, Beit Yerah; 4–6, 8–9, Yarmouth [Rosen 1988b, pl. 51]; 7, Hartuv [Rosen n.d.b])*

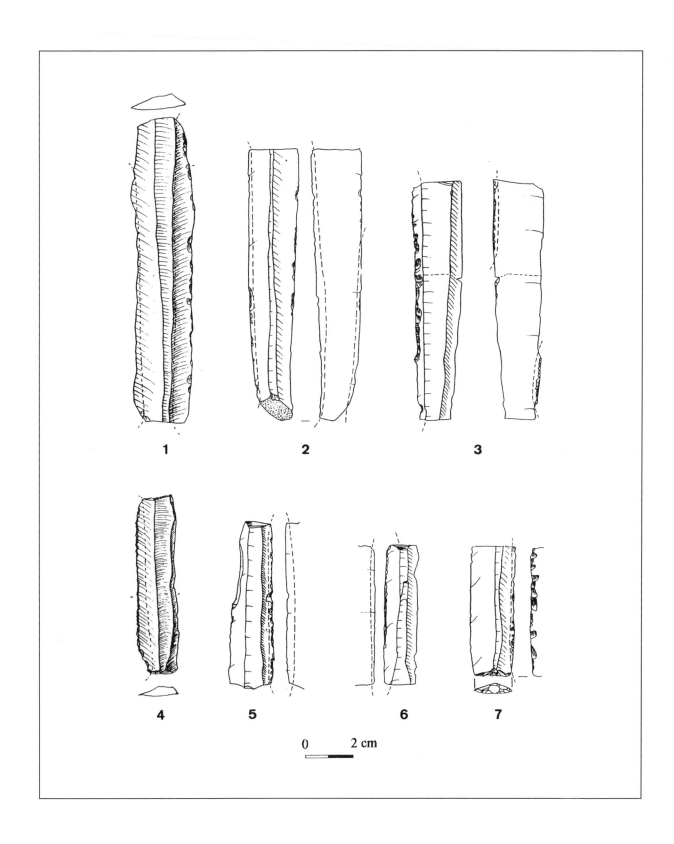

FIG. 3.14. *Canaanean sickles. 1–3, reaping knife fragments; 4–7, sickle segments. (1, Sha'ar Hagolan; 2–3, 5–7, Beit Yerah; 4, Hesi)*

Large Geometric sickles (figs. 3.15–3.16), based on flake/blade technology, are divided by geometric shape, determined by the direction of the truncations (see typological list). Variation occurs especially in the presence or absence of backing and the occasional exploitation of natural cortical backing. Triangles show oblique backs, obviating the need for truncation on one edge. There is some overlap between types since truncations are not always straight, nor are angles always consistent.

Other sickles are those which do not fall into the categories listed above.

FUNCTION

The artifacts classified here as sickles are identified as such on the basis of the presence of sickle gloss (luster, sheen, polish) on the working edge of the tool and a general morphology appropriate to reaping. Sickle gloss as characteristic of reaping grasses has been recognized as such at least since the 1930s (e.g., Curwen 1930), and controversies over interpretation date to the same period (Neuville 1934–35; Curwen 1930, 1935). There is a general consensus that reaping of grasses results in sickle gloss (e.g., Anderson 1980; Unger-Hamilton 1984; Witthoft 1967; Semenov 1976, 115–22), and may form in as little as a few hours of work, although accumulating enough to preserve archaeologically may require more time (Unger-Hamilton 1989). However, it has also been recognized that lustrous edges may result from other actions as well, including cutting of canes and reeds, woodworking, and perhaps even hoeing or digging (cf. discussions in Curwen 1930, 1935; Neuville 1934–35; Anderson 1980; Unger-Hamilton 1984, 1991). In some cases, it may be possible to distinguish the different types of gloss, either macro- or microscopically. The actual formation of sickle gloss (as opposed to other polishes) has also been the subject of debate, the question focusing on whether gloss results from the abrasive polishing of the silica inherent in the flint artifact (Meeks et al. 1982) or is a silica coating, added from the silica in the grasses harvested (Anderson 1980; Unger-Hamilton 1984). Anderson and Inizan (1994) have also recently suggested that some gloss

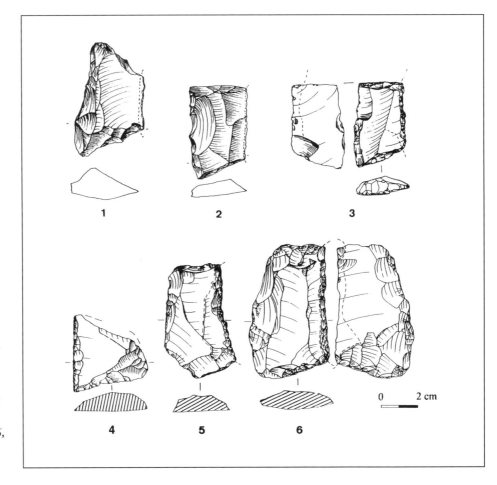

FIG. 3.15.
Large Geometric sickles.
1–3, trapezoids;
4, triangle (nonglossy);
5–6, quadrilaterals.
(1, Deir el Balah; 2, Tell Hesi; 3, Qasis; 4, Gezer [Rosen 1986, fig. 1]; 5–6, Ashdod [Rosen 1993c, fig. 49])

FIG. 3.16. *Large Geometric sickles. 1–4, incomplete or
unused (nonglossy); 5–6, parallelograms; 7–9, rectangles.
(1, 6–7, Qasis; 2–4, 8, Gezer [Rosen 1986, fig. 1];
9, Ashdod [Rosen 1993c, fig. 49])*

may derive from use as threshing teeth. The hypothesis still remains to be confirmed in more studies.

Much of this debate on the meaning of sickle gloss seems directed at understanding the rise of agriculture and the use of sickles as indicators of reaping grasses in Epipaleolithic and early Neolithic societies (e.g., Unger-Hamilton 1989). In post-Neolithic societies, where agricultural economies are well documented from a wide range of types of evidence, the problem seems less pronounced. These groups unquestionably engaged in agriculture using sickles, as documented from the texts, if nothing else. The identification of the artifacts described here as sickles seems eminently sound.

However, the equation *gloss + morphology = sickle* leaves open the question of morphologically appropriate pieces without gloss. Thus, Gilead (1973) identified nonglossy backed blades at the Middle Bronze I site of Har Yeruham as sickles, as did Noy and Cohen (1974) at the PPNB site of Nahal Boker. The fact that gloss does *not* seem to require a great amount of reaping before it begins to appear suggests that such identifications are suspect. However, archaeological context may also play a role here. At sites where glossy blades of a particular morphology are found, it is reasonable to assume that there will be sickles that have been used for differing lengths of time. This can also be seen, for example, in the differing degrees of working edge retouch, actually a measure of resharpening. Unused sickles, in small quantities, should be expected to form one end of a spectrum. Thus, morphological sickles lacking gloss, if found in small numbers or in contexts suggesting production (e.g., Gezer [Rosen 1986]), can be identified as incomplete or unused sickles. Obviously, such information can be of great significance in economic reconstructions. On the other hand, the total absence of glossy blades at Har Yeruham suggests that Gilead's (1973) identification of nonglossy backed blades as sickles is inappropriate (and similarly for Nahal Boker PPNB [Noy and Cohen 1974]). Notably, assemblages with glossy blades and high numbers of morphologically similar blade tools lacking gloss probably reflect multiple functions, as at Tel Erani (Rosen 1988a) and Uvda Valley (e.g., Rosen n.d.a).

Beyond identifying glossy blades as sickles used in reaping, different forms of sickles probably functioned differently. The morphologies of the different composite sickles can be reconstructed on the basis of truncation shape, direction and location of gloss along the working edge (Cauvin 1973), and presence of adhesive on a few rare pieces (e.g., Marder et al 1995; Schick 1978). If the precise difference in functions cannot be identified without experimental work, certainly the differences in form are recognizable and may correspond, at least partially, to functional variability.

All the sickles from these periods seem to have been hafted along their backs, parallel to the working edge, and not daggerlike, with a proximal handle. This is a logical necessity for segments that require parallel haft to be held in place. Backing retouch probably facilitates this type of hafting. Furthermore, the presence of bitumen along the back edge of long Canaanean reaping knives (Schick 1978) indicates that these pieces too were hafted along the edge. Bitumen has also been found on the edges of Canaanean segments (Schick 1978, Marder et al. 1995) and possible other adhesives have been found on the backs of Large Geometric segments (e.g., Deir el Balah [Rosen and Goring-Morris n.d.a]). Additionally, the Solferino sickle (Curwen 1930; Gilead 1973) preserved large geometric segments intact in a haft. Notably, Natufian (e.g., Garrod and Bate 1937, plate XIII:1,3) and PPNB (Bar-Yosef and Alon 1988, 16–19, pl. V) examples are also known.

Placement of the segments in the haft can be reconstructed by reference to truncation angles and direction of gloss lines relative to the working edge (e.g., Cauvin 1973, 1983b). The first point to be considered is that gloss lines rarely penetrate more than 0.5 cm onto the face of the segments. This, combined with the remains of adhesive quite close to the gloss lines on a few pieces, indicates that in most cases from one-half to three-quarters of the width of any blade was embedded in the handle or covered by adhesive, thus ensuring a tight-fitting blade. Cauvin (1973) has demonstrated the likelihood of a toothy haft design for at least some Neolithic sickles, based on diagonal appearance of gloss lines. Later period sickles do not show such patterns, and gloss lines run almost invariably parallel or near parallel to working edges.

Truncation angles on large geometric sickles indicate clearly that these were mounted in a crescent shape, a classic sickle. Triangular segments probably functioned as end pieces of such sickles, and this is supported by a relatively constant ratio of triangles to other shapes of between 1:5 and 1:8. Such a ratio would produce composite blades of roughly 30–40 cm in length, the generally expected length of sickles as based on those found intact at Solferino (Curwen

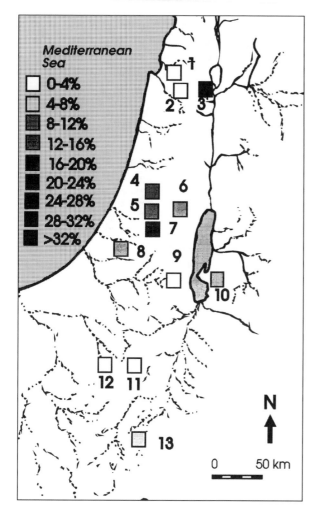

FIG. 3.17. *Map showing sickle percentages at selected Early Bronze Age sites. 1. Yiftahel (Rosen and Grinblatt n.d.); 2. En Shadud (Rosen 1985); 3. Beit Yerah (Rosen, unpublished); 4. Lower Horvat Illin (Marder et al. 1995); 5. Hartuv (Rosen n.d.b); 6. Ir David (Rosen n.d.d); 7. Yarmouth 1982 (Rosen 1988b); 8. Hesi (Rosen 1983d); 9. Arad K (Schick pers. comm., cited in Rosen 1983b); 10. Bab edh Dhra (McConaughy 1979); 11. Camel Site (unpublished); 12. Har Horsha (Rosen 1991); 13. combined Early Bronze Age Uvda Valley sites (Rosen 1983d).*

1930; Gilead 1973) and nearly intact at Lachish (Mozel 1983). The introduction of this type of curved sickle is probably a significant innovation.

Straight truncated segments, i.e., Canaanean sickle segments and non-Canaanean prismatic types, were probably also hafted in a crescent or sickle shape, since otherwise there would be little need for truncated elements. The long Canaanean reaping knives were probably hafted in a straight line, perhaps only one to a sickle. The angled truncations of the Large Geometrics may have provided a tighter fit or match in the curved haft than straight truncations.

Hafting of arched backed blade sickles is difficult to reconstruct. Speculating, the haft notch in the handle may have been filled with adhesive, and these blades pressed in place. In such a case, composite blade shape is not reflected in truncation angle.

GEOGRAPHY

The geographic frequency distribution of sickle segments corresponds to the practice of agriculture using sickles. Thus, fig. 3.17 shows how Early Bronze Age assemblages from desert areas generally show proportionally fewer sickles than those from the Mediterranean zone. Variability in frequencies within agricultural regions, such as the difference between the Beersheva Basin Chalcolithic and the Besor variant (Gilead 1988, 1989; Rosen 1987) may well reflect different intensities of agricultural practices. Similarly, in the desert regions, in the Early Bronze Age, Arad (Rosen 1983b for percentage data from T. Schick, pers. comm.) and the Uvda Valley sites show similar frequencies of sickle segments, but in the intervening Negev Highlands frequencies are much lower. Again, this probably reflects degrees of agricultural exploitation.

Typological contrasts exist between the north and south as well (fig. 3.18). In the Early Bronze Age, the areal extension of Canaanean technologies extends as far south as Arad and the Beersheva Basin, but does not extend into the Negev Highlands or farther south (discounting the occurrence of a few "Canaanean" blades, probably trade items, at Uvda Valley and at Maadi, in Egypt [Rizkana and Seeher 1985]). Interestingly, Canaanean technology is apparently rare at Bab edh Dhra (McConaughy 1979, 218), although present at Numeira (McConaughy 1980a, 1980b). Remaining in the Early Bronze Age, the presence of backed blade and arched backed blade sickles in the Negev complements the absence of Canaanean sickles. This probably is a reflection of differences in production-distribution systems (Chapter 4).

In the Middle Bronze I, Canaanean sickles are again restricted to the Mediterranean zone. Although sickles in general are unknown from the Negev Middle Bronze I, in North Sinai, backed blade sickles have been recovered from Middle Bronze I sites. However, given the surface nature of the sites and the absence of information on Egyptian sickle segments from the First Intermediate period, it is not yet certain that these are not intrusive from the Chalcolithic, also known in the area.

A similar desert-Mediteranean zone contrast occurs in the Iron Age, with Large Geometric sickles extending to the Beersheva Basin, but backed and arched backed blade sickles dominating the south, as at Qadesh Barnea (Cohen 1986, pl. 140:6–7, 10–13; also Haiman 1986, 93; 1988, fig. 55).

CHRONOLOGY

Sickles are the longest-lasting lithic type in the post-Paleolithic Levant. Lustrous blades are known as early as the Epipaleolithic and continue into the Iron II. The precise date of cessation of flint sickle production is difficult to pin down, but data from Batashi,

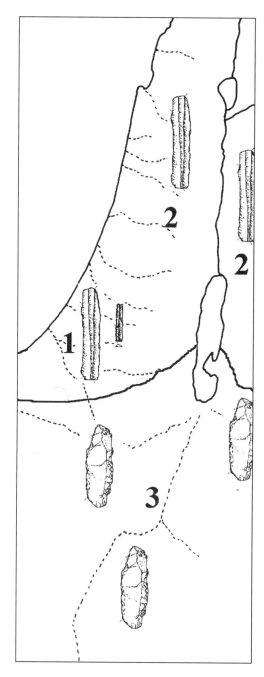

FIG. 3.18. *Summary map of sickle type distribution in the Early Bronze Age. Area 1 shows both Canaanean sickles, as well as Egyptian types. Area 2 shows only Canaanean sickles, and Area 3 shows simple backed and nonbacked sickles, when they are present at all.*

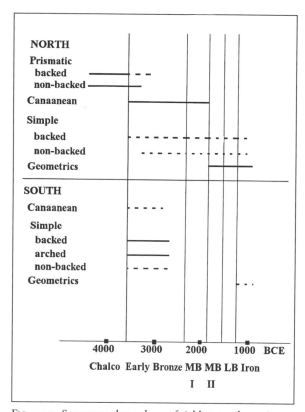

FIG. 3.19. *Summary chronology of sickle types by region.*

one of the few well-collected and stratigraphically closely controlled excavations for which data are available, suggest that by the eighth century B.C.E. at the latest, flint sickles have dropped out of the Iron Age material culture repertoire (see Chapter 7). The apparent presence of flint sickles in later horizons, as at Persian Period Hesi (Bennett et al. 1989) is almost undoubtedly the result of mixing and intrusions from earlier strata.[1]

Typologically there are clear chronological patterns, summarized in fig. 3.19 (also fig. 3.3). The Chalcolithic period all over the Southern Levant is dominated by non-Canaanean prismatic backed blade sickles.[2] Canaanean sickles dominate the areas north of the Negev in the Early Bronze Age, and backed blade sickles, especially arched backed blade sickles, are diagnostic of the south. Canaanean sickles continue into the Middle Bronze I/Early Bronze IV horizon in the north and cease with the Middle Bronze II (*contra* Jacobs 1984 and Warburton 1980, again with problems of stratigraphic mixture [see Seger et al. 1990 for general discussion of the Lahav stratigraphy]). The Middle Bronze I/Early Bronze IV horizon in the south lacks sickles. Canaanean sickles are replaced by Large Geometric sickles in the Middle Bronze II. In the Negev, Iron Age sickles are on backed and arched backed blades. Notably, simple backed or truncated sickles appear in all periods, probably on the edge of general typological variation, and also functioning as *ad hoc* substitutions for more standardized and specialized types.

Several attempts have been made to refine within period dating of sickles using intra-type attribute analysis. Thus, Waechter (1958) suggested that MBI/EBIV Canaanean sickles were wider than their Early Bronze Age predecessors. Hanbury-Tenison (1986, 148) adopted this idea and extended it as a general trend toward increasing width through the Early Bronze Age, from early to late, and Betts (1992a) makes a similar claim based on the material from Um Hammad. However, the trend is confounded the moment one extends the analysis to data beyond two or three sites. Thus, for example, the Canaanean sickles of Arad Early Bronze I–II (e.g., Schick 1978) are wider than those of Hesi EBIII (Rosen 1983a). Raw materials clearly play a major role here. Dever's (1973) reference to "decaying" Canaanean blades in the MBI at Jebel Qa'aqir is simply inappropriate, conveying no information.

Although Large Geometric sickles seem to show a general trend toward declining length from the Middle Bronze II period to the Iron II (Rosen 1982), the variability in the samples is great, and there are too few assemblages from the MBII. Although there are obvious metric differences between sites and levels, it is not clear how much these really constitute a chronological trend. For example, there are clear metric/shape differences between strata XII and XIII at Ashdod, but these should probably be interpreted as reflecting a specific event, a new knapper perhaps, and not a general trend (Rosen 1993c).

C. Backed and Retouched Blades

(Figs. 3.20–3.23)
1. retouched Canaanean blades and blade segments
2. backed blades
    a. straight backed blades
    b. arched backed blades
3. bitruncated blades (no backing)
4. simple retouched blades

TECHNOLOGY

The basic technologies used to produce backed and retouched blades are those same technologies described for sickles and will not be reiterated here. In general, it is likely that many of the blade tools described here were by-products of sickle manufacture. Exceptions are the bitruncated blades (and backed bitruncated blades) associated with the Egyptian materials from Early Bronze Age Erani (Rosen 1988a), and the arched backed blades found in abundance in Early Bronze Age sites in the Uvda Valley.

Retouch type varies with tool type. In general, backing retouch, when present, is abrupt and occasionally bipolar. Truncations are abrupt to semi-abrupt. Working edge retouch ranges from edge damage and nibbling to irregular denticulation. The regular serration common to sickle blades is virtually absent from backed and retouched blades.

Raw materials vary. The Canaanean blade tools, like the Canaanean sickles, are produced on relatively fine-grained, brown Eocene flint. The Egyptian backed/truncated blade segments at Erani were manufactured, for the most part, from a coarser, gray flint. Other types seem to reflect the availability of local materials.

FIG. 3.20. *Backed and retouched blades. 1–3, 5–6, retouched Canaanean blades and segments; 4, atypical retouched Canaanean blade; 7–11, backed truncated blade segments (Egyptian). (1–2, Beit Yerah; 3, Sataf; 4, Yarmouth [Rosen 1988b, pl. 52]; 5–6, Hartuv (Rosen n.d.b]; 7–11, Erani [Rosen 1988a, fig. 3])*

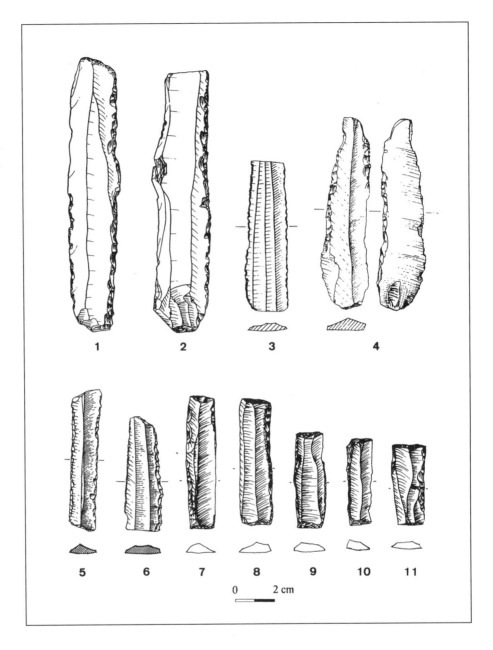

TYPOLOGY

Retouched Canaanean blades and segments (fig. 3.20:1–6) are defined by their technology, the presence of retouch, and the absence of gloss that would define them as sickles. There is little standardization in retouch. These pieces are rarely truncated or backed.

Backed blades are divided into two types, straight backed (figs. 3.20:7–11; 3.21:1–4) and arched backed (fig. 3.21:5–9). Straight backed blades can be divided on the attribute level according to metric attributes and the presence/absence of truncations. Thus, the backed truncated blades[3] from Early Bronze Age Erani (fig. 3.20:7–11) fall into a group with the bitruncated

(non-Canaanean) blades from the same site (fig. 3.22:1–7) and can be attributed to the Egyptian presence there (Rosen 1988a; also Yeivin 1976; Gophna and Friedmann 1993 for other sites, and Schmidt 1992a, 1992b for Egypt). They contrast technologically with the Canaanean materials on the site and with the backed blades from the Negev Early Bronze Age, as from the Uvda Valley, in their standardization in truncations, and metrics, being significantly shorter.[4]

Arched backed blades (macrolunates) are crescent shaped and therefore lack truncations. Cross sections are quadrilateral or triangular in shape. Backing is usually abrupt, sometimes bipolar. Edge retouch is

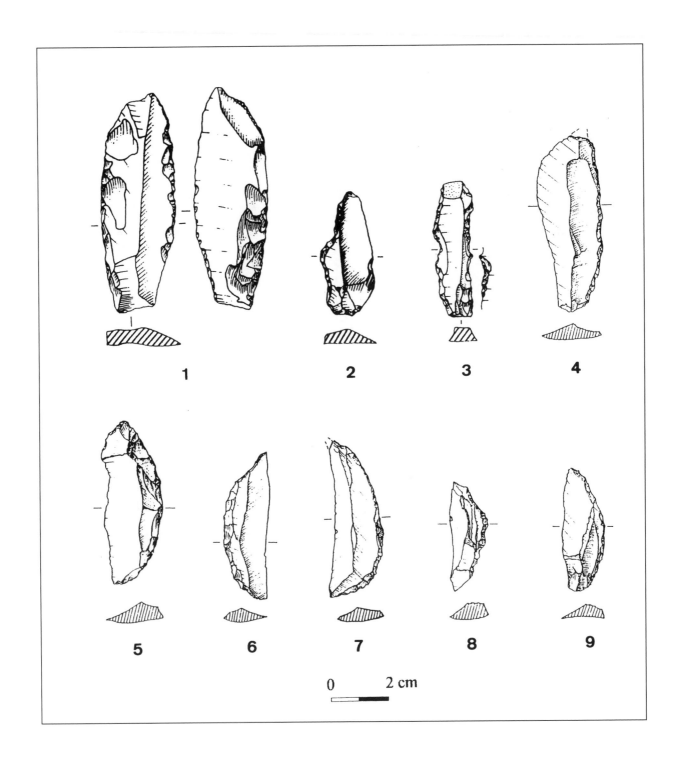

FIG. 3.21. *Backed and retouched blades. 1–4, backed blades; 5–9 arched backed blades. (1–3, Mitnan [Rosen 1993b, figs. 1–2]; 4–9, Uvda Valley 16 [Rosen n.d.a])*

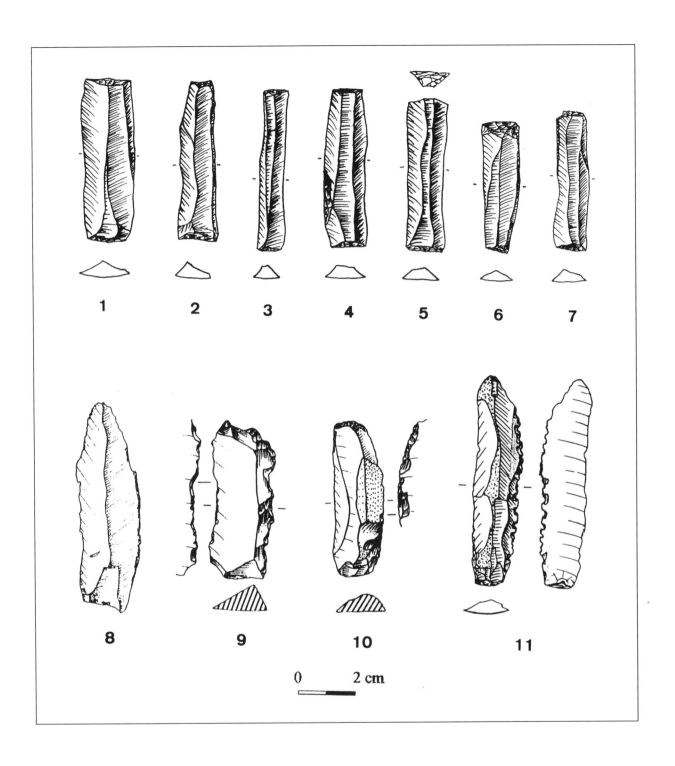

FIG. 3.22. *Backed and retouched blades. 1–7, bitruncated blades (nonbacked, Egyptian); 8–11, simple retouched blades. (1–7, Erani [Rosen 1988a, fig. 2]; 8, Uvda Valley 16 [Rosen n.d.a]; 9–10, Mitnan [Rosen 1993c, fig. 2]; 11, En Besor, Gophna and Friedman 1993, fig. 5])*

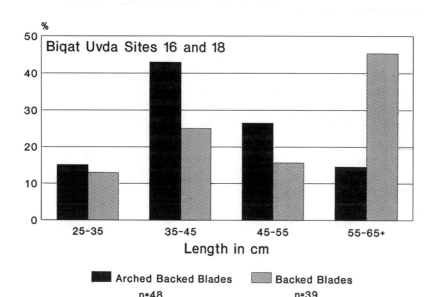

FIG. 3.23. *Length frequencies of arched backed blades and straight backed blades from Uvda Valley 16 and 18 (combined).*

rare. Although in the wider scheme, arched backed blades can be seen as part of the spectrum of variability in backed blades, under certain circumstances they indeed seem to constitute a distinct type. Thus, at the Early Bronze Age Uvda Valley sites, aside from morphological distinctiveness, there is a clear metric distinction between the backed blades and the arched backed blades (fig. 3.23), the arched pieces being shorter.

Bitruncated blades usually seem to be a variant of backed truncated blades, but are included as a distinct type because they are found in large numbers at Early Bronze Age Erani, where they seem to be associated with an Egyptian presence (Rosen 1988a). At Erani these pieces are highly standardized, measuring roughly 4–5 cm in length, 1.2–1.8 cm in width, and 0.2–0.5 cm in thickness, the standardization supporting the idea of a distinct type. Of course, they constitute a distinct type within Egyptian lithic assemblages of this period as well (Schmidt 1992a).

Beyond these relatively standardized types lies a wide range of simple retouched blades (fig. 3.22: 8–11). These can be divided according to specific attributes, but in fact show little standardization and great variability.

FUNCTION

Specific functions of the backed and retouched blade class are difficult to ascertain. Certainly in some cases these tools are simply unused sickles, unidentified because they represent morphologically atypical variants. However, edge damage and retouch on many of these pieces indicate other uses. McConaughy's (1979, 250–51) microscopic analyses of damage and polish on backed and retouched blades at Bab edh Dhra, on the eastern shore of the Dead Sea, suggests their general use as knives. Backing suggests hafting, indicating longer, composite blades, suggesting slicing and cutting. Notably, the hafts would prevent deep cutting; these are not saws as we recognize in metal tools.

GEOGRAPHIC DISTRIBUTION

As a general class, backed and retouched blades are found throughout the Levant. However, intraperiod type distributions are more restricted.

As with Canaanean sickles, retouched Canaanean blades are more or less restricted to the Beersheva Basin and north. The type, and the technology, extends throughout the Near East. As noted for sickles, the discovery of a few of these in Egypt (Rizkana and Seeher 1985) has been attributed to exchange, and the same is likely for the few retouched Canaanean blades found in the Uvda Valley.

Backed blades as a general class also appear throughout the Levant. During the Chalcolithic, they appear to be an adjunct to sickle manufacture. In the Early Bronze Age, they are eclipsed by Canaanean technology in the Mediterranean zone, but are very common in the desert. Arched backed blades are especially common in the Uvda Valley in this period, although they also appear earlier, seemingly as a variant of general Chalcolithic backed blades.

Bitruncated blades, along with the related backed truncated blades discussed above, seem to be an Egyptian type. They are found specifically in Early Bronze I contexts in the southern Shephela (foothills) and Coastal Plain of Israel, as well as, of course, in Egypt. Along with other elements of the material culture, such as pottery (e.g., Brandl 1989), they represent an Egyptian presence in Canaan during this period (Rosen 1988a).

CHRONOLOGY

As discussed earlier, Canaanean technology appears in the earliest stages of the Early Bronze Age and continues through the Middle Bronze I. In the Mediterranean zone, backed blades are more or less restricted to the Chalcolithic period, with the exception of the Egyptian types dated securely to the Early Bronze I at Erani and other sites (Rosen 1988a; Gophna and Friedmann 1993). Arched backed blades occur as a variant of straight backed blades in the Chalcolithic, but constitute a diagnostic type in the Early Bronze Age in the Negev, especially in the Uvda Valley. Bitruncated blades are an Egyptian type, seemingly restricted to the Early Bronze I in the southern Shephela. Simple retouched blades occur in all periods.

D. Bladelet Tools

(Figs. 3.24–3.25)
    1. microendscrapers
    2. retouched twisted bladelets
    3. retouched bladelets

TECHNOLOGIES

Two basic technologies were exploited for the production of bladelets. During the Chalcolithic and Early Bronze I Ages in the Mediterranean zone, regular prismatic bladelets were struck from single platform prismatic bladelet cores (fig. 3.24:1–6), usually conical or pyramidal in shape. Relatively small translucent chalcedony nodules, grayish in color, were often deliberately selected for these cores (e.g., Roshwalb 1981, 58; Gilead 1984). The twisted bladelet tools (cf. Roshwalb 1981, 282; Yeivin 1976; Baumgartel 1960, 42) seem to show almost a plunging bladelet aspect to them.

The second technology, more prominent in the desert regions, is more *ad hoc*, reflected in mixed flake-bladelet cores (fig. 3.24:7–8), with one or more striking platforms. In these desert assemblages, it is often difficult to distinguish between blade and bladelet production. Raw materials do not reflect special selection.

TYPOLOGY

The class has been divided into three types, which overlap to a significant degree. Gilead (1984) defined the microendscraper (fig. 3.25:1–4) on the basis of the presence of nibbling "retouch" on the distal and sometimes lateral edges of bladelets, superficially resembling miniature endscrapers on blades.

Retouched twisted bladelets, and twisted bladelets in general (fig. 3.25:5–6), were defined by Roshwalb (1981, 282) based upon identical Egyptian types (e.g., Baumgartel 1960, 42) and indeed were assumed to reflect Egyptian presence (also Rosen 1988a; Yeivin 1976). Their key diagnostic feature is a lateral twist in the profile of the bladelet. Retouch is, in fact, varied.

In addition to the above two types, bladelets appear with simple retouch and edge damage in various locations (fig. 3.25:7–8). Abrupt retouch and backing are virtually absent, except on microlithic lunates, transverse arrowheads, and microlithic drills, incorporated into other classes.

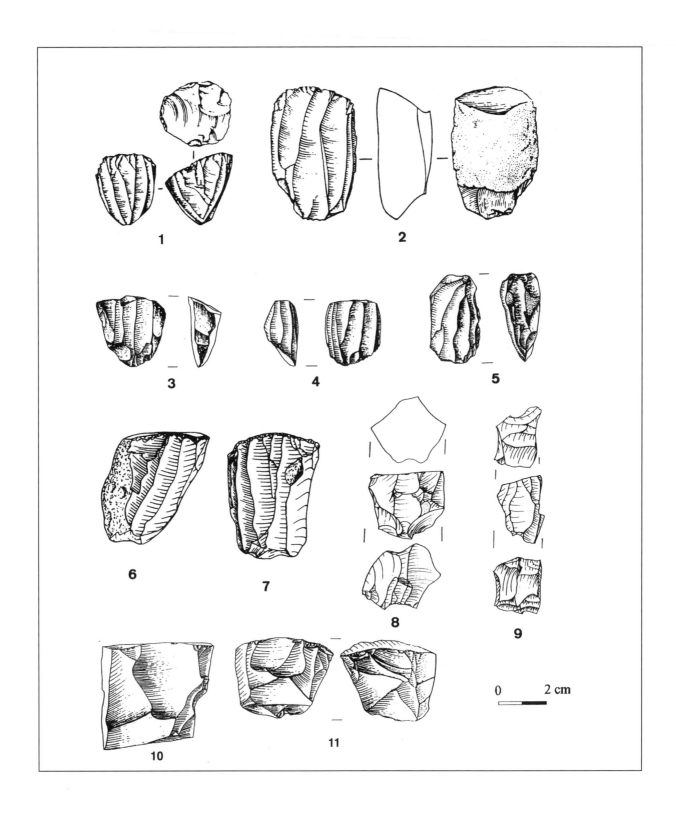

FIG. 3.24. *Bladelet and mixed bladelet cores. 1–7, bladelet cores; 8–11, mixed flake-bladelet cores. (1–2, Gaza A [Roshwalb 1981, fig. A.9]; 3–5, Grar [Gilead et al. 1995, fig. 5.8]; 6–7, En Besor [Gophna and Friedman 1993, fig. 5]; 8–9, Kvish Harif [Rosen 1984b, fig. 12]; 10–11, Camel Site)*

FUNCTION

Aside from the assumption that these tools were used for cutting, based on morphology and the existence of a sharp edge, little can be said concerning bladelet tool functions.

GEOGRAPHICAL DISTRIBUTION

Bladelet tools exhibit a sporadic geographical distribution during the Chalcolithic. They are common in some of the Wadi Gaza sites, and in North Sinai, and seem to be typical of what Gilead (1988) has termed the Besor-Grar Cluster of the Beersheva Chalcolithic. On the other hand, they are rare in the classic Beersheva Chalcolithic, as at Shiqmim, Abu Matar, Safadi, and Horvat Beter. They seem to be common at Ghassul (e.g., Neuville 1934b; Mahan 1940) and in the Jerusalem area (e.g., Nasrallah 1936; Rosen n.d.a), but are absent from the Golan Chalcolithic, and from Tell Teo and Fasael, in the Upper and Middle Jordan Valley, respectively. In desert sites they seem to occur only in low frequencies, as at the Uvda Valley sites (e.g., Rosen 1983d), although bladelet technology is present in other tool types, i.e., microlithic lunates, microdrills, and transverse arrowheads.

CHRONOLOGY

Bladelet technologies are well known in the Pottery Neolithic, for example in the Qatifian (Gilead 1990), and microendcscrapers are most likely derived from that tradition. Although Gilead (1984) has suggested the type as diagnostic of the Chalcolithic, Early Bronze I Gaza H (Roshwalb 1981, 282; Macdonald 1932, pl. xxiv) also shows the type. Also, the Egyptian Nagada-type twisted bladelets (Roshwalb 1981, 282; Rosen 1988a) known from the southern Shephela and Coastal Plain in the Early Bronze I overlap typologically with the microendscraper. As with the Egyptian sickles and blade segments, these too probably reflect an Egyptian presence (Rosen 1988a). Following this earliest subphase of the Early Bronze Age, the bladelet tools described in this section seem restricted to *ad hoc* elements.

Within the Chalcolithic, relative frequencies of bladelet tools may have chronological significance if the different "subcultures" of the Chalcolithic are chronologically patterned. That is, if the Besor phase (Gilead 1988) sites, with relatively numerous bladelets, are chronologically later (or earlier) than the Beersheva phase sites, with few bladelet tools, then the bladelets are reflective of the chronological difference. However, at this stage of research, chronological differentiation within the Chalcolithic remains problematic.

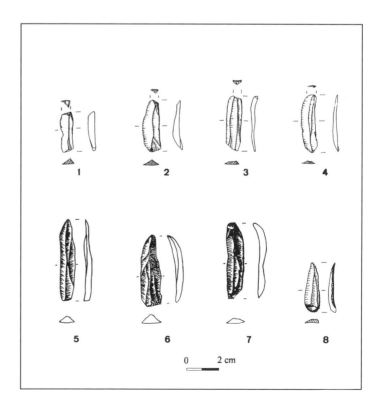

FIG. 3.25. *Bladelet tools. 1–4, microendscrapers; 5–6, retouched twisted blades; 7–8, retouched bladelets. (1–4, Grar [Gilead et al. 1995, fig. 5.22]; 5–7, Erani [Rosen 1988a, fig. 5]; 8, Sataf)*

E. Borers

(Figs. 3.26–3.27)

    1. awls
    2. drills
    3. microlithic drills
        a. single shoulder
        b. double shoulder
        c. straight
        d. triangular
        e. narrow
    3. miscellaneous points

TECHNOLOGY

The tools classed as borers crosscut technological categories. Awls were manufactured on nonstandardized flakes, often elongate. Drills were manufactured on simple blades, and microlithic drills, on bladelets. With the exception of the microlithic drills, the technological base for these tools is *ad hoc* and unstandardized.

The bladelets used for microlithic drill production seem to derive from two different core types. In the Early Bronze Age, as at the Camel Site (Rosen 1995), the cores are mixed flake/bladelet cores, with one or two striking platforms. Bladelets are relatively short and wide. For the Chalcolithic there is no direct association between the tools and the by-products of their manufacture, but bladelet cores in the Chalcolithic, as especially from Gaza A, are single platform prismatic cores, and bladelets are long and relatively thin.

Retouch varies greatly with tool type. Coarse abrupt and semi-abrupt retouch are typical of awls and some drills, which usually show finer work. Nibbling may be present on all tools, and fine abrupt retouch, probably accomplished using pressure techniques, is typical of the microlithic drills.

TYPOLOGY

Awls (fig. 3.26:1–8) are manufactured by single-notching a flake against a corner or double-notching a flake to produce shoulders and a point between the two notches. Drills (fig. 3.26:9–14) show bits longer, narrower, and thinner than those of awls, with a tendency toward more regular and abrupt retouch. There may be some overlap between the types, as when awl bits are longer and more finely manufactured. McConaughy's (1979, 257–58, 270–71, 306–7) "beaked denticulates" and perhaps his "chiseloids" seem to correspond to borers and drills. Neither type

resembles the fine delicate awls typical of the Pottery Neolithic (Stekelis 1972, pls. 25–30; Payne 1983, fig. 340), and which are absent from the lithic repertoire in the periods under discussion here.

Microlithic drills (fig. 3.27, 1–14) are considerably more standardized. Four basic subtypes are recognized, as listed above. The primary difference seems to be the presence/absence of distinct shoulders. Bits are uniformly narrow and long, showing fine abrupt retouch. Although some of the typological variation is probably determined by technological base, the presence of distinct shoulders as opposed to gradual reduction from base to bit may have temporal or geographic implications, as indicated by the typological contrasts between the Early Bronze Age Camel Site in the Central Negev and the Chalcolithic sites of the western and northern Negev (Rosen 1995). Narrow bits (e.g., Burian and Friedman 1987) seem to lack a wider base. It is difficult to know if this is simply the result of breakage, or whether they ought to be considered a separate subtype. However, established examples of narrow bits are known from other regions, in both the Old World (e.g., Piperno 1973, figs. 9.1–3, pl. 9.1, 121–25) and the New (e.g., Yerkes 1983, fig. 5, 509).

In addition to the relatively set types outlined above, flakes or blades may be minimally retouched to exploit the natural shape of the blank (fig. 3.27: 15–18). Small notches may be produced, resulting in a short protuberance; convergent blades may be nibbled to accentuate the point; and a variety of pointed or beaked pieces may be modified to emphasize the natural shape. Although these cannot be easily placed in one of the above categories, the pointed aspect suggests that they be placed in the general borer class, and they may be classified as miscellaneous points (cf. Betts 1991).

FUNCTION

Although the fact that the borer class is pointed suggests that these tools share a common function of piercing or producing holes, McConaughy's (1979, 257–58) microwear analysis of points of beaked denticulates, more or less corresponding to the awls, did not reveal any evidence of rotary motion. In fact, comparison with his controlled experiments indicated use on hard materials like bone or wood, and he suggests they were used as engraving tools.

Aside from McConaughy's work, there is no direct evidence for function of awls or drills, in spite of the names, and functional interpretation is difficult.

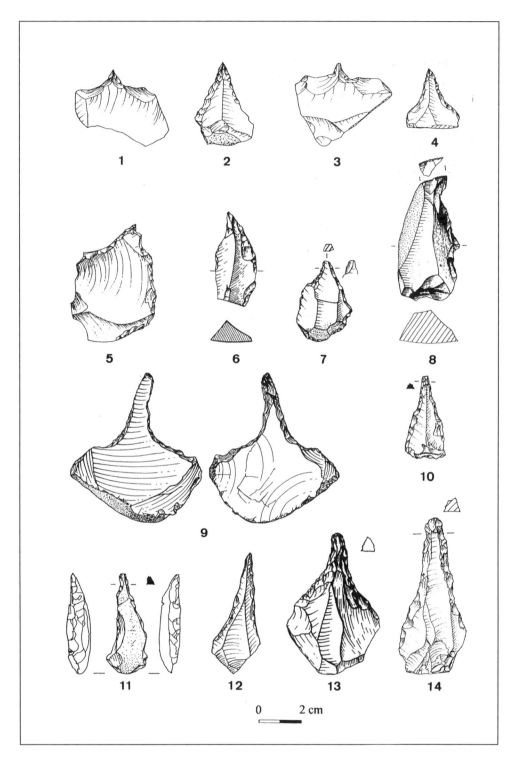

FIG. 3.26. Borers (awls and drills). 1–8, awls; 9–14, drills.
(1–4, Kvish Harif [Rosen 1984b, fig. 3]; 5, Har Qeren 15
[Rosen and Goring-Morris n.d.b]; 6, Hartuv [Rosen n.d.b];
7, Mitnan [Rosen 1993c, fig. 3]; 8, Sataf; 9, Shiqmim [Levy
and Rosen 1987, fig. 10.11]; 10, 14, Nahal Nizzana 103
[Burian and Friedman 1987, figs 6, 7]; 11, Gebel Gunna
[Bar-Yosef et al. 1986, fig. 11]; 12, Sha'ar Hagolan;
13, En Besor [Gophna and Friedman 1993, fig. 4])

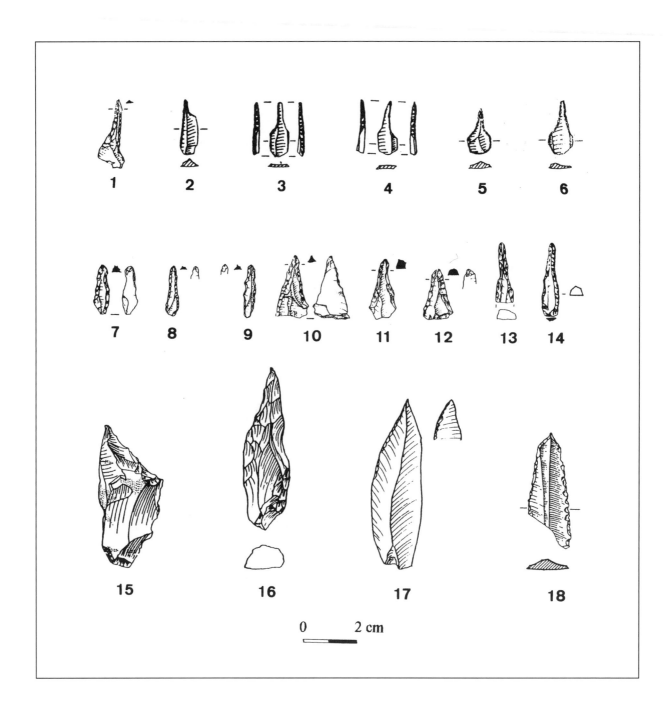

FIG. 3.27. *Borers (microlithic drills and miscellaneous points). 1–2, single shoulder microlithic drills; 3–6 double shoulder microlithic drills; 7–9, straight microlithic drills; 10–12, triangular microlithic drills; 13–14, narrow microlithic drills; 15–18, miscellaneous points. (1, 7–12, Nahal Nizzana 103 [Burian and Friedman 1987, figs. 2–3]; 1, 2–6 Camel Site [Rosen 1995, fig. 2]; 13, Gaza M [Roshwalb 1981, fig. M.2]; 14, Yarmouth [Rosen 1988b, fig. 50]; 15–16, Hartuv [Rosen n.d.b]*

Microlithic drills have been found in good association with bead manufacture at a number of sites, including Nahal Nizzana 103 (Burian and Friedman 1987), Gaza M (Roshwalb 1981, 166–70), and the Camel site (Rosen 1995). Microscopic examination of bit ends indicates wear which is probably indicative of drilling abrasion (Roshwalb 1981, 166–70; Burian and Friedman 1987). They were undoubtedly hafted onto the shafts of bow drills (e.g., Burian and Friedman 1985).

GEOGRAPHY

Awls, drills, and miscellaneous points are found throughout the Levant, a part of the general *ad hoc* tool kit that dominates post–Neolithic chipped stone industries. Microlithic drills have been recovered exclusively from the southern areas, Gaza and the Negev, and are found in specialized contexts such that they are lacking in most sites, but are present in large quantities in a few sites. Given that these tools are microliths, it is difficult to determine how representative absence may be from early excavations; however, even recent well collected assemblages show this pattern.

CHRONOLOGY

All types show antecedents in the Neolithic. The awl class seems to continue through the Early Bronze Age and into the Middle Bronze I and II. It is not unlikely that it continues into the Late Bronze Age, but there is difficulty in accounting for the problem of intrusions in these later sites. Drills are present at least through the Middle Bronze I, as at Sha'ar HaGolan, in the Jordan Valley (Rosen 1983d, 274–75), but seem to be rare in later contexts.

The latest occurrence of microlithic drills is from the Camel Site, with a C14 date and material culture attributable to Early Bronze II. Earlier assemblages are Chalcolithic. A possible chronological distinction can be drawn between the dominant shouldered types of the Early Bronze Age Camel Site and the earlier Chalcolithic straight and triangular types. Obviously, the sample of assemblages is far too small to establish this "trend" with any reliability.

F. Tabular Scrapers

(Figs. 3.28–3.37)
1. round
2. oval
3. elongate
4. fanscrapers
5. knives
6. irregular

TECHNOLOGY

Tabular scrapers are large retouched flakes showing intentional retention of cortex on virtually all of the dorsal surface. Cores (figs. 3.28–3.29), recovered from a few manufacturing sites in the Negev and Sinai (Rosen and Goring-Morris n.d.b; Rosen 1983b; Kozloff 1972–73), are large nodules with flat cortical surfaces, sometimes as large as 60 cm in length, but usually averaging around 20 x 15 x 10 cm in dimensions. At Har Qeren 15, a small quarry site in the western Negev, they show removals from one or more surfaces and seem to have been little exploited beyond initial removal of cortical flakes. Beyond occasional platform preparation, there is little evidence for elaborate core preparation, such as present in the Middle Paleolithic Levallois technique or some for sophisticated blade production. Raw materials are brown fine-grained flints, in the Negev sites associated with Eocene outcrops. Notably, raw material is not vein or tabular flint.

Flakes are both endstruck and sidestruck. Bulbs of percussion are pronounced, although some of the more carefully worked pieces show deliberate bulbar thinning. Some pieces show striking platform facetting. This facetting superficially resembles that on Canaanean blades, and Hennessy (1967, 41–44; also Betts 1991, 1992a) has thereby suggested a close relationship between the technologies. Indeed, at Lahav, Futato (1990) has documented what appears to be a tabular scraper blank, apparently resulting from cortical removal in the preparation of a Canaanean blade core. However, the dissimilarities in other elements of the technologies, geographic distributions, chronologies, and (sometimes) raw materials indicate that this connection was not the rule.

Flake removal at Har Qeren 15 (Rosen and Goring-Morris n.d.b), the only site for which data are available, seems to have been accomplished using a block-on-block technique, as reflected especially in light of the absence of hammerstones on the site. Some

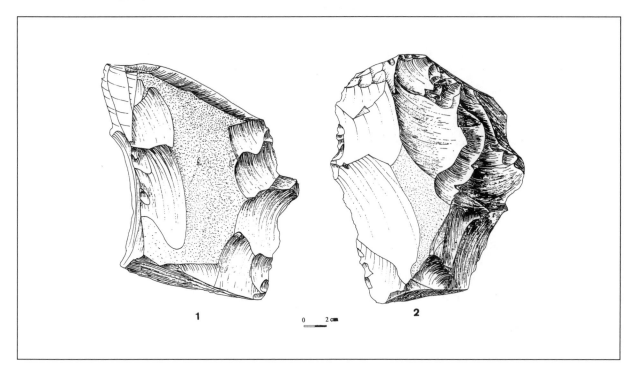

FIG. 3.28. *Tabular scraper cores. (Har Qeren 15 [Rosen and Goring-Morris n.d.b])*

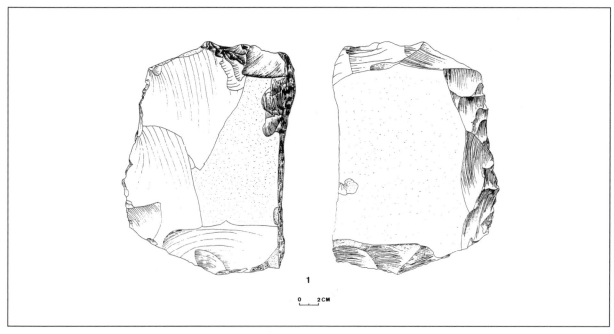

FIG. 3.29. *Tabular scraper core. (Har Qeren 15 [Rosen 1983b, fig. 3])*

FIG. 3.30. *Tabular scrapers—fanscrapers. (1–2, Uvda Valley 16 [Rosen n.d.a]; 3, Mitnan [Rosen 1993c, fig. 2]; 4, Mitzpe Shalem [Greenhut 1989, fig. 13])*

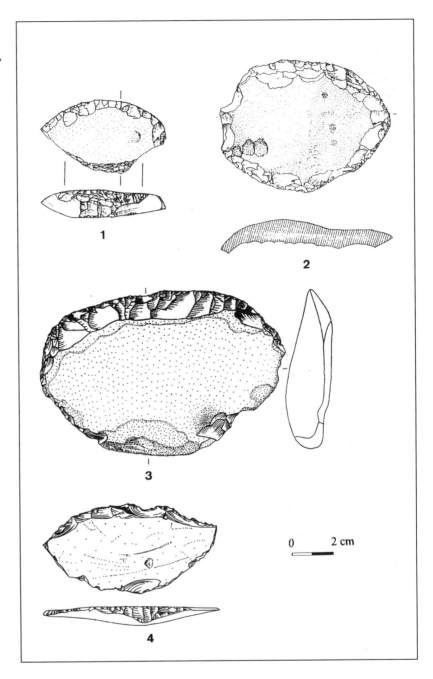

pieces may have been manufactured using indirect percussion, since the precision of some of the manufacturing seems too fine for block-on-block. The large size of the flakes and their bulbs of percussion indicates that a great deal of force was required.

Tamar Noy (pers. comm.) has noted that types lacking cortex, especially from the Golan Chalcolithic, seem to reflect repeated exploitation of tabular scraper cores, beyond the initial removal of the cortical flakes.

Retouch is hard hammer direct percussion, and informal replication experiments show it can be accomplished with virtually any kind of hammerstone. In addition to simple untreated cortex, two types of cortical treatment are known. On some pieces, cortices are deliberately ground to produce a smoother, more uniform surface. Striations are usually evident, even without the use of a microscope. On others, design motifs are incised into the cortex using a strong pointed tool. Replication shows that this can be accomplished using flint borers. The two types of treatment are not mutually exclusive.

TYPOLOGY

The vast majority of tabular scrapers recovered from well-collected excavations are fragments, often identifiable as tabular scrapers by reference to retention of cortex, retouch type, and general morphology, but unclassifiable to subtype. With respect to complete tools, excepting the fanscraper, the typological distinctions drawn here are based on shape (figs. 3.30–3.34), specifically L/W ratios, as reflected in a weak polymodality when complete pieces are graphed (figs. 3.35–3.36). Whether the modes present in the graph represent some typological reality beyond the archaeological construct is unclear, and assigning meaning to this range of variability is difficult. Much of it may simply relate to original flake shape, as determined by core-nodule size and shape. For example, the thirty-eight tabular scrapers measured from Tumulus 1/5 at Ein Yarka (Sinai) show an average L/W ratio of 1.61±0.31 and in a range of features clearly reflect a single manufacturing event. Given that the tumulus seems to have been a grave, it is likely that the cache of scrapers is some kind of mortuary offering. Yet, the shape distribution (fig. 3.37) crosscuts all the shape categories. If all the scrapers from this site were intended as a single type with similar function, then it stands to reason subtype variation be considered more in the nature of modalities than defined types, and that it may not be appropriate to assign too much meaning to variability in shape.

Furthermore, in addition to the problem of core variation, the high rate of breakage and apparent repair suggests that many shorter pieces, i.e., the round and oval types, may once have been elongate and reduced to shorter types. Dibble (1987) has suggested a similar phenomenon for Middle Paleolithic scrapers.

The classic fanscraper (*grattoir en éventail*), as especially described by Neuville (1930, 1934a,b) are "fan"-shaped, transverse flakes (i.e., sidestruck) (fig. 3.30). They seem more often to show platform facetting and bulbar thinning than the other types, but high rates of breakage and low numbers of tools in general make this difficult to quantify.

In addition to these types, many irregular types, not fitting these categories, have been recovered (fig. 3.28). For example, occasionally large flakes that are recovered show smooth, noncortical, dorsal surfaces, otherwise technologically and morphologically similar to tabular scrapers. Furthermore, sometimes simply oddly shaped tabular scrapers are recovered, the shapes perhaps due to breakage and repair or idiosyncrasies in raw material (e.g., holes). The pieces from the Golan also show more invasive retouch. Many of the pieces are also deliberately holed and may be classified with the discs and holed pieces. Tabular knives, dealt with in the next section, are technologically similar to tabular scrapers, but are often lacking cortex, as in many pieces recovered from the Golan Chalcolithic.[5]

FUNCTION

Although the term *tabular scraper* implies scraping, possibly hideworking as a primary function of these tools, microwear analyses conducted by McConaughy (1979, 304) indicated that these pieces from the Early Bronze city at Bab edh Dhra were, in fact, used as butchering knives. This seems especially reasonable in regard to fanscrapers, with their long transverse edges. Henry (1995, 372–73) has suggested that the tools were used as wool shears by early pastoralists, and experimental work by Bennett et al. (1989) has indicated that this is possible, although it was unsupported by wear analysis. However, the wool-shearing theory seems speculative at best, with little hard evidence in its favor. Microscopic examination of a single tabular scraper from Jawa by Unger-Hamilton (1991) suggested the possibility of its use to scrape reeds.

Tabular scrapers also seem to have had some ritual function. McConaughy (1979, 304; 1980a, 1980b), based on Elliot's (1977) discussion of Chalcolithic ritual, draws this conclusion from the physical association between these tools and the Bab edh Dhra temple area and speculates on the possibility of their use as knives in ritual sacrifice. Notably, tabular scrapers were also recovered from the Megiddo Early Bronze temple district, and a tabular scraper was the only tool recovered from the Uvda Valley 6 open-air shrine (Yogev 1983). The site of Mitzpe Shalem, in the Judean desert (Bar Adon 1989; Greenhut 1989), interpreted by the authors as a ritual or ceremonial center, included hundreds of tabular scrapers among the finds (and few other lithic artifacts). Finally, the presence of incised motifs on so many pieces, especially those in the north, suggests symbolic loading, according well with the idea of at least some ritual function. This is not to deny other functions, but to indicate the ritual function as well.

Tabular scrapers in the southern regions, closer to the source areas, are found in greater numbers and seemingly greater variability, with less care in manufacture, less standardization, and fewer incised motifs. Although in some cases, as at Uvda Valley 6 (Yogev 1983) and Ein Yarka, in South Sinai, a ritual interpretation may be indicated, the tools at most sites do not seem to be associated with ritual or symbolic functions. They probably served a general range of domestic tasks, indeed perhaps including domestic ritual.

The function of the cortical incisions (fig. 3.33:2; fig. 3.34) found on some tabular scrapers has not been systematically addressed. The clear repetition of a few motifs, such as that described by Macalister (1912, 125–26, pl. 139:16) as a proto-aleph, sometimes on pieces from different sites, suggests a meaning which transcends idiosyncrasy. That is, it seems unlikely that these are ownership (*per contra* Macalister 1912, 125–26) or manufacturer's marks. Furthermore, the absence of incisions on the pieces at the quarry sites, and the near absence from desert sites in general, suggests that they were marked after acquisition. It is tempting to correlate these incised symbols with early writing, which appears at just about the same time in Uruk region. More work is clearly in order.

GEOGRAPHY

Tabular scrapers in various forms have been found at sites throughout the Levant (Rosen 1983b), as far south as South Sinai (e.g., Milstein 1981; Kozloff 1972–73), in the Nile Delta (Rizkana and Seeher 1985), and in southeast Turkey and northeast Syria (Algaze 1989, 581). They seem to be rare occurrences in Egypt and Turkey, and researchers have suggested that in these areas they should be seen as Levantine imports.

Within the Levant, although information is more limited for the north, distribution seems proportionally skewed to the south, especially the southern regions of the Negev and Sinai. Quarry sites, with cores for tabular scraper manufacture, are known exclusively from these areas, and sites in these regions show consistently higher proportions of tabular scrapers in their tool assemblages than do sites from other regions. In fact, a distance-percentage graph measured from the western Negev, the apparent focus of at least some of the tabular scraper manufacture, shows a logarithmic falloff of tabular scraper frequency with distance from this source area (Rosen 1983b, 1989a). Although some sites do not fit the falloff model, for example, the Beersheva Chalcolithic sites and Tell Um Hamad (Helms 1987), it does seem to account for a surprising amount of variability. Changes in exchange patterns between periods, and additional sources of tabular scrapers, perhaps in eastern or southern Jordan (e.g., Muheisen et al. 1988, 482–83), probably account for much of the remaining variability.

CHRONOLOGY

Tabular scrapers are known from Late Neolithic sites (Moore 1973) and may have developed from the production of Late Neolithic bifacial knives, whose quarry sites are found in the same locales in the western Negev as the tabular scraper quarry sites (Goring-Morris and Rosen 1986; Goring-Morris et al. 1994). They are especially common in the Chalcolithic and Early Bronze Ages and disappear with the end of the Early Bronze III. The precise date of disappearance is problematic. Kozloff (1972–73) indicated the presence of tabular scrapers in MBI sites in Sinai, but footnotes the problematic nature of mixed surface assemblages. In a later, unpublished manuscript, he suggested that the initial evaluation was premature. This accords well with the apparent absence of tabular scrapers from MBI sites in the Negev (e.g., at Yeruham [Gilead 1973] and other sites examined by the author), and other MBI sites in Sinai. On the other hand, recent data from North Sinai (pers. obs.) suggest at least the possibility that the type may continue into the earliest phases of the MBI. However, here too there is a problem with surface sites, at least some of which are mixed. No tabular scrapers were recovered from the MBI layers of Sha'ar Hagolan (Rosen 1983d, 273–76) or Um Hammad MBI (Betts 1992a), or apparently from Djebel Qa'aqir (Dever 1973). There is no good evidence for the continuation of the type into the Middle Bronze II (noting the problem of intrusion on tell sites).

The only clear chronological patterning within this fifth–third millennium span is the appearance of incised tabular scrapers exclusively in the Early Bronze Age. To date, incised motifs are absent from Chalcolithic tabular scrapers, although cortical grinding is present. Ultimately it may be possible to distinguish between tabular scrapers from different periods using detailed attribute analyses, but to date no systematic synthetic attempts have been made.

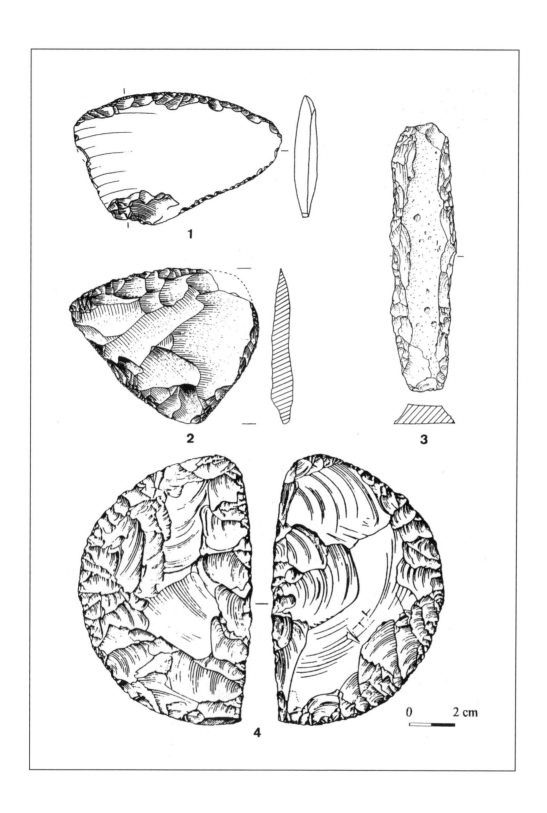

FIG. 3.31. *Tabular scrapers—others. (1, Mitnan [Rosen 1993c, fig. 2]; 2, Sataf; 3, Nahal Nizzana 103 (Burian and Friedman 1987, fig. 2]; 4, Gaza A [Roshwalb 1981, fig. A.4])*

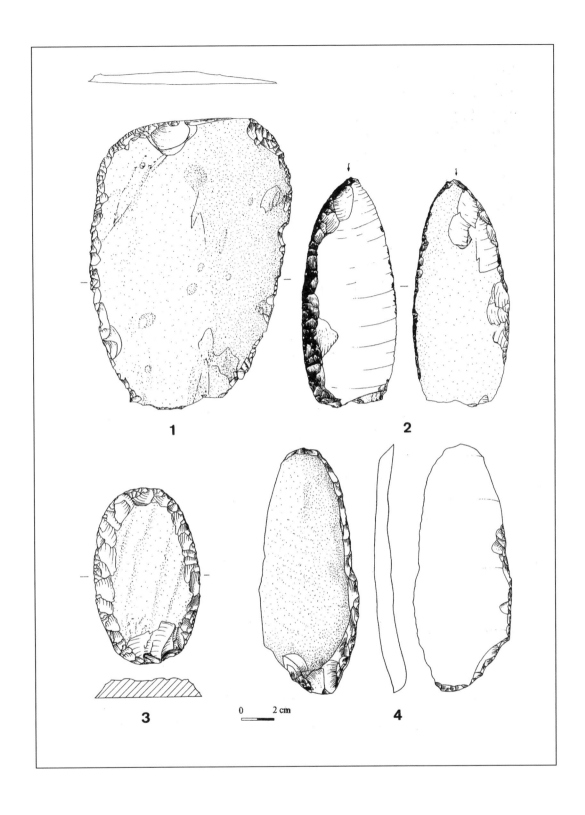

FIG. 3.32. *Tabular scrapers. 1, oval; 2–4, elongate.*
(1, Har Qeren 15 [Rosen and Goring-Morris n.d.b];
2, Shiqmim [Levy and Rosen 1987, fig. 10.5]; 3, Gebel
Gunna [Bar-Yosef et al. 1986, fig. 9]; 4, Beit Yerah)

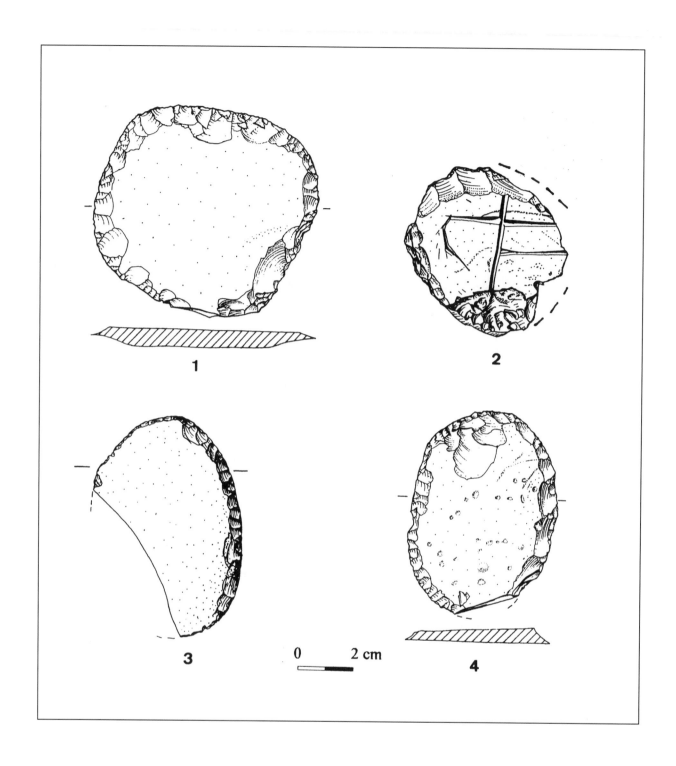

FIG. 3.33. *Tabular scrapers. 1, round; 2, round with incisions; 3–4, oval. (1, 4, Nahal Nizzana 103 [Burian and Friedman 1987, fig. 2]; 2, Mitzpe Shalem (Greenhut 1989, fig. 12]; 3, Shiqmim [Levy and Rosen 1987, fig. 10.5])*

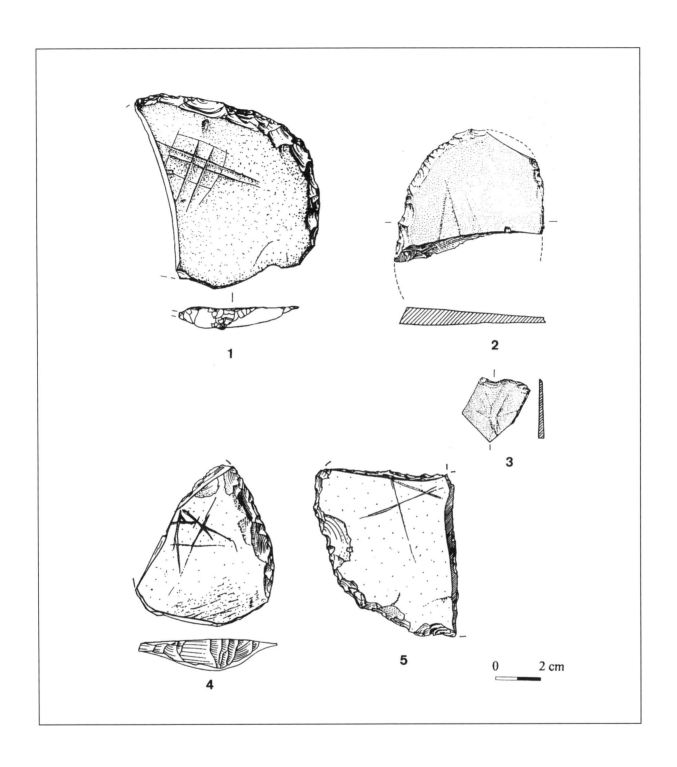

FIG. 3.34. *Tabular scrapers with incisions. (1, Qasis; 2–3, Yarmouth [Rosen 1988b, pl. 53]; 4–5, Mitzpe Shalem [Greenhut 1989, fig. 8])*

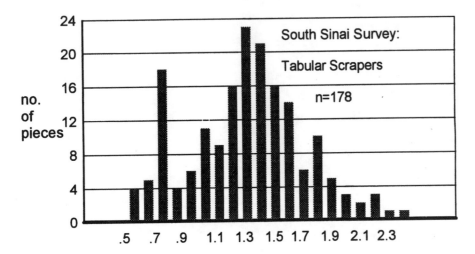

FIG. 3.35. *Histogram of tabular scraper length/width ratios from South Sinai Survey. Note clear bimodality, reflecting endstruck versus sidestruck pieces, and possible additional modes. Interval widths are in ratio units of 0.1.*

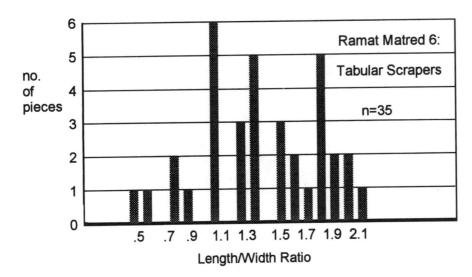

FIG. 3.36. *Histogram of tabular scraper length/width ratios from Ramat Matred 6. Note apparent polymodality. Interval widths are in ratio units of 0.1.*

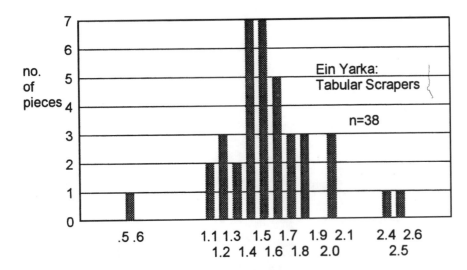

FIG. 3.37. *Histogram of length/width ratios of tabular scrapers from Ein Yarka. Note the generally great range in shape in spite of the techno-typological homogeneity of the assemblage. Interval widths are in ratio units of 0.1.*

G. Bifacial Knives and Invasively Retouched Pieces

(Figs. 3.38–3.40)
  1. roughouts
  2. bifacial knives
  3. unifacial knives

TECHNOLOGY

Bifacial knives were manufactured on large flat flakes, removed from large cores using either the block-on-block technique or indirect percussion, depending on the specific type. Blank production is akin to that of tabular scrapers, and Pottery Neolithic knives may be the technological precursors to tabular scrapers. Quarry sites, probably dating to the Pottery Neolithic, are known from Har Qeren, in the western Negev (Goring-Morris et al. 1994; Rosen and Goring-Morris n.d.b). Preliminary retouch was accomplished using direct percussion, leaving roughouts with large invasive flake scars. Final retouch was accomplished using smaller scale direct percussion and pressure retouch, resulting in straight, flat lateral edges. Some pieces show fine ripple pressure retouch (e.g., Crowfoot Payne 1978). Retouch may be unifacial or bifacial. Detailed replication experiments of Egyptian ripple flake knives (Kelterborn 1984) suggests that this retouch is not bladelike, but consists of overlapping oval shaped flake removals. Furthermore, grinding of the blanks seems to have been an intermediate stage in production.

TYPOLOGY

The three types defined here do not exhaust the typological variability in the class. Egyptian bifacial knives come in a wide range of forms (cf. Baumgartel 1960, 27–34; Holmes 1989, 400–11), and this variability would probably be reflected at least somewhat in the Levantine assemblages were the pieces unbroken and the assemblages larger. However, the class is rare, and detailed exposition based on Egyptian typologies seems pointless.

Roughouts (fig. 3.38:1–2) are found only at quarry sites at Har Qeren (Goring-Morris et al. 1994; Goring-Morris and Rosen 1986). They are larger, cruder, and with larger removals than the final products. The sites at Har Qeren probably date to the late Pottery Neolithic and thereby do not strictly fall into the chronological range covered by this study, but they provide our only Levantine case study of the manufac-ture of these tools.

Bifacial (figs. 3.38:3; 3.39; 3.40:2) and unifacial knives (fig. 3.40:1) are distinguished by location of retouch, as evident in the names. Forms include fish-tails, ripple knives, ovals, leaf shapes, dagger shapes, etc. (cf. Baumgartel 1960, 24–34; Holmes 1989, 400–11). Most of the knives recovered from excavations are fragmentary and cannot be further classified.

FUNCTION

Aside from the assumption, based on morphology and edge shape, that most of these pieces were used as knives, no work has been conducted to determine their function. Funerary contexts of some of the types in Egypt (e.g., Baumgartel 1960, 28) suggest ritual and symbolic function. This is supported by the heavy investment in pressure retouch of entire dorsal faces of such items as ripple knives, which seems to have little utilitarian function. In fact, some of these tools seem to be far too delicate to have been used in day-to-day utilitarian context, and ritual/symbolic context is almost undoubted (cf. Holmes 1989, 282; also Keltenborn 1984). On the other hand, given the difficulties of establishing good intrasite context for many of these pieces in Levantine sites (cf. Rosen 1988a), assumptions based on Egyptian contexts need not apply. Certainly not all the tools were ritual in use.

GEOGRAPHIC DISTRIBUTION

Bifacial knives are found throughout the Levant, but for the most part relate to Pottery Neolithic assemblages, beyond the scope of this study. There is some difficulty in distinguishing Egyptian Early Bronze Age types from those of the Pottery Neolithic, especially since in most cases we are dealing with fragments. Thus, for example, Payne (1978) suggested Egyptian affinities for "Chalcolithic" knives recovered from the Besor region of the western Negev, although she recognized that they were locally produced.

Within the Early Bronze Age, geographic distribution of the class is restricted to the southern Shephela, up as far north as the Azor tombs (Ben-Tor 1975), but restricted to the foothills and coastal plain. This distribution seems to correspond to areas of Egyptian presence, although trade in these pieces cannot be ruled out. Indeed, at least one piece from the Early Bronze I Egyptian settlement at Erani is clearly imported flint (Rosen 1988a).

CHRONOLOGY

Egyptian bifacial knives are restricted to the Early Bronze I (cf. Weinstein 1984), and there is virtually no evidence for either manufacture or import of these items after this period. Late Pottery Neolithic assemblages also contain similar pieces, but they are rare in Beersheva-Ghassul Chalcolithic assemblages.

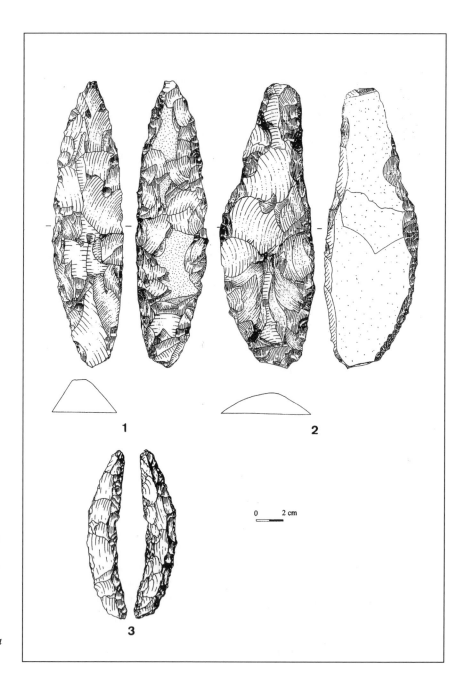

FIG. 3.38. *Bifacial knives and invasively retouched pieces. 1, bifacial knife; 2, cortical knife (unifacial); 3, bifacial crescent-shaped knife (Egyptian). (1, Har Qeren V [Goring-Morris and Rosen 1986, fig. 2.5E–A-11]; 2, Har Qeren XIV [Goring-Morris and Rosen 1986, fig. 2.5E–A-6]; 3, En Besor [Gophna and Friedman 1993, fig. 4])*

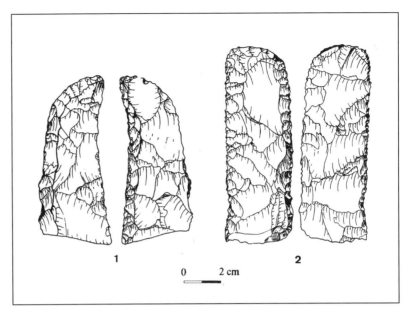

FIG. 3.39. *Bifacial knives and invasively retouched pieces.*
1–2, Egyptian bifacial knives. (1–2, Erani [Rosen 1988a,
fig. 1])

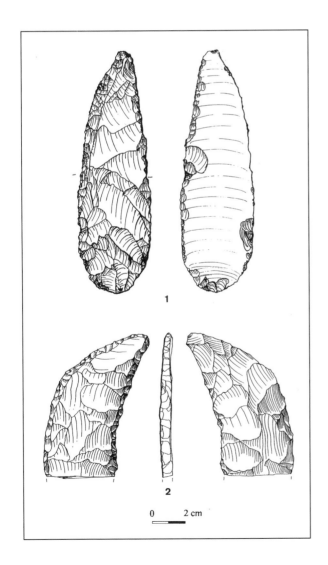

FIG. 3.40. *Bifacial knives and invasively retouched pieces.*
1, unifacial knife (Egyptian); 2, bifacial knife (Egyptian).
(1, Erani, drawing by Efrat Yeivin; 2, Lower Horvat Illin
[Marder et al. 1995, fig. 10])

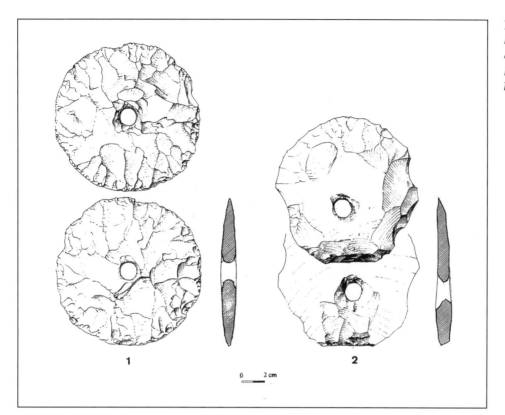

FIG. 3.41. *Discs and holed tools. Holed discs. (1–2, Neve Ur [Perrot et al. 1967, figs. 2, 8])*

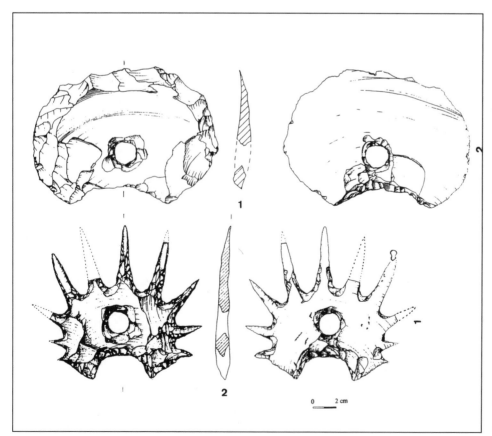

FIG. 3.42. *Discs and holed tools. 1, holed disc; 2, star. (1, Golan [Epstein and Noy 1988, fig. 4]; 2, north Jordan, unprovenanced [Epstein and Noy 1988, fig.2])*

H. Discs and Holed Tools

(Figs. 3.41–3.42)
  1. discs
  2. holed discs
  3. stars

TECHNOLOGY

These tools are made on large flakes, reminiscent of tabular scrapers, retouched unifacially or bifacially with large invasive removals (Perrot et al 1967). Most show total removal of cortex. Tamar Noy (pers. comm.) has suggested that these are the result of repeated removals from tabular scraper-type cores, after initial cortex removal. Holes, roughly a cm in diameter, are pecked through from one side and show microflaking on the reverse side. Often one blunt edge will show pecking or abrupt retouch. Protrusions or points on the stars show bifacial retouch and are not blunted. No cores or other waste products from the manufacture of this class have been recovered.

TYPOLOGY

Three types are defined. Discs are round or oval, flat flakes, with invasive retouch usually restricted to the dorsal surface. Holed discs (figs. 3.41; 3.42:1) are similar, with the hole usually somewhat off center. Stars (fig. 3.42:2) are similar to holed discs, but show multiple rays extending outward from the central portion of the tool. The number of points vary, but usually range from seven to eleven, depending on which protuberances are counted as "rays." There may be as few as three. Variation in all three types may occur on the butt or base, which may be straight, concave, or, in some discs, simply rounded as with the rest of the disc. It is clear that numerous subtypes exist.

FUNCTION

The function of these tools has yet to be ascertained. Epstein and Noy (1988) have suggested that the central hole allowed insertion of a finger and that the blunted edge found on most pieces fit into the heel of the hand, thus assuming a handheld manual function. Given the small size of many of the holes, the effort required to drill them, and the limited increase in efficiency of use that would be engendered by such a grip, this reconstruction seems strained. Hafting of some kind seems a more likely explanation for the hole.

Wool carding has been suggested as a function for the stars (The Abbe Breuil, cited in Nasrallah 1948).

This too seems a questionable interpretation in that the sharp edges of the flint tool would tend to shred any wool fibers stretched against them. Also, far more effective wool cards could be produced more easily from other materials like wood.

The effort invested in these tools along with their unusual shapes, especially in the case of the stars, suggest some symbolic functions. Given this, it is perhaps not inappropriate to suggest that the similarity in shape between the stars and the wall paintings of "rays" discovered at Chalcolithic Ghassul (Mallon et al. 1934) is not coincidental. Epstein and Noy (1988) have noted the relative abundance of stars in Golan Chalcolithic sites, but this need not suggest utilitarian function. Instead, it might indicate the pervasiveness of some associated rite.

GEOGRAPHIC DISTRIBUTION

These tools are generally rare, such that geographic distribution is difficult to define. However, their scarcity in the Beersheva and Gaza sites and their discovery at sites in the Jordan Valley and the Golan (e.g., Perrot et al. 1967; Epstein and Noy 1988) suggest an eastern orientation. Meaning cannot yet be assigned to this phenomenon. Noy (pers. comm.) connects them to the Chalcolithic tabular knives and suggests a general northern distribution.

CHRONOLOGY

These tools are restricted to the Chalcolithic period. Within the period, their attribution depends on our ability to define subphases, and as yet no clear subdivisions are possible.

I. Scrapers

(Figs. 3.43–3.45)
1. endscrapers
    a. simple endscrapers
    b. tongue-shaped endscrapers
2. sidescrapers
3. steep scrapers
4. small scrapers
5 massive scrapers

TECHNOLOGY

Scrapers as a class are variable technologically, as reflected in the range of types listed above. With the possible exception of tongue-shaped endscrapers, technologies for scraper manufacture are *ad hoc*. Cores are amorphous (fig. 3.43), and reduction is based on direct percussion, probably using a hard hammer. There is no evidence for regular core preparation, either on the cores or on flake striking platforms. Flakes vary greatly in size and show numerous "errors" in production, as per the retouched flake class. Retouch is varied, from rather ephemeral to somewhat invasive. Raw materials vary and show no evidence for selection of specific flint types (e.g., Hammond 1977). Gilead (1989) has documented a major set of Chalcolithic scrapers (as well as other tools) on hard limestone.

The issue of hafting (cf. Keeley 1982) is difficult. The *ad hoc* nature of so many of these tools, and the scarce evidence for long-term resharpening, seems to suggest immediate use and discard, with no hafting. On the other hand, some of the more formal scrapers may well have been hafted.

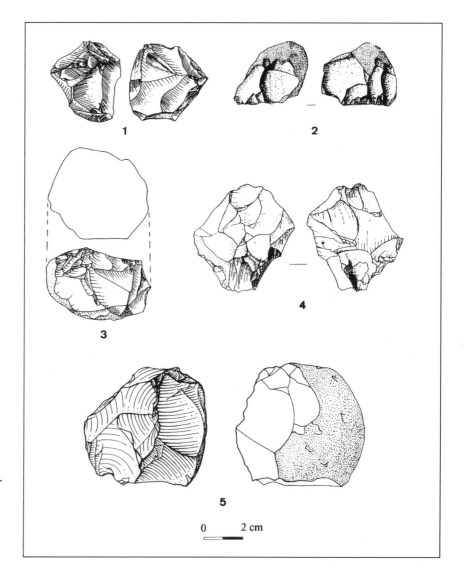

FIG. 3.43. *Amorphous flake cores. (1, Camel Site; 2, Grar [Gilead et al. 1995, fig. 5.3]; 3, Beit Yerah; 4, Uvda Valley 16 [Rosen n.d.a]; 5, Shiqmim [Levy and Rosen 1987, fig. 10.21])*

TYPOLOGY

With the exception of tongue-shaped endscrapers and perhaps to a lesser extent, steep scrapers, the types listed represent a range of variability rather than distinct types; they nonetheless provide a convenient descriptive device. Egyptian endscrapers on blades (e.g., Petrie 1902, pl. xiv, 1904; pl. vii, 48–51; Reisner 1908, pl. 40c; Rizkana and Seeher 1985, figs.5:4–8) are another more formal tool, but are rare in south Levantine contexts. As in the Paleolithic, the difference between end- and sidescrapers lies in the location of retouch, either distal (fig. 3.44) or lateral (fig. 3.45:1–2). Pieces showing both are classified as endscrapers with additional retouch. Retouch is varied, and may be dorsal or in some cases ventral. It tends to be less regular than that on Paleolithic scrapers.

Tongue-shaped endscrapers (fig. 3.44:5), the only type showing real similarity to Upper and Epipaleolithic types, were manufactured on oval flakes, average 5–10 cm in length, 4–5 cm in width, and 0.5–1.5 cm in thickness. They show regular dorsal retouch in an arc on the distal end. They constitute perhaps the only formal type in the general class.

Steep scrapers (fig. 3.45:3–6) are similar to steep denticulates and notches, but lack the concavities present in the latter. Retouch is abrupt and semi-abrupt, on thick flakes.

Small scrapers (fig. 3.45:7–8) are analogous to Upper Paleolithic thumbnail scrapers, but are not as regular or standardized. Massive scrapers (fig. 3.45:9) show scraper retouch on large flakes, usually greater than 10 cm in length.

Different types of scrapers clearly overlap with types from other classes. Thus, flat notches and denticulates, retouched flakes, and simple endscrapers, sidescrapers, small scrapers, and massive scrapers are difficult to truly justify as distinct types, at least in the classical template concept (e.g., Deetz 1967, 43–52). The divisions here should be seen as providing a descriptive range. The same applies to steep notches, denticulates, and scrapers, forming a continuum whose primary characteristic is a thick, abruptly retouched end, usually denticulated.

FUNCTION

Explicit functional definition of the class is not possible due to its great variability, but McConaughy's (1979, 292, 334–44) analyses indicate a range of functions, especially scraping of hard and soft materials (cf. Rowan and Levy 1991).

GEOGRAPHY

The scraper class is found throughout the study region. Tongue-shaped end scrapers were present in Chalcolithic sites and in the Early Bronze sites from the Uvda Valley, but have not been recovered from northern Early Bronze Age sites. Steep endscrapers are common throughout the region, but seem especially typical of southern industries (cf. Kozloff 1972–73).

CHRONOLOGY

As a general class, scrapers seem to follow a frequency trajectory similar to that of the retouched flakes and notches and denticulates. They are present in Chalcolithic and Early Bronze Age industries in fair quantities, but decline in post Early Bronze Age times. The *ad hoc* nature of the tool types makes precise chronological definition difficult. The more formal tongue-shaped endscrapers (where they are really the standard type) are more prominent in the Chalcolithic (e.g., Rowan 1990; Rowan and Levy 1991) and occur later only in the Uvda Valley Early Bronze Age sites. Steep scrapers seem to be hallmark of the Timnian industries of the desert regions (Kozloff 1972–73), corresponding to the terminal Neolithic, Chalcolithic and early part of the Early Bronze Age, and the type may continue into the Middle Bronze I in the Negev.

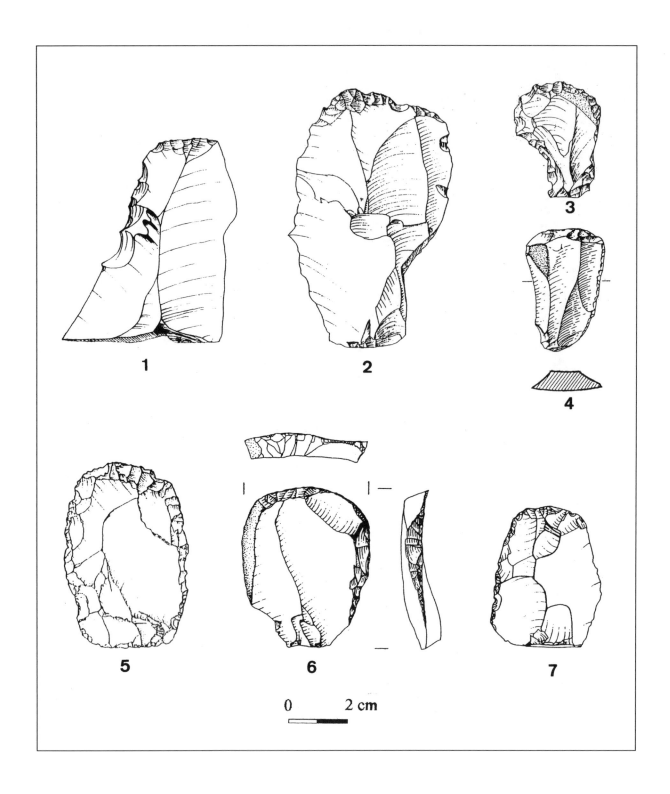

FIG. 3.44. *Scrapers. 1–4, 6–7, simple endscrapers; 5, tongue-shaped endscraper. (1, Deir el-Balah [Rosen and Goring-Morris n.d.a]; 2–3, Har Qeren XV [Rosen and Goring-Morris n.d.b]; 4, Hartuv [Rosen n.d.b]; 5, Uvda Valley 16 [Rosen n.d.a]; 6, Grar [Gilead et al. 1995, fig. 5.10]; 7, Beit Yerah)*

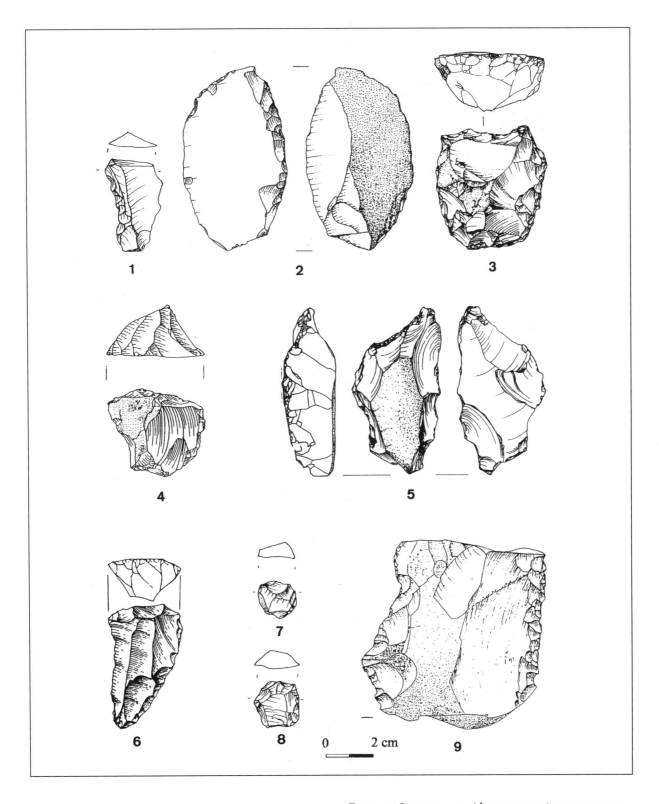

FIG. 3.45. *Scrapers. 1–2, sidescrapers; 3–6, steep scrapers; 7–8, small scrapers; 9, massive scraper (broken). (1, 7–8, Kvish Harif [Rosen 1984b, figs. 4, 5]; 2, Grar [Gilead et al. 1995, fig. 5.10]; 3, 5 Qasis; 4, Yarmouth [Rosen 1988b, pl. 50]; 6, Hartuv [Rosen n.d.b]; 9, Har Qeren 15 [Rosen and Goring-Morris n.d.b])*

J. Notches and Denticulates

(Fig. 3.46)

    1. flat
        a. notches
        b. denticulates
    2. steep
        a. notches
        b. denticulates

TECHNOLOGY

Notches and denticulates constitute a variable class manufactured from a wide range of flakes, generally from *ad hoc* flake cores. The steep variety requires thicker flakes, and sometimes chunks and decortication flakes were utilized. They are clearly an expedient type showing virtually no technological or typological standardization. Retouch is almost always direct percussion, consisting of notching or repeated notching. This crude denticulation is not to be confused with the regular serration seen on sickle blades, or with the regular deep denticulation found on Pottery Neolithic sickles.

Raw materials are varied, seemingly related simply to the locally available flint types.

TYPOLOGY

The primary levels of differentiation within the general class are blank thickness/retouch angle and the repetition of notching. Basically, any piece on a thick flake with abrupt or semi-abrupt retouch is a steep notch (fig. 3.46:6) or denticulate (fig. 3.46:7–8) and any piece with more than two notches is classified a denticulate. Notches vary considerably in size and regularity. At Har Qeren 15, depth of notches varied from 2 to 10 mm, and the length of the notches from 15 to 50 mm. Other assemblages show shorter notches (i.e., finer denticulation). Number of teeth on denticulates at Har Qeren 15 varied from three to seven. General size of these pieces ranged from 31 mm to 140 mm. Some notches and denticulations are single blow removals, whereas others show internal retouch. Clearly blank size dictates many of the notch size attributes. There is obviously a gradation between the two types, and for that matter between notches and denticulates and other tools, specifically scrapers and retouched flakes. It is undoubtedly possible to distinguish a series of subtypes based on various specific attributes, but the analytic value of such distinctions is unclear. Simple attribute analyses, based for example on edge angles (cf. Speth 1972) might indeed prove to be of use, but have not yet been conducted (but see McConaughy's [1979, 42] detailed typology).

FUNCTION

McConaughy's (1979, 288–89, 317–18, 324, 334) microwear analysis on flat notches and denticulates (or their equivalents in his typology) from Bab edh Dhra indicated their use as general all-purpose implements. Notches were probably used for light scraping of hard objects, like wood or bone, and denticulates may have been cutting implements or used for plant processing. The steep denticulates, not studied by McConaughy, may also have been used for working hard objects, but identifying function is speculative. The great variability in this class, the *ad hoc* nature of the tools, and the likelihood of multiple uses preclude reliable functional generalizations based on examination of limited samples.

GEOGRAPHIC DISTRIBUTION

Notches and denticulates as a general class are a dominant type throughout the Levant in the Chalcolithic and Early Bronze Ages. Steep notches and denticulates are especially common in the desert regions, and Kozloff (1972–73) has included them as a diagnostic element in his description of the Timnian culture of Sinai and the southern Negev.

CHRONOLOGY

Notches and denticulates are found in all periods, but their frequencies seem to vary chronologically. They rise in frequency to become one of the dominant classes in lithic assemblages sometime in the Late Neolithic and continue as such through the Early Bronze Age and seemingly into the Middle Bronze I, perhaps into the Middle Bronze II. By the Late Bronze Age, they have clearly declined in frequency such that they constitute only a small proportion of any assemblage. Given the problems of intrusion, it is even possible that they were no longer in use by this period.

Steep notches and denticulates are especially common in the Chalcolithic and Early Bronze Age cultures of the southern region, such as the Timnian. They too decline in the post–Early Bronze Age.

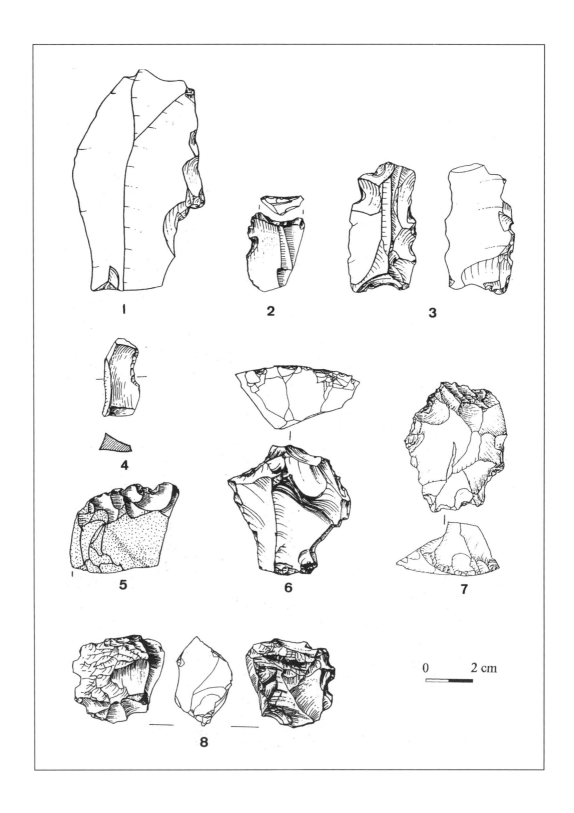

FIG. 3.46. *Notches and denticulates. 1–3, flat notches; 4–5, flat denticulates; 6, steep notch; 7–8, steep denticulates. (1, 4, Beit Yerah; 2, Sataf; 3, Hartuv [Rosen n.d.b]; 5, Mitnan [Rosen 1993c, fig. 1]; 6, 8, Qasis; 7, Uvda Valley 16 [Rosen n.d.a])*

K. Retouched Flakes and Pieces

(Fig. 3.47)

TECHNOLOGY

These pieces are the products of simple retouch on a wide range of *ad hoc* or expedient flakes and even chunks. There is no standardization in technique. Cores are amorphous. In general, the technology shows a high number of errors, such as hinged flakes, and shattered or broken flakes. Raw materials are varied, and unlike some of the more formalized tools, there seems to be little deliberate selection of specific materials.

TYPOLOGY

This category acts as a catchall for many pieces that do not fall into recognizable types, but which nevertheless show retouch (fig. 3.47). Variability is great. Although it may be possible to subdivide the class into types according to specific attributes, such as size, the utility of such types has not been demonstrated. The typological overlap with scrapers and notches and denticulates is recognized. One of the primary differences between these classes is intensity of retouch, and certainly in some cases the typological distinction is the result of greater reduction.

FUNCTION

The great variation evident in this class renders functional definition problematic. Presumably the sharper flakes were used for cutting, whereas blunter pieces might have been used for scraping or whittling (cf. McConaughy 1979, 347, 357).

GEOGRAPHY

These pieces are found throughout the Levant, with no discernible variation in frequency of types. Notably, assemblages from earlier excavations show many fewer of these tools, the result of selective recovery. As with notches and denticulates, the few well-collected assemblages from Mesopotamia (e.g., Caneva 1993) seem to show proportionally fewer retouched flakes than those of the Levant.

CHRONOLOGY

As with notches and denticulates, retouched flakes rise in frequency in Late Neolithic assemblages and continue as a dominant class through the Chalcolithic, Early Bronze, and Middle Bronze I periods. Sometime post-MBI, their importance declines so that by Late Bronze and Iron Age times they are scarce.

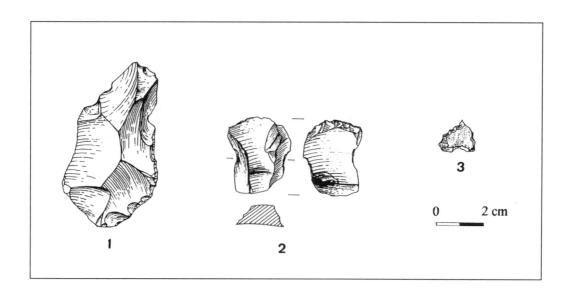

FIG. 3.47. *Retouched flakes and pieces. (1, Hartuv [Rosen n.d.b]; 2, Camel Site; 3, Yarmouth [Rosen 1988b, pl. 50])*

L. Celts

(Figs. 3.48–3.51)

    1. axes
        a. straight edge
        b. rounded edge
    3. adzes
    4. chisels
    5. picks
    6. votive axes
    6. miscellaneous
        a. roughouts
        b. other

TECHNOLOGY

Celts were manufactured on large flakes or, perhaps, flat nodules. The tools were usually modified such that original blank type is impossible to ascertain. Although roughouts have been identified, for example at Gaza A (Roshwalb 1981, 58), the complete reduction sequence has yet to be documented. Most analyses have not identified roughouts since it is difficult to distinguish them from broken pieces or simply crude pieces.

After the initial set of direct percussion large flake removals from the blank, smaller and thinner removals, also using direct percussion, shaped the implement. Distal working edges usually show longitudinal removals, although these are not always elongate or blade shaped. Repair of the tool often entailed a transverse blow across the working edge (cf. Olami 1970). Of course, distinction between original working edge and transverse repair is problematic. Many of the axes at Shiqmim (Levy and Rosen 1987, figs. 10:14.2, 17.2) show transverse blow working edges. Retouch on lateral edges either is invasive direct percussion or in some cases consists of battering, depending on the preform shape and lateral angles.

Many pieces show ground or polished working edges. Within the exception of votive axes, polishing is almost always restricted to the working edge, with occasional facets on the dorsal or ventral surfaces, probably by-products of the grinding of the working edge or as a result of use. Votive axes show polish over their entire surface.

Celts are unquestionably hafted, but no handles have been recovered. Reconstructions have been based on tool morphologies, assumed functions, and ethnographic analogies (e.g., Lee 1973; cf. Semenov 1976, 126–35; also Petrie 1917, 5–22, for metal equivalents).

Raw materials are varied. However, the more standardized types seem to require higher quality flint such as the brown Eocene material or the fine-grained translucent materials. Some picks were manufactured on coarse conglomerates. Votive axes were manufactured on magmatic stones of various types (e.g., Schick 1978).

TYPOLOGY

The types presented here are based on simple criteria (cf. Olami 1970). The primary characteristic distinguishing axes/adzes from chisels (fig. 3.48:4, 6) is tool width (fig. 3.51), chisels being significantly narrower than axes and adzes. The difference between axes (fig. 3.49) and adzes (fig. 3.48:1–3, 5) lies in the cross-section symmetry of the working edge (e.g., Lee 1973, 248; Semenov 1976, 126–35; also see Petrie 1917, 5, for metal equivalents). An axe shows a working edge bisecting the tool in cross section, whereas an adze shows a working edge skewed toward the ventral surface. Adzes are usually trapezoidal in cross section, sometimes trihedral. Axes are either lens shaped or trapezoidal. Chisels are usually, but not always, trihedral. Axes can be further subdivided, by shape of working edge, into rounded-end versus straight-ended tools. The lens-shaped sections are usually associated with the rounded ends, and lateral edges tend toward smooth convexity. The straight-ended axes tend to be trapezoid in section, and lateral edges are either parallel or diverge.

Picks (fig. 3.50:3) are large crudely worked celts, usually trihedral in section. They are often manufactured on poor quality lithic materials, such as those from Shiqmim, made on Mishash (conglomerate) flint.

Votive axes (fig. 3.50:2) show grinding or polish over both dorsal and ventral surfaces. They are made on different raw materials, usually identified in the literature as jadeite, diorite, or basalt. They are not of flint. Votive axes are lens shaped in section.

The necessity for a "miscellaneous" subtype stems from the variability evident in numerous pieces, probably caused by breakage, repair, or poor execution. Roughouts (fig. 3.50:1), that is, incomplete tools, can be considered here too.

Neuville (1934b), and Lee (1973) following him, distinguished another type, the gouge. This is essentially an axe or adze with a concave working edge. The utility of the type is questionable; the concave edge probably reflects damage and/or repair.

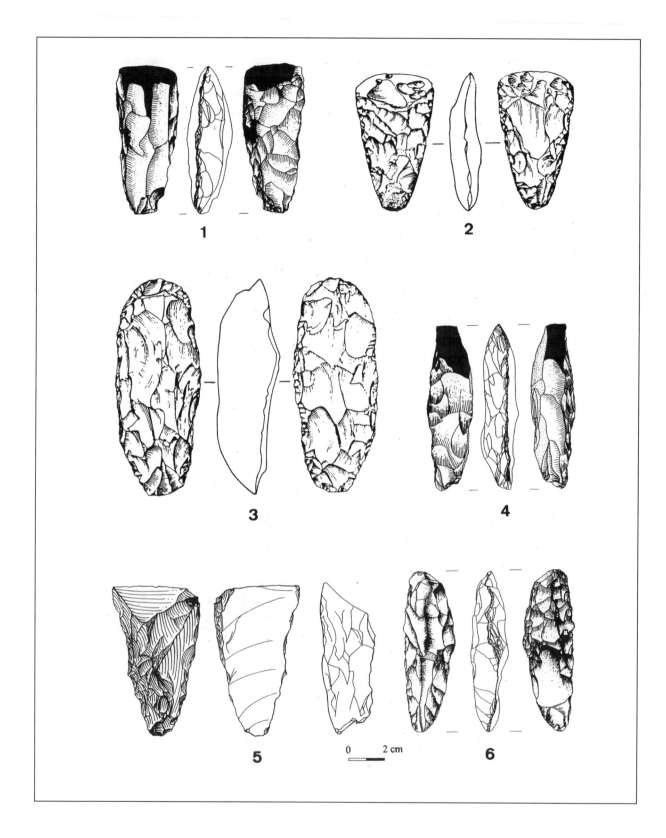

FIG. 3.48. Celts. 1–3, 5, adzes; 4, 6, chisels. [1, 4, Sataf;
2–3, Gaza M, Gaza A [Roshwalb 1981, figs. M.2, A.7];
5, Shiqmim [Levy and Rosen 1987, fig. 10.13]; 6, Grar
[Gilead et al. 1995, fig. 5.26])

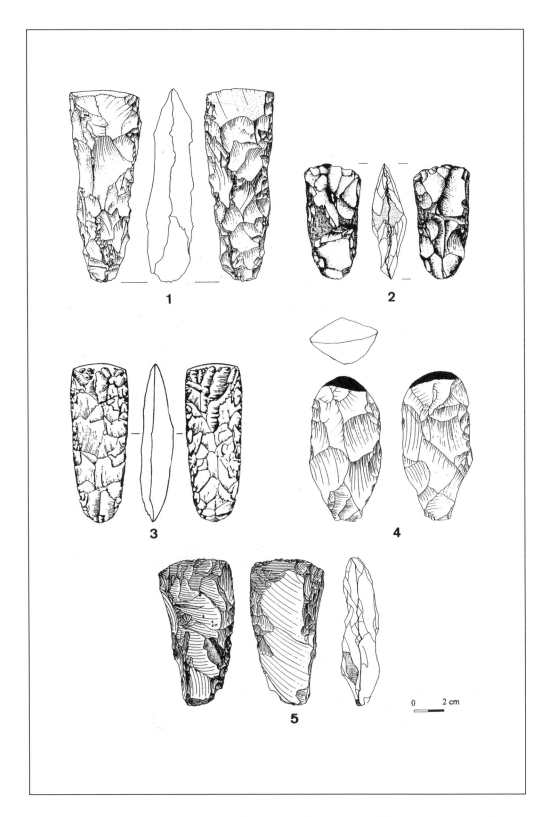

FIG. 3.49. Celts. 1–3, 5, straight-edged axes; 4, round-edged axe. (1, Nahal Nizzana 103 [Burian and Friedman 1987, fig. 4]; 2, Grar [Gilead et al. 1995, fig. 5:26]; 3, Gaza A [Roshwalb 1981, fig. A.7]; 4, Sha'ar Hagolan; 5, Shiqmim [Levy and Rosen 1987, fig. 10.13])

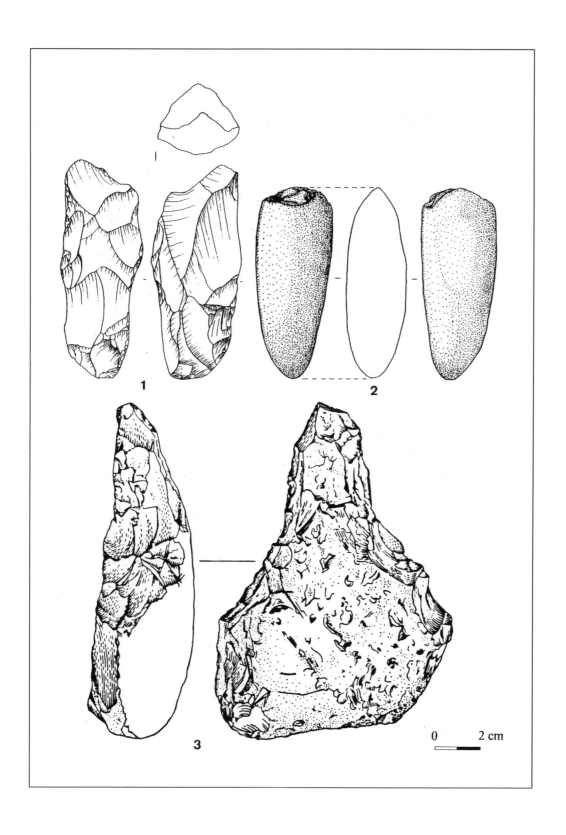

FIG. 3.50. *Celts. 1, roughout or broken axe; 2, votive axe; 3, pick. (1, Kvish Harif [Rosen 1984b, fig. 12]; 2, Mitnan [Rosen 1993c, fig. 1]; 3, Gaza H [Roshwalb 1981, fig. H.3])*

FUNCTION

The specific functions of celts have not been satisfactorily determined. Although woodworking and tree clearance are assumed from experimental work on similar tools (e.g., Semenov 1976, 126–35; Coles 1979), from ethnographic analogy (e.g., Carneiro 1979), and from microwear studies (e.g., Keeley 1983), other ethnographic studies show greatly varying uses (e.g., Dickson 1981, 6–9; Hayden 1977). Furthermore, the discovery of celts in regions where trees were probably always a rarity, such as the southern and Central Negev and south Sinai, also suggests that these tools were put to other uses. For example, Gazit (1986) has shown that edge polish develops when celt tools are used for excavation in the silt terraces of the Negev. In this connection, some of the subterranean rooms in Chalcolithic Beersheva indeed seem to show gouge marks, presumably from the use of these tools in their excavation. Alternatively, the use of celts as hoes for agriculture cannot be discounted either.

The distinct morphologies of axes, adzes, and chisels suggest to different functions as well. Lee (1973), like Semenov (1976, 126–35) suggests that the difference in edge symmetry distinguishing axes from adzes reflects different patterns of use and hafting (also Petrie 1917, 5). Axeheads, with symmetric working-edge placement, were mounted with blade parallel to the plane of the haft. A blow from an axe strikes the intended object straight on. In contrast, the adzehead,

with a skewed working edge closer to the base of the tool, was mounted with blade transverse, at 90° to the plane of the haft. The blow is struck at an arcing oblique angle. Given such reconstructions, chisels may have been hafted straight on, although this is speculative.

However, there are several practical problems with this reconstruction. First, use, reuse, and repair modify precisely the edge used for classification. A single transverse repair blow across the working edge can conceivably change an "axe" to an "adze" by modifying edge symmetry (cf. Dibble 1987 for similar typological change caused by use and repair of scrapers). Second, given such a functionally differentiated system, one would expect to find both types represented at most sites, assuming that both functions were common. This is often not the case. Simply put, function is still a difficult problem.

Votive axes are assumed to be ceremonial or ritual in use, based on archaeological contexts. For example, they have been recovered from tumuli in the Central Negev (Rosen 1993b) and other southern sites (e.g., Beit Arieh 1986; Beit Arieh and Gophna 1976; Bar-Yosef et al. 1986; Schick 1978), but are rare in domestic contexts. The fully polished surfaces of these tools indicate much effort to nonutilitarian purposes, suggesting value not associated with utilitarian function.

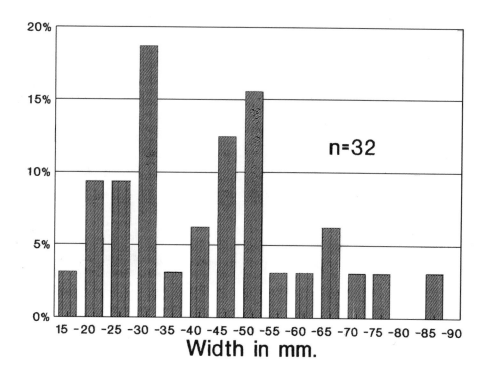

Fig. 3.51. *Histogram of axe/chisel width frequencies from Yiftahel (Neolithic). Left mode is chisels (narrow), and right mode is axes/adzes.*

GEOGRAPHY

Celts in their various forms are found throughout the Levant, from South Sinai and the southern Negev, up into Syria and Lebanon. It is difficult to discern any geographic patterns of association with specific types, especially in light of difficulties in chronological control.

CHRONOLOGY

Celts derive clearly from Late Neolithic predecessors. In the case of the round-ended axes, chronological distinction is virtually impossible to achieve. With the exception of votive axes, the entire class disappears totally with the beginning of the Early Bronze Age. The precise chronological definition of this disappearance is difficult to establish since so many of the earliest Early Bronze Age sites lay above earlier horizons, resulting in problems of intrusions. Given the virtual absence of celts at single period occupations early in the Early Bronze Age (e.g., En Shadud [Rosen 1985], Hartuv [Rosen n.d.b], Yarmouth [Rosen 1988b], En Besor [Gophna and Friedmann 1993], and Nizzanim [Yekutieli and Gophna 1994]), claims for their presence in Early Bronze Age assemblages deriving from complex stratified sites (e.g., Shuneh [Baird 1987]) need to be examined very carefully. Regardless of the precise date of disappearance, it is clear that the process was a rapid one, which was completed during the Early Bronze Age.

Within the Chalcolithic, data are chronologically problematic, and geographically skewed to the south. It is possible that round-ended axes chronologically precede straight-ended axes and adzes. Certainly, the latter types dominate the assemblages from the Beersheva sites and seem less dominant at Ghassul, which may be earlier. On the other hand, the presence of late Neolithic at Ghassul complicates the picture, and Roshwalb (1981) was unable to distinguish subtype variation between late Neolithic and Chalcolithic horizons from Wadi Gaza.

In contrast to utilitarian types, votive axes continue in use through at least the Early Bronze II and perhaps as late as the Iron Age. However, the problems of intrusions of rare artifacts, or for that matter reuse of curated or found pieces, render post–Early Bronze Age attributions problematic, although not to be rejected outright.

M. Choppers

(Fig. 3.52:1–2)
  1. cobble choppers
  2. other choppers

TECHNOLOGY

Cobble choppers were manufactured by opening wadi cobbles, either through flaking angled edges or by splitting, followed by the removal of a few flakes, either bifacially or unifacially, to form a sharp edge. Most are roughly fist sized and show cortex over most of the "dorsal" surface. Other choppers show similar techniques of manufacture, but may be manufactured on nodules or chunks. The expedient nature of the technology is to be noted.

TYPOLOGY

It is possible to adopt Leakey's (1971) system for typological classification of choppers, dividing them into side-, end-, pointed-, chisel-ended, and so forth, as based on her work at the Lower Paleolithic site of Olduvai Gorge in Kenya. The analytic utility of these types seems questionable since morphology seems dictated by cobble or nodule shape and location of suitable edges for flaking. The distinction between cobble choppers and others is made because of the large number of choppers made on locally available wadi cobbles in the Beersheva Chalcolithic sites. The type seems characteristic of the assemblages from this area (cf. Yeivin 1959).

As in the Lower Paleolithic, and other periods, distinguishing between choppers and the preliminary stages of core reduction can be problematic. Edge damage on many choppers and the relatively large number of these tools suggest that they are more than partially reduced cores, but the possibility cannot be excluded. Choppers, especially in the Beersheva Chalcolithic, also overlap typologically with some scrapers, especially those on cortical flakes.

FUNCTION

As mentioned above, some choppers may be preliminary cores, not reduced beyond the initial stages of decortication. However, McConaughy (1979, 273–74) found signs of plant processing—pounding and shredding—on the edges of chopperlike tools from Bab edh Dhra.

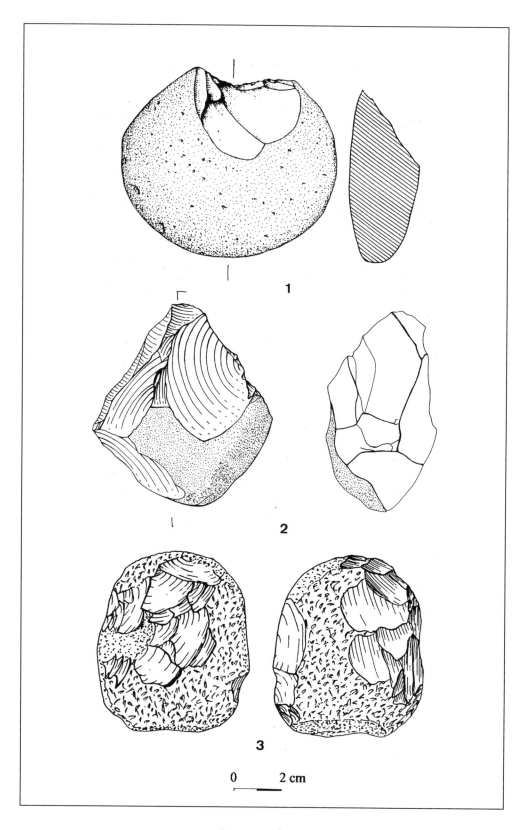

FIG. 3.52. *Choppers and hammerstones. 1–2, choppers;*
3, hammerstone. (1, Grar [Gilead et al. 1995, fig. 5.4];
2, Shiqmim [Levy and Rosen 1987, fig. 10.21];
3, En Besor [Gophna and Friedman 1993, fig. 3])

GEOGRAPHICAL DISTRIBUTION

Choppers as a class appear in low numbers in all areas under study. Cobble choppers seem to be especially common in the Beersheva Chalcolithic (e.g., Yeivin 1959; Levy and Rosen 1987).

CHRONOLOGY

Choppers are especially common in the Chalcolithic of the Beersheva Basin (Schick 1978; Yeivin 1959; Levy and Rosen 1987; Rosen and Eldar 1993), but they occur in low numbers, as *ad hoc* tools, during Early Bronze times as well. As with other expedient tools, they seem to decline in the post–Early Bronze Age. Notably, such a simple technology may appear with little connection to previous lithic traditions, especially in association with flake oriented reduction.

N. Ephemeral Types

1. burins
2. threshing teeth

BURINS

Burins are pointed tools manufactured by a longitudinal blow or blows down the edge of a flake, leaving a chisellike end (e.g., Semenov 1976, 94–99). Although common from Upper Paleolithic through the Middle of the Pottery Neolithic, they are extremely rare in post-Neolithic contexts. In fact, it is likely that burins appearing in post-Neolithic assemblages are either (1) chance occurrences caused by manufacturing mistakes, (2) misidentified snaps (sometimes on truncations!), or (3) intrusions.

THRESHING TEETH

The *tribulum,* or threshing sledge, has been studied ethnographically (Whallon 1978; Ataman 1992; Bordaz 1965, 1969) and is known from classical period texts from the Near East (e.g., Adams 1975). A threshing sledge is a board with stone or metal teeth inserted underneath, which is run over a threshing floor with unseparated cereal grains. The threshing teeth thus break open the glumes, releasing the cereal seeds, and winnowing then separates the chaff from the seeds. Flint threshing teeth are usually medium-sized flakes, rarely larger than 5 cm in length. Whallon (1978) indicates clear wear patterns, in the form of polish and facetting on the working edge of these pieces, derived from contact with the grains and threshing floor. Basalt teeth, common in nineteenth and early twentieth century Palestine, are usually similarly sized pebbles, and also show clear facets and polish (pers. obs.).

No unequivocal threshing teeth have yet been recovered from archaeological contexts. Claims for their presence at Early Bronze Age Uvda Valley (Avner 1990, 130) are speculative, and the artifacts lack the facetting described by Whallon (1978) as diagnostic. Anderson and Inizan (1994) have suggested that some Canaanean blades may have functioned as threshing teeth. Their microwear analogues are important, but still require confirmation.

O. Hammerstones

(Fig. 3.52:3)
 1. spheroids
 2. pecked stones

TECHNOLOGY

Hammerstones are often excluded from studies of chipped stone, because although they are made of stone, they are generally not the products of conchoidal fracture. However, as they are often incorporated into lithic assemblages, they are included here. They are manufactured through the crushing and pecking of cobbles, usually ranging in size from 5 to 10 cm in diameter. Many pieces show crushing on all sides and are quite rounded. Some preserve the original shape of the stone, showing pecking on only one edge or end, and may thereby be longer. Some pieces show what appear to be flake scars, but striking platforms are absent. Raw materials vary, but flint is common.

TYPOLOGY

Hammerstones can be divided into two general categories, spheroids and pecked stones. The spheroids are round, ball-like stones, with pecking and crushing on all surfaces. The standardization in their size and shape suggests that they were intentionally manufactured as such. Pecked stones show only limited evidence of use (or manufacture), and the pecking is probably the result of use rather than intentional modification.

FUNCTION

Although the term *hammerstone* has been retained for these pieces, their use as hammerstones in the manufacture of other flint implements is *not* to be assumed. The spheroids probably functioned as pounding stones, perhaps in the preparation of food. Other possible functions include use as projectile weapons and, perhaps, crude weights. Of course, a subsidiary function as hammerstones should not be excluded. The pecked stones show more limited use and are more likely to have been used as hammerstones.

GEOGRAPHICAL DISTRIBUTION

This type is found throughout the Levant.

CHRONOLOGY

Spheroids and hammerstones are known from the earliest prehistoric times (e.g., Willoughby 1985) and continue through the Bronze Age and into the Iron Age.

NOTES

1. The lithic assemblage from the Persian stratum at Hesi (Bennett et al. 1989) contains Pottery Neolithic arrowheads and sickle segments (showing classic Pottery Neolithic A deep denticulation), Early Bronze Age Canaanean sickles, and typical Large Geometric Iron Age sickles. These have all been classified as Persian. No distinctive Persian types were defined. It would be interesting to see if the ceramic assemblage were as mixed as the lithic.

2. A recent claim for Canaanean technology in the Chalcolithic of Shiqmim (Rowan and Levy 1994) is problematic. Essentially a group of thirteen fine-grained brown prismatic blade tools were identified as significantly contrasting with standard Chalcolithic technology. A superficial similarity based on raw material and cross-section shape suggested "proto-Canaanean" to the authors. Canaanean technology is defined on the basis of assemblages and a range of attributes, and includes recognition of a range of variability. The tools identified by Rowan and Levy are not sickles, the primary and nearly exclusive products of Canaanean technology. The identification seems premature. Notably, the identification of Canaanite (sic) technology at Fasael (Milstein and Ronen 1985) is clearly mistaken, and the blades do not conform to Canaanean attributes.

3. Gophna and Friedmann (1993) claim that these are best classified as sickles, but the absence of sickle gloss on so many pieces cannot be ignored.

4. E.g., modal length for backed blades at Uvda 16 and Uvda 18 is 55–65 mm; modal length for backed blades at Erani is 40–50 mm.

5. I am grateful to Tamar Noy for showing me the results of her forthcoming research on these materials from the Golan Chalcolithic. The detailed publication of these materials will provide important insights in the regionalization of the different techno-typological variants of tabular scrapers.

4 The Organization of Production and Distribution

Introduction

The structure of lithic systems in the protohistoric and historic periods in the Levant is fundamentally different from that of the Paleolithic. The greater complexity of post-Paleolithic economies is well reflected in the lithic systems, and their essential feature is their multiplicity. Different tool groups are the products of different production/distribution systems, which can be reconstructed by reference to differential distribution of diagnostic waste and comparison to the distribution of resulting tools.

Diachronically, several trends can be traced effecting the differentiation seen in these later assemblages. Increasing specialization in lithic production for some tool groups can be seen, beginning probably in the Neolithic (e.g., Rosen 1989b) and culminating in the Bronze and Iron Ages. There is also increasing specialization in use, corresponding to the production specialization. On a lower level, an unspecialized mode of expedient production and use continues as well and, in fact, numerically dominates the lithic systems of these periods.

The final trend to be noted is the rise of metallurgy as a technology, which slowly, over the course of several millennia, ultimately replaces lithic technology in most of its functions. This apparently was behind some of the increasing restriction in lithic types in the later periods (Chapter 7).

The Chalcolithic Systems (FIG. 4.1)

During the Chalcolithic period in the settled zone, modes or patterns of production-distribution can be defined incorporating sets of tools and varying degrees of specialization. These economic structures undoubtedly originated earlier, in the late Pottery Neolithic (e.g., Qatifian and Wadi Raba cultures), but data for the Neolithic are limited at best and beyond the scope of this work. In the desert periphery, these production-distribution modes seem less pronounced and less discrete, probably reflecting a general economic system

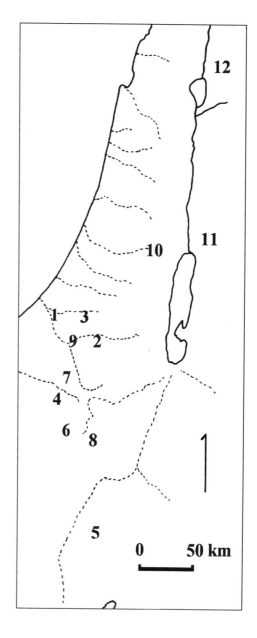

FIG. 4.1. *Map of Chalcolithic sites mentioned in Chapter 4.*
1. Gaza sites, especially Gaza A and Gaza M; 2. Beersheva sites: Abu Matar, Safadi, Horvat Beter; 3. Grar; 4. Nahal Nizzana 103; 5. Uvda Valley sites; 6. Nahal Mitnan; 7. Har Qeren 15; 8. Kvish Harif; 9. Shiqmim; 10. Sataf and Ir David; 11. Ghassul, 12. Golan Sites.

more based on domestic modes of production (cf. Sahlins 1972). Social groups in the desert are also significantly more mobile than those of the agricultural zones.

The Chalcolithic lithic production-distribution system shows minimally a two-tiered hierarchical structure, consisting of *ad hoc* tools manufactured on-site by nonspecialist users for a range of domestic tasks, and semispecialized manufacture of blade-bladelet tools and celts, centered at production sites like Gaza A, one of a series of small Chalcolithic and Late Pottery Neolithic sites along the Wadi Gaza (the southern Coastal Plain), and excavated by Macdonald in the late 1920s, under Petrie's patronage (Macdonald 1932; Roshwalb 1981). A third mode of manufacture-distribution can be tentatively identified for tabular scrapers, which seem to show at least the initial stages of production in the pastoral periphery, possibly with later reduction occurring at lithic production centers, again like Gaza A. In terms of structure, microlithic drill production and use seem to fall between the blade-bladelet and tabular scraper systems.

BLADE AND BLADELET TOOLS

Increasing specialization in the manufacture of sickle blade segments, microendscrapers and other retouched bladelets, and perhaps microlithic drills can be reconstructed from the discovery of a major workshop at Gaza A (Macdonald 1932, 10, pls. xvii and xxii:2; Roshwalb 1981, 58; Gilead [pers. comm.] has identified another smaller sickle production workshop at Safadi, as yet unpublished), and blade core:blade tool ratios at other sites (table 4.1), especially in comparison with the domestic expedient system of tool manufacture (see below). In essence, blade and bladelet tools seem, at least in part, to have been manufactured in workshop sites and transported from these centers to other sites. In the absence of excavation of complete sites, it is obviously impossible to determine whether each site included a specialized production area or whether production occurred primarily at manufacturing centers. However, the marked contrast between Gaza A and other sites, and the relatively large exposures at numerous sites in the Beersheva Basin (e.g., Abu Matar, Horvat Beter, Safadi, Shiqmim) suggest the latter. It is also clear that some on-site manufacture occurred at virtually all sites, to judge by the presence of blade and bladelet cores in small quantities all over. It is difficult to ascertain whether the local production was based on imported prepared blade cores or whether local craftspeople manufactured the local blades from scratch. Given the availability of raw material, in the form of banded high-quality flint wadi cobbles at all the Beersheva sites, the presence of mixed blade-flake cores as well as the blade cores, and the evidence for their reduction in the manufacture of choppers and scrapers, it seems reasonable to assume that blade tools may well have been manufactured in small numbers from local cobbles at most sites, in addition to being imported. With respect to bladelet tools, the nonlocal raw materials (chalcedony) suggest that cores may well have been imported along with bladelets.

Given the presence of some local manufacture, it is impossible to determine whether the specialists at the different manufacturing centers (and one can assume more than a single center given the raw material variability between blade tool assemblages from different sites [e.g., Gilead et al. 1995] and the distance between sites) produced complete composite tools (including hafts), retouched but unhafted blade and bladelet segments, or simple blades and bladelets to be modified by the user. No caches or packets of unretouched blades have been recovered from Chalcolithic sites (as have been found in the Early Bronze Age), and Gaza A was excavated too long ago, with methods too imprecise by modern standards, to be able to reconstruct the final on-site products of the reduction process.

The relationships between the different tool types are not clear either. Although the Gaza A workshop contained large numbers of both blade and bladelet cores, proportions of blade to bladelet tools, notably microendscrapers and other retouched bladelets versus sickle segments, vary considerably from site to site and region to region (table 4.1; cf. Gilead 1988, 1989; Rosen 1987). To a degree, this variability is probably functional, relating to factors such as intensity of agricultural exploitation (see Chapter 5) as it might affect sickle blade frequencies. However, the difference in frequencies also suggests that at least in some cases the production of the different types may have been undertaken by different people. That is, in spite of similarities in the structure of the distribution systems, the actual systems themselves were not identical. The geographic differences in frequency distribution between bladelet tools and sickles supports this, and the possibility of chronological variation between the types also accords well (cf. Levy 1995; Gilead 1990).

This is also apparent from examination of the microdrill systems. Microlithic drills are virtually unknown at most Chalcolithic village sites, yet are abundant at Gaza M, also excavated by Macdonald in the 1920s, and at (apparently) Chalcolithic sites[1] in the western Negev, such as Nahal Nizzana 103, collected by Burian and Friedman (1987). Although these tools are made from bladelets roughly similar to those of microendscrapers, they are found in greatest numbers in the western Negev sites. Although some of these sites seem to show local manufacture of drills, as for example in the presence of incomplete drills, Nahal Nizzana did not contain near enough cores to account for the six thousand drills recovered, and primary manufacture of the drills must have occurred elsewhere, presumably at a site similar to Gaza A.

These patterns also indicate at least some specialization in use, as well as in lithic manufacture. It is clear that Gaza M was a major bead production site, exporting to other sites where there is no evidence for bead manufacture at all, in spite of the discovery of beads on many sites. The site was also an occupation site, a village. It is difficult to characterize Nahal Nizzana 103 as a bead production site *per se* since it may be drop site or some such, but it certainly reflects specialized manufacture. No architectural remains were discovered there at all.

The desert sites, as at the Uvda Valley, Kvish Harif, and Nahal Mitnan, show fundamentally different production-distribution structures for blade and bladelet tools. Virtually all these sites show evidence for on-site manufacture of transverse arrowheads, in the form of small mixed blade-flake cores and blades/bladelets (table 4.1). Those sites with little evidence

for on-site manufacture of blade/bladelet tools contained few such tools, so that import when it does occur can easily be accounted for by tool curation, i.e., manufacture, transport, and use by the same person or persons. There are no indications of specialized manufacture.

TABULAR SCRAPERS

The tabular scraper system seems to differ significantly from the blade-bladelet system. Although the presence of seventy-seven tabular scrapers (Roshwalb 1981, 39) in varying states of completion at Gaza A suggests that the site functioned as a secondary workshop, the apparent absence[2] of cores and appropriate core waste indicates that the site did not function as a primary workshop, as it did for the blade and bladelet tools. Instead, quarry sites and primary workshops are known only from the desert regions farther south, in the western Negev (Rosen 1983b; also Perrot 1955) and South Sinai (Kozloff 1972–73). Although a geometric falloff curve has been constructed for the general tabular scraper system (Rosen 1983b, 1989a), it appears that this system is primarily Early Bronze Age in date (Rosen 1989a). There is little discernible geographic pattern to the frequency distribution of Chalcolithic tabular scrapers, except insofar as Central Negev and Sinai sites show generally higher proportions than heartland sites. Within the settled zones, however, the Beersheva sites show remarkably few tabular scrapers when compared with assemblages from the center and north of the country (table 4.1), in spite of their greater proximity to the apparent sources.

	Blade Cores	Tools	C:T	Bladelet Cores	Tools	C:T	Flake Cores	Tools	C:T	Tabular Cores	Tools	C:T
Sataf-Chal	0	38	0.00	5	22	0.23	7	29	0.24	0	4	0
H. Beter	9	23	0.39	3	2	1.50	162	193	0.84	0	2	0
Grar	11	248	0.04	10	30	0.33	190	366	0.52	0	7	0
Shiqmim	2	299	0.01	2	24	0.08	1029	5500	0.19	0	8	0
Gaza A*	450	92	4.89	950	263	3.61	20	126	0.16	0	77	0
Gaza B	11	16	0.69	17	2	8.50	2	25	0.08	0	12	0
Gaza D	5	62	0.08	5	13	0.38	2	50	0.04	0	6	0
Gaza O	16	29	0.55	5	2	2.50	2	64	0.03	0	0	0
Gaza M (F.2)	33	10	3.30	17	211	0.08	6	27	0.22	0	1	0
H. Qeren 15	0	3	0.00	0	0	**	6	176	0.03	25	25	1
K. Harif	1	7	0.14	8	18	0.44	49	245	0.20	0	32	0

TABLE 4.1. Core:tool ratios from Chalcolithic sites. *Estimated **Undefined

Examination of Har Qeren 15,[3] a small quarry site in the dunes of the western Negev and the only one of its kind analyzed (Rosen 1983b; Rosen and Goring-Morris n.d.b), indicates that tabular scraper manufacture, or, perhaps better, at least the production of tabular scraper blanks, does not appear to have been an intensive operation. Only twenty-four cores, representing at most a few dozen tabular scrapers, were recovered from the site. The rest of the lithic assemblage from the site, consisting of scrapers, notches, denticulates, and other *ad hoc* elements, suggests a range of other activities not related to lithic manufacture. Thus, the site seems to be a semispecialized activity site, probably attached to a larger settlement or settlement system in the general area. In turn, this system is most likely a pastoral adjunct to the Chalcolithic heartland, representing either seasonal occupation by shepherds coming south from the Beersheva or Lower Besor (Wadi Gaza) Basins (cf. Gilead and Goren 1986), or a perhaps more independent pastoral system operating on the fringes of the agricultural region farther north. Regardless, the absence of all evidence for manufacture on all the more northern sites except Gaza A indicates import of these artifacts. The source area seems to be in the desert pastoral periphery, notably a prime source for the appropriate raw materials. It is likely that at least some of the distribution of these artifacts was mediated through secondary processing centers, such as Gaza A.

CELT TOOLS

Evidence for the manufacture of celt tools, axes, adzes, chisels, etc., is more subtle than for the previous tool groups. In the absence of detailed technological studies, the flake debitage from the manufacture of these tools is indistinguishable from other flake waste, and the only indicator of celt manufacture is the presence of roughouts, i.e., incomplete tools. Given the high instances of breakage and repair, even these may be difficult to identify. In general the Gaza sites seem to show higher proportions of celt roughouts than others, especially Gaza A (Roshwalb 1981, 45–52). Notably, data from the other sites are problematic. A production-distribution system similar to that of blade tools seems reasonable since there is little evidence for manufacture of celt tools in the Beersheva Basin sites. The manufacture of celt tools on more or less local raw materials, as opposed to the imported Eocene flint used for tabular scrapers, more or less supports the idea of Gaza A as a primary workshop site for these

tools. Although some celt tools (perhaps most) were produced from large flakes (as opposed to the reduction of nodules as in classic core tools), the absence of diagnostic cores may be the result of further reduction, since similar raw materials were used for blade production. That is, unlike tabular scrapers, the absence of cores need not imply that the initial stages of production occurred off-site.

Celt tools are rare in the desert sites. There is little evidence available for reconstruction of production-distribution patterns.

AD HOC TOOLS

This general class, consisting of notches, denticulates, borers, retouched flakes, choppers, awls, and, to a lesser extent, scrapers, shows little evidence for specialized manufacture, import/export, or exchange, either in the settled regions or in the desert, in marked contrast to the tool systems described above. The abundance of simple expedient flake cores, and large quantities of flake waste at virtually all sites and most especially village and hamlet sites, indicates the predominance of on-site manufacture (table 4.1). This is supported by the use of local raw materials for all of these tools, the general lack of standardization in their manufacture, and the simple technologies used.

The quantitative dominance of the *ad hoc* tool complex is also important (table 4.1). Although perhaps a partial result of more activities in which these tools were used, the minimal retouch on many *ad hoc* tools, especially the numerically dominant retouched flakes, notches, and denticulates, indicates only minimal efforts in manufacture and probably fairly rapid discard (since greater use would presumably require resharpening). This suggests that in general these tools were made quickly by the users (or by people in close association), used, and discarded, with little effort toward conservation or curation. The possible exceptions include some of the more finely made scrapers and borers, constituting a low proportion of the complex. Of course, expedient production and rapid discard would create archaeological abundance (cf. Shott 1989).

The Early Bronze Age (Fig. 4.2)

The Early Bronze Age assemblages of the settled zone can be divided into three basic industries, excluding the intrusive Egyptian elements (see Chapter 6). These are the Canaanean sickle industry, the tabular scraper industry, and the *ad hoc* industry, each one exhibiting discrete patterns of production and distribution. The desert Early Bronze Age assemblages show additional components that have little in common with the settled zone, with the exception of the tabular scraper industry. The lithic industries are notable for their differences in geographic scale and degree of specialization. The Canaanean system is based on specialized or semispecialized production, local distribution and exchange networks, and curated use and reuse. Tabular scrapers are longer distance trade items than Canaanean blades, deriving primarily from the desert, and were probably part of the peripheral pastoral economic system. The *ad hoc* system is an unspecialized, intrasite industry and can be characterized as expedient in production, use, and discard. The desert lithic systems are more akin to those of the preceding Stone Age, reflecting minimal specialization and exchange in lithic artifacts, in general accord with the pastoral nomadic systems from which they derive.

CANAANEAN SICKLES AND BLADES

Specialized production of Canaanean blades can be postulated on the basis of three primary sets of data. First, although these sickles are abundant in virtually all Early Bronze Age settlements in the settled zone, diagnostic cores are absent from the vast majority of sites (table 4.2). The absence of cores and the almost exclusive exploitation of relatively source-restricted fine-grained brown Eocene flint for the manufacture of these tools indicate that they were imported to most sites. Notably, even excavations with large exposures, such as Arad and Yarmouth, have failed to recover Canaanean cores, again indicating that the blades were indeed imported and not merely produced in specialized activity areas.

Second, caches or packets of unmodified Canaanean blades, consisting of eight to fifteen blades, each deriving from the same core, have been recovered from four sites, Beit Yerah (Rosen n.d.a), Motza (Eisenberg 1993), Lower Horvat 'Illin (Marder et al. 1995), and Nizzanim (Yekutieli and Gophna 1994). These seem to represent exchange packets. The fact that they are not physically associated with cores suggests import and not on-site production. The lack of modification indicates that the sickles themselves were probably manufactured by the users.

Finally, evidence for manufacture, in the form of cores and in some cases associated blades and decortication blades, has been discovered at a few sites, including Saida Dakkerman, in Lebanon (Hours

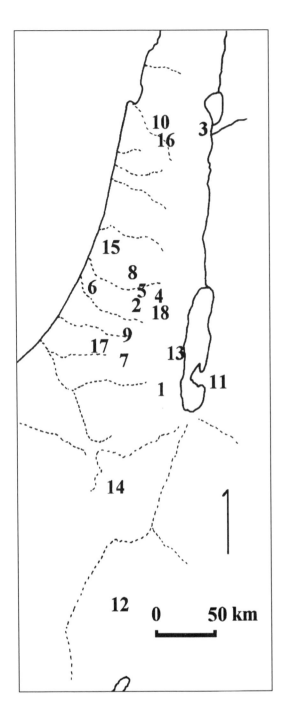

FIG. 4.2. *Map of Early Bronze Age sites mentioned in Chapter 4. 1. Arad; 2. Yarmouth; 3. Beit Yerah; 4. Motza; 5. Lower Horvat Illin; 6. Nizzanim; 7. Lahav (Tell Halif); 8. Gezer; 9. Erani and Gat-Guvrin; 10. Har Haruvim and Qasis; 11. Bab edh Dhra; 12. Uvda Valley sites; 13. Mitzpe Shalem; 14. Camel Site; 15. Azor; 16. En Shadud; 17. Hesi.*

	Canaanean Cores	Tools	ratio	Blade Cores	Tools	ratio	Flake Cores	Tools	ratio	Tabular Cores	Tools	ratio
Arad	0	73	0	0	17	0.00	13	83	0.16	0	64	0
Hartuv	0	16	0	0	34	0.00	10	97	0.10	0	3	0
Beit Yerah	0	83	0	0	33	0.00	9	42	0.21	0	10	0
Yarmouth	0	54	0	0	9	0.00	17	43	0.40	0	20	0
Shadud	0	47	0	0	14	0.00	75	336	0.22	0	2	0
Hesi EB	0	50	0	4	33	0.12	87	243	0.36	0	5	0
Qasis EB	0	82	0	1	14	0.07	17	101	0.17	0	7	0
Malha	0	22	0	1	75	0.01	48	179	0.27	0	0	0
B. edh Dhra	0	0	**	2	97	0.02	29	222	0.13	0	14	0
BU16	0	0	**	1	55	0.02	52	141	0.37	0	6	0

TABLE 4.2. Core:tool ratios from Early Bronze Age sites. **Undefined

1979); Lahav (Futato 1990; Forshey 1987) and Gat-Guvrin (Perrot 1961),[4] both in the northern Negev; Gezer, in the center of the country (Macalister 1912, II:126, fig. 300); and Har Charuvim, in the Galilee (Meyerhof 1960). Only Har Charuvim and Gat Guvrin (and perhaps Lahav) seem to show more than a few cores, although none have been fully investigated or reported, so that evaluation is difficult. It is notable that of these sites only Lahav (Tel Halif) can be classified as a town or a city. They seem to be Early Bronze Age villages (although in the case of Gezer, it is impossible to characterize the site for this period).

In an earlier study, I measured the widths of Canaanean sickles (Rosen 1983a) and showed that the averages and width distributions differed in assemblages from different sites. This suggested that the individual assemblages derived from different populations of blades, i.e., different sources. Although the methodology was flawed since retouch was not taken into account, the conclusions are probably valid anyway. Variability in raw materials between sites (as in the coarser grained raw material of the blades from Beit Yerah) and the existence of several apparent workshop sites do indeed suggest multiple sources (cf. Cauvin 1968 for an opposing view; also see Betts 1992a for brief discussion). Thus the Canaanean system can be viewed as one based on specialized or semi-specialized production in village centers, with local distribution of unmodified blades, later snapped or truncated and hafted by the user.

One qualification needs to be noted. Both Saida Dakerman and Gat Guvrin are dated to the Early Bronze I, a preurban phase. The presence of nine cores at Tel Halif in the urban Early Bronze III (Futato 1990) suggests the possibility of a shift from village to city production with the rise of urbanism. Other sites cannot be characterized adequately. In short, data are simply insufficient to test this as yet.

The presence of low frequencies (10–30%) of unstandardized non-Canaanean sickle segments at many sites (table 4.2) and some evidence for their manufacture (cores, decortication blades) suggests the additional existence of an on-site adjunct industry. These may have served for expedient sickle repair or some such.

The local or cellular nature of this exchange system is to be emphasized. The near absence of Canaanean blades at Bab edh Dhra (McConaughy 1979, 218), replaced by simple blade and backed blade sickles, but lacking evidence for manufacture, again supports the idea of local networks. That is, Bab edh Dhra, located just east of the Dead Sea and clearly contemporary with such sites as Arad and Jericho, was nonetheless part of a different sickle distribution system, in spite of its geographic proximity.

In this context of technological variability from site to site, the Egyptian presence during the Early Bronze I horizon at Tel Erani, in the Shephela, also requires comment. As is the case for Canaanean blades, there are not enough simple blade cores to account for the large number of Egyptian style sickles and blade tools at the site. Whether the Egyptian knapper worked at Erani itself, and his workshop has not yet been exposed, or whether the blades are imports is a moot point. The real issue is that there was apparent specialization in the production of these blades, so much so that there was an Egyptian knapper on the site (see Chapter 6). Furthermore, the Egyptian materials are contemporary with Canaanean blades, so that in fact there are two specialist knapper systems intersecting at this site in the Early Bronze I.

The general Canaanean blade system was also limited geographically, not extending into the desert regions, and not even into those where agriculture was a common practice, as at the Uvda Valley sites in the southern Negev (table 4.2). On one hand, this may be a direct consequence of the nature of a system based on specialists in villages supplying larger urban zones. On the other, as noted above with respect to Bab edh Dhra, there may also be geographic borders to the distribution of the type, perhaps based on "traditions" of flint working (see Chapter 6). Regardless, the economic systems linking the desert with the Mediterranean or urban region were not all encompassing, and the lack of Canaanean blades in desert agricultural sites is indicative of the fact that economic integration between the desert and the sown was not complete. Detailed exploration of this lack of integration is beyond the scope of this work, but the lithic production systems can be used as one line of evidence in reconstructing economic asymmetries between heartland and periphery, as well in delineating more precise mechanisms of exchange between the systems.

THE TABULAR SCRAPER SYSTEM

The tabular scraper exchange system in the Early Bronze Age is a direct descendent of the Chalcolithic system. No sites north of the western Negev show evidence for tabular scraper production, with the only possible exception being at Lahav (Futato 1990), showing a Canaanean blade core with large primary decortication removals matching the general shape of fanscrapers[5] (table 4.2). As per the Chalcolithic, and in fact indistinguishable from it, quarry sites are known from the Negev and Sinai (Rosen 1983b; Kozloff 1972–73; Perrot 1955, 179), but do not seem to reflect intensive exploitation. No known secondary production sites comparable to Chalcolithic Gaza A are known.

During the Early Bronze Age, the Negev and Sinai are clearly part of a pastoral nomadic zone (e.g., Haiman 1992; Rosen 1988c). It is reasonable to attach the nonintensive production of tabular scrapers to part of the pastoral round, a system that undoubtedly incorporated a wide range of activities beyond animal husbandry (e.g., Betts 1989, 1992b; Rosen 1993a; Saidel 1995).

Distribution frequency of tabular scrapers closely follows a geometric decline with distance from source when measured from the western Negev (Rosen 1983b, 1989a). Deviations from this curve need not imply rejection of the trade model (e.g., Helms 1987), but rather suggest additional factors that ought to be considered. Thus, although the model as originally suggested utilizes only a single point of origin, in the western Negev, for tabular scrapers, it is clear that other sources were also exploited. Beyond the already known quarry sites in Sinai, it should not be surprising if additional workshops are discovered in eastern Jordan and Syria.

The problem of complex sampling and sample size also affects our understanding of the frequency distribution. In particular, since tabular scrapers, especially in the north, seem to have some ritual function, higher numbers can be expected to be recovered from ritual loci, as indeed has been demonstrated by McConaughy (1979, 304; 1980a; 1980b) at Bab edh Dhra (also see Elliott 1977). Thus, excavation strategies can significantly affect sampled populations since tabular scrapers are not distributed evenly over the sites. At small sites, site function may have even greater effect. The presence of over four hundred tabular scrapers at Mitzpe Shalem (Greenhut 1989) is not a refutation of the trade model, but an indication of the special function of the site. Similarly, central places in general may affect frequency distributions (e.g., Fry 1980).

Variable function and value of tabular scrapers may also affect distribution patterns. The greater number of incised scrapers and apparently greater standardization in manufacture in northern assemblages suggests a higher symbolic loading and greater value for those pieces than for tabular scrapers found in the Negev and Sinai. Proximity to sources may render the raw material less valuable, allowing its use for a wider range of activities, resulting in relatively greater numbers of tools in the southern regions.

| | Blade | | | Flake | | |
	Cores	Tools	ratio	Cores	Tools	ratio
Hesi Iron	0	132	0	52	200	0.26
Gezer	0	212	0	0	3	0.00
Qasis MB-Ir	0	116	0	3	44	0.07
Batashi MB2-Ir	0	86	0	2	22	0.09
Wawiyat	0	66	0	3	17	0.18
D.el Balah	0	219	0	10	64	0.16

TABLE 4.3. Core:tool ratios from post–Early Bronze Age sites.

AD HOC TOOLS

These tools, consisting of retouched flakes, notches, denticulates, borers, crude scrapers, and a range of other miscellaneous trimmed pieces, numerically dominate virtually all Early Bronze Age assemblages. As in the preceding Chalcolithic, there is abundant evidence, in the form of numerous expedient cores, flakes, and other waste (table 4.2), that this general complex was produced on-site with no specialization in manufacture nor exchange. Raw materials are varied and usually local in origin, reflecting exploitation of whatever flint was on hand. The complex can be characterized in a word—*expedient*.

DESERT SYSTEMS

Assemblages from the Negev and Sinai show a fair amount of typological and technological variability, encompassing at least four distinct technological modes: blade tools (sickles, backed blades, retouched blades, arched backed blades), bladelet tools (arrowheads, microlithic lunates, microlithic drills, retouched bladelets), tabular scrapers, and *ad hoc* flake tools (types as above). However, unlike northern assemblages, where the technological modes seem to correspond to discrete modes of production and distribution, tabular scrapers constitute the only class for which there is evidence for off-site manufacture (table 4.2). Cores and waste appropriate to all other classes are found on most sites, and there is little evidence for specialized manufacture.

The presence of numerous microlithic drills and evidence for their manufacture, at the Camel Site, and the absence of similar phenomena at other sites can be interpreted as a kind of specialization in drill production, as well as bead making (Rosen 1995). However, this is clearly of a different order than the specialization-distribution system of the Canaanean blades in Mediterranean zone. At the Camel Site, the drill makers were also the drill users. Furthermore, bead making based on fifty microlithic drills in a small pastoral encampment cannot be interpreted as an intensive specialized activity, but is better seen as a kind of specialized cottage industry.

As mentioned above, there is some evidence for regional overlap between the desert and the Mediterranean zone in the lithic systems. This is most obviously evident in the tabular scraper system, whose sources seem to be in the pastoral periphery. The presence of microlithic lunates in some sites in the north (e.g., Azor [Rosen 1983c]) may also be a reflection of

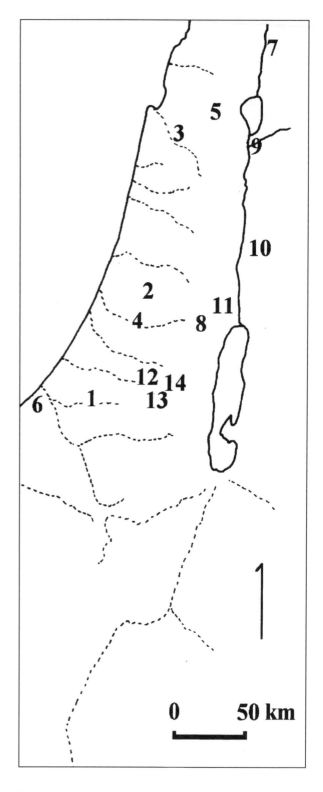

FIG. 4.3. *Map of post–Early Bronze Age sites mentioned in Chapter 4, including the Middle Bronze I.*
1. Hesi; 2. Gezer; 3. Qasis; 4. Batashi; 5. Wawiyat;
6. Deir el Balah; 7. Dan; 8. Ir David (Jerusalem);
9. Sha'ar Hagolan; 10. Umm Hamad; 11. Jericho;
12. Lachish; 13. Beit Mirsim; 14. Djebel Qaaqir.

desert connections. Alternatively, these may also be the result of Egyptian influences.

The Middle Bronze I (Intermediate Bronze Age)
(FIG. 4.3)

The Middle Bronze I lithic systems in the north are similar to those of the Early Bronze Age, but lack the tabular scraper system. The desert assemblages show a much more restricted set of types and technologies, but are similar in the dominance of on-site production by nonspecialists. Of especial importance here is the fact that the Middle Bronze I represents the period of major urban decline, usually characterized as collapse, following Early Bronze Age civilization. On one hand, the economic continuity reflected in the uninterrupted production of Canaanean sickles points to underlying economic continuities, in spite of the urban collapse. This continuity is also reflected in the ceramics, although to a lesser degree. On the other hand, the disappearance of the tabular scraper system may well reflect these changes. Perhaps the distribution networks from source to consumer, desert to Mediterranean zone, were disturbed. Alternatively, if the tabular scraper system was indeed connected to cult practices, changes in those practices may have reduced demand for the pieces.

CANAANEAN BLADES

The Canaanean exchange network apparently survived the collapse of Early Bronze Age urban civilization since these blades continue to dominate the sickle assemblages from virtually all Middle Bronze I sites (e.g., Lachish [Waechter 1958], Beit Mirsim [Albright 1936–37, 12, 23, 27], Sha'ar Hagolan [Rosen 1983d, 273–76], Qa'aqir [Dever 1970], Malha [pers. obs.], Jericho [Payne 1983], and Um Hammad [Betts 1992a]). Similar to the preceding period, evidence for manufacture is absent from virtually all sites, and in fact, no Middle Bronze I lithic workshops have been discovered, although Har Charuvim, the largest Early Bronze Age workshop, also shows Middle Bronze I occupation. Data are too scant for interassemblage comparisons or for more detailed reconstruction of the exchange system.

AD HOC TOOLS

The *ad hoc* tools from Middle Bronze I sites have been little studied. In general, they are similar to those of the Early Bronze Age. The few sites that have relatively well collected, such as Malha, near Jerusalem, or Sha'ar Hagolan, also show evidence for on-site manufacture of these tools in the form of flake cores and waste.

DESERT SYSTEMS

Reliable data from desert Middle Bronze I sites are scarce. In light of the general absence of tabular scrapers and sickles (in the desert) from the lithic assemblages of this period, there is no evidence for import of chipped stone tools, nor for specialization in production. Tool assemblages are basically *ad hoc*, with abundant evidence for on-site manufacture. Unfortunately, little data beyond the impressionistic are available (but see Gilead 1973).

The Middle Bronze II, Late Bronze, and Iron Age Systems (FIG. 4.3)

These periods show decline in the use of flint as a raw material (Chapter 7), as well as typo-technological change from the preceding periods. Canaanean sickles are replaced by Large Geometric sickles, which appear to be associated with an exchange system structured somewhat differently from the former. *Ad hoc* tools continue to be produced, in decreasing numbers, but problems of archaeological intrusion and attribution make detailed study of this system difficult. This long period of more than a millennium is examined as a unit since both technologically and typologically the lithic systems within it seem stable. Culturally, if not politically, one can also make a case for fundamental continuities.

LARGE GEOMETRIC SICKLES

Although Large Geometric sickle segments have been recovered from virtually every site dating from the Middle Bronze II through the ninth/eighth centuries B.C.E. (early Iron II), no cores appropriate to the manufacture of these tools have ever been reported. To a degree this may reflect simple lack of archaeological recognition. Nevertheless, the total absence of cores, along with the presence of hundreds of sickle blades at some sites, strongly suggests off-site production (table 4.3). On the other hand, other remains of the reduction process have been recovered: unused sickle segments, unfinished segments, and unretouched flakes appropriate for segment manufacture. Specifically, unused sickle segments show backing and truncations, but lack sickle gloss, and almost always show fresh, unretouched working edges. Unfinished sickle segments show one or more attributes usually associated with sickle segments, such as truncations or backing, but also lack some, as well as lacking gloss, indicating that they were both incomplete and unused. Unretouched flakes appropriate for sickle manufacture are relatively standardized in dimensions (slightly larger than the sickle segments themselves), usually showing a pronounced bulb of percussion.

The flint caches from Iron Age Gezer (Rosen 1986) constitute the most important assemblage of this material. These caches, consisting of hundreds of flakes, incomplete sickle segments, unused segments, and a very few used sickles, were discovered in shallow pits in an Iron Age courtyard on the site. No cores were recovered, but it is clear from the uniformity in raw materials that artifacts from individual caches derive from the same core (or cores). An antler, clearly used as a hammer and perhaps for pressure flaking, was also recovered. The materials are similar in configuration to those of Tel Dan (pers. obs.) whose associations are less well preserved.

Thus the Large Geometric sickle system contrasts with that of Canaanean blades. Although both are products of specialist manufacture, Canaanean blades seem to have been traded in small packets from workshop sites which included primary reduction. Large Geometric sickles seem to have been distributed from secondary specialist workshops after initial reduction elsewhere. Admittedly, samples are inadequate, but the differences between the Gezer caches and the Canaanean blade workshops and trade packets are striking enough to warrant such a reconstruction, at least as a working hypothesis.

AD HOC TOOLS

As mentioned above, in these periods it is difficult to determine to what extent *ad hoc* tools were still in use, given the problems of archaeological intrusions in tells and cultural attribution of these nondiagnostic elements. Assuming that at least some of the materials recovered from stratified tell sites like Ir David (Rosen n.d.d) are associated with the Middle Bronze II or perhaps the Late Bronze Age, then the presence of cores and flake waste indicate nonspecialized on-site production (table 4.3). This mode of production/distribution seems to be similar to those of the preceding periods.

DESERT SYSTEMS

There is a near total absence of lithic assemblages available for analysis from the Middle and Late Bronze Ages in the desert regions, even from the few sites in the southern Negev and Sinai which can be dated to this period. Flint sickle blades have been recovered from Iron Age sites (Cohen 1986, pl. 140:6–7, 10–13; also Haiman 1986, 93; 1988, fig. 55), but evidence for reduction is lacking. The techno-typological distinctiveness of the desert Iron Age sickle segments, arched backed blades, indicates a network distinct from that of the central region. However, in the absence of better data, no conclusions concerning specialization or off-site production can be drawn.

The Rise of Specialization: An Alternative Perspective

The rise of craft specialization has been tied to numerous factors, including ranking and power structures (e.g., Renfrew 1982; Shennan 1982), the rise of urbanism (e.g., Childe 1951a, 35; 1951b, 24), elite and/or ritual goods (e.g., Adams 1966, 127; Champion 1982), restricted access to raw materials (e.g., Chapman 1982; Zeitlin 1982), trade and exchange systems (e.g., Earle 1977; Morris 1978), and elite control of markets and allocation of resources (e.g., Tosi 1984). It has often been tied directly to metallurgy (e.g., Redman 1978, 270; Childe 1951a, 95–99, 114–42; Renfrew 1984; Zaccagnini 1983). Nevertheless, although most scholars agree that specialization is part and parcel of the rise of social complexity, there is no consensus on the precise mechanisms involved in the rise of this phenomenon.

Defining specialization may be part of the problem. In his study of early craft specialization in the Balkans, Evans (1978) used four criteria in his definition: (1) specialists constitute only a small proportion of the community, (2) they work at their crafts during their productive time (i.e., during "work hours"), (3) consequently they withdraw from basic subsistence tasks during that time, and (4) they receive goods in exchange for their products. Few would argue with these, although some scholars might add other, perhaps more restricting criteria. For example, Childe (1951b, 24) defined specialization as full-time occupation. However, even given this, there seems to be a wide range of variation in features of those activities that can be classified as specialization. Besides the question of full- or part-time occupation (which can vary either daily or seasonally), variation can also occur in the materials exploited, ease of access to them, complexity of the manufacturing process, availability of general knowledge of that process, tools or installations required for that process (capital investment), numbers of objects produced, type of consumer, utilitarian and symbolic functions of the manufactured goods, size of the goods, and physical and social requirements for distribution. In a general review of the evidence for early specialization on the Turanian Plateau in Iran, Tosi (1984) suggested that such variability may be the result of a specialization spectrum, that specialization is a matter of degree or intensification, depending especially on elite control. Notably, he concludes that the archaeological evidence to support such a framework is equivocal.

Alternatively, craft specialization need not be examined as a single monolithic phenomenon. Although Evans' (1978) criteria allow us to view many forms of production as "specialized," beyond an assumed theoretical framework, there is nothing requiring that origins and development of different crafts be dictated by the same factors, nor that they be on the same developmental trajectory.

The lithic systems described above are a case in point. They do not seem to represent a *developmental* spectrum ranging from nonspecialization to specialization. Rather, although all began from the same Paleolithic baseline, they seem to represent specific socioeconomic adjustments to a complex set of factors. There is no *a priori* reason to assume that intensification of factors leading to increased specialization in one system would lead to a similar result in another. In fact, the reasons for specialization or semi-specialization seem to differ from system to system. Accepting an elite-power-control role for the rise of specialization in some commodities, like metals, examination of the lithic systems suggests that there may be more than one path leading to the phenomenon we call specialization.

The first issue here is to what degree the different lithic systems indeed can be classified as specialized. Unfortunately, Evans' (1978) criteria are difficult to actually use in an archaeological context: how can one really determine what hours of the day a craftsperson worked, and whether he or she participated in subsistence activities at other times, or received goods in exchange for the products of his or her trade? Ultimately he bases most of his conclusions on the existence of workshops. Tosi (1984, 23) concludes that archaeologically the primary identifying characteristics of craft specialization are "differences in spatial distribution of different manufacturing processes." Additionally, there should be evidence for distribution of products beyond the use of the manufacturer or his close kin. Limited distribution of objects exhibiting restricted manufacture, while suggesting perhaps a low-level division of labor, does not imply the same set of social relations connoted by the term *craft specialization*. In a sense, one is distinguishing between the domestic economy and some type of redistribution economy (cf. Sahlins 1972), not necessarily associated with a central redistributing agency.

Finally, in order to distinguish between crafts and craft specialization, it is also worth differentiating between different types of activity areas (cf. Tosi 1984). Specifically, it is important to distinguish between workshops, sites, or loci where a wide variety of activities occurred, including the production of the hypothesized specialized goods, and workshops, sites, or loci where only the specialized production is represented. In a sense, this is a correlate of Childe's "full-time specialization."

Based on these definitions and criteria, the sickle systems outlined above describe a pattern of increasing specialization in production. The first hints of specialized or expert manufacture of sickle blades occurs in the Pre-Pottery Neolithic B (Rosen 1989b), where sites show considerable variability in core:sickle ratios. Although all PPNB sites seem to show some on-site production of sickles, and there is as yet no evidence for intensively exploited workshops or quarries, some sites seem to reflect some import of sickles, at least as reflected in the scarcity of cores. Alternatively, given limited exposures, variability in waste:tool ratios may indicate intrasite distributional differences in waste and/or tools. Data for evaluating this are not available. Regardless, both interpretations suggest incipient expert modes of production. They need not qualify as true craft specialization, but given later developments, the beginning of these trends can be traced at least to this period.

In the Chalcolithic, the large concentration of cores and other diagnostic lithic waste at Gaza A (and perhaps other sites), and the apparent import of axes, adzes, sickles, and bladelet tools at many sites, suggest some form of specialization or near specialization in some aspects of lithic manufacture. The presence of some blade manufacture at most Chalcolithic sites renders the differential spatial distribution of manufacturing somewhat less contrastive than might be required to assume some "true" or "pure" craft specialization. However, it adds to the contrast with the succeeding Early Bronze Age Canaanean system, which shows a total absence of sickle manufacturing residue at the vast majority of sites, with concentration of production at only a few centers. Both the Chalcolithic and Early Bronze Age systems show fairly widespread distribution of sickles and other specialized lithic products, certainly beyond the confines of close kin. Gaza A, or at least part of it, seems to be a true lithic workshop, reflecting a major activity and not some minor subsidiary craft. The same is probably true of Har Charuvim and perhaps Gat Guvrin, although data here are simply inadequate. Canaanean blade production in the Early Bronze Age certainly fits the archaeological criteria for specialization, and Chalcolithic sickles (and perhaps celt tools and microliths as well) also seem to fit, on perhaps a lesser level.

The Large Geometric system also seems to represent a fairly specialized mode of manufacture, perhaps in this case focused in the cities. The absence of evidence for primary manufacture at all sites, the abundance of sickles at all sites, and the apparent concentration of secondary manufacture at a few centers, as at Gezer, certainly reflect differences in spatial distribution of manufacturing. The absence of an example of a primary reduction site does not diminish this variability; it only makes the specifics more difficult to document.

Unlike most commodities used in discussions of the rise of specialization, like metal goods, it is difficult to associate sickle segments in the Levant with elite control of resources, chiefdom redistribution, class structure, or the symbols of power. These are tools manufactured in large numbers in villages, for farmers. Although the specifics of the technology may have been somewhat esoteric, it required little investment in terms of site furniture; no truly restricted raw materials, although the appropriate flint is not found dispersed uniformly over the landscape (at least not in the Levant—Mesopotamia presents a different situation with apparently genuine lithic scarcity); and no special tools not available to the general populace. Aside from the absence of archaeological evidence for the role of power or elites in the rise of this form of specialization, it seems difficult to even place the sickle systems in such a framework theoretically. In this context, the specialized manufacture of flint tools differs in kind from that of specialized obsidian manufacture in Greece (e.g., Torrence 1986) and in Mesoamerica

(e.g., Johnson 1996), where truly restricted sources result in different patterns in the organization of production and distribution.

The gradually increasing specialization in sickle segment production from the Neolithic through the Bronze and Iron Ages thus represents a fundamentally different path toward economic complexity. The Neolithic experts in blade production seem to have gradually expanded their "market" beyond near kin, eventually to villages and afterward to regional supply zones, perhaps because it proved advantageous to all sides. In Service's (1962) conception, the sickle systems may be an example of economic integration, without the imposition of hierarchy.

The tabular scraper system exhibits some of the characteristics of specialization, but seems to lack others. Although clearly reflecting "spatial differentiation in manufacture," the primary workshops do not suggest intensity of exploitation or activity exclusivity. It is interesting to note that Torrence (1986) comes to similar conclusions regarding what appear to be intensively exploited workshops in the Greek Islands in the Bronze Age. The secondary production center at Gaza A suggests a higher order of exploitation than do the primary sites, but again does not reflect exclusivity of manufacture, unless a wide range of chipped stone tools are classed together as a single craft (not necessarily inappropriate).

While these differences alone need not indicate any fundamental contrasts with the sickle systems, and clearly there is some overlap, there are basic differences in function and end user which suggest basically different developmental trajectories. Unlike sickles, tabular scrapers were not produced in large numbers for mass consumption.[6] Instead, the high symbolic value of these pieces and their apparent association with ritual indicate a different stimulus and a different structure to the production of these artifacts. Sickle manufacture must have met certain minimum (large) numbers to satisfy basic subsistence needs. Demand on that minimum level was inflexible. On the other hand, demand for tabular scrapers was not. If the primary role of these tools was indeed ritual, and the symbolism arbitrary, then the ritual authorities could alter the ritual if need be. Even assuming some more utilitarian function to these tools (shearing?), they are easily replaceable by less formal and/or specialized types.

Although the presence of low numbers of non-Canaanean sickles in most assemblages indicates that they too were replaceable, the much higher number of sickles in general suggests that this would be a much more difficult process. Furthermore, blade production is, in itself, a more esoteric technology than flake production. Almost any flake can be used as a cutting edge to replace a tabular scraper in a utilitarian sense. Insertion into a sickle haft requires a specific shape, not readily achievable using an expedient technology. In short, tabular scrapers seem much more to conform to the classic argument that specialization arose in response to the demands of the elite, even if in this case the specialization was marginal and nonintensive. The two systems seem to be fundamentally distinct in their structure and function within Early Bronze Age society.

The third primary mode of manufacture reviewed here, that of expedient manufacture, also requires some discussion in the context of specialization. Parry and Kelly (1987) have argued that the rise of expedient core technologies in the New World during the Archaic is a result of decreasing mobility and increasing need to more intensively exploit raw materials. A similar argument has been made for Natufian industries in the Levant, in the sense of greater core reduction (Bar-Yosef and Belfer-Cohen 1989, 468). However, the real rise of expedient cores and tools in the Levant begins sometime in the Pottery Neolithic (Rosen 1996) and continues as the numerically dominant industry at least through the Early Bronze Age. This considerably postdates the sedentarization processes associated with the earlier stages of the Neolithic and the rise of agriculture, but coincides well with increasing specialization in some components of lithic production. That is, the rise of *ad hoc* or expedient lithic production in the Levant is the complement of specialization. It arises as the more sophisticated and perhaps more esoteric technologies concentrate in the hands of the specialists. It is likely that early Pre-Pottery Neolithic farmer-hunters made their own sickles and arrowheads, and that mastery of blade production was a prerequisite to farming and hunting. Thus, knowledge of blade production was common, and general skills in lithic reduction acquired through learning blade production would be equally applicable to other modes. With increasing specialization, the knowledge of the more complex reduction modes became more restricted, effectively reducing overall skill levels in lithic production. Other tasks and tools not requiring special skills in manufacture, nor specific raw materials, could continue to be produced in expedient fashion as the need rose.

Conclusions

The above materials suggest that different lithic systems developed and operated in quasi-independent ways, converging at particular points in time and space. Even given this framework, however, it is important to consider that "convergence in time and space" is not an abstract concept, but in fact means that the people ultimately producing and using these tools were not operating independently of one another. Thus, blades in the Neolithic were manufactured for both sickles and arrowheads, and it can be no accident that the workshop at Chalcolithic Gaza A contained hundreds of blade and bladelet cores, blanks for tabular scraper manufacture, and roughouts for celt production. Thus, even when the origins and endpoints of specific lithic complexes differed, the people involved in lithic production may well have been the same, perhaps playing different roles within the structure of the system. Similarly, at Lahav, tabular scrapers may well have been by-products of Canaanean sickle manufacture (Futato 1990), even if not the primary source of these tools. And again at Tel Dan, the areal coincidence of sickle manufacture and other industrial activities suggests that lithic manufacture was tied into other systems.

Although beyond the scope of this book, the lithic systems may also be compared with other systems like metallurgy, ground stones, lapidary, etc. (cf. Tosi 1984; Rosen 1993a). If the lithic systems exhibit multiple pathways to specialization, then examination of a wider range of technologies and artifacts may result in even better understanding of this complexity.

NOTES

1. The discovery of microlithic drills and bead manufacture in the well-dated Early Bronze Age Camel Site in Mizpe Ramon opens the question of chronological attribution of some of these sites, since in some cases the only artifacts recovered were drills and beads, neither yet typologically diagnostic. Some of the sites may be Early Bronze Age, not Chalcolithic.

2. "Apparent absence" because it is difficult to evaluate how much was saved/recovered from excavations conducted in the 1920s. Still, the recovery of numerous blade and bladelet cores (on a different raw material from the tabular scrapers, meaning that these were not merely reduced versions of the larger tabular scraper cores) suggests that Macdonald would have recognized tabular scraper cores if they had been present.

3. The site of Har Qeren 15 (Rosen and Goring-Morris n.d.b) cannot be precisely dated and may be as early as the terminal Neolithic or as late as the Early Bronze Age. The absence of earlier period diagnostics suggests a later date, but this is by no means strong evidence.

4. Perrot (1961) does not mention the existence of numerous Canaanean blade cores in the publication, but has been kind enough to show me the collection.

5. This connection between Canaanean technology and tabular scrapers was suggested initially by Hennessy (1967, 41–44). Although clearly not fortuitous, the distinct chrono-cultural trajectories of the types suggest that this convergence of the two technologies is not a primary factor in their development, and that they should still be treated as fundamentally distinct.

6. Although large numbers of these tools can be found in some desert sites, the apparent association of tabular scraper manufacture with mobile pastoralists suggests that southern production is not specialized in the senses discussed above.

5 A Study of Function

Introduction

Functional analysis of stone tools is far more complex than implied by common English usage. The mere fact that most type names imply a single use or pattern of use, as in *scraper, knife, drill*, etc., serves as a stumbling block to comprehension of how these tools actually functioned within a given society. Beyond the fact that it seems likely that many stone tools and tool types had more than a single utilitarian function, restriction of the analysis to the mere utilitarian seems ultimately a sterile exercise, resulting in a list of activities with little attached social or cultural context. That is, even given our often dubious abilities to determine how a stone tool was used, or what it was used for, the uses and activities themselves need to be placed in some larger context.

Archaeologically, the problem of determination of (utilitarian) function can be tackled on several scales. On the smallest, use wear analysis can often determine the particular activities resulting in a polish, wear, or fracture pattern on a specific edge of a tool. Usually this can be extended to a general functional interpretation of the tool itself as a unit, especially when integrated with morphology and other attributes (edge angle, size, etc.). Beyond the level of the individual tool, general types or type classes can be examined for variability in use defined on the single artifact level, and site assemblages can be studied for patterns defining complex sets of activities requiring sets of tools. Finally, on the highest level, one can compare and contrast industries, cultures, and complexes, in some attempt to characterize them functionally. Such characterizations by no means preclude other perspectives, nor are they precluded by them. The multifaceted nature of material culture is a given.

The modern argument over the function of stone tools can, to a great extent, be traced to the debates stimulated by the Binfords' interpretations (e.g., Binford and Binford 1966; L. R. Binford 1973; S. R. Binford 1968) of Mousterian facies variability as reflecting task-specific tool kits. They proposed that the typological configuration of different Mousterian lithic assemblages represented the remains or discards of different activities performed at different sites and explicitly rejected Bordes' (e.g., 1972, 146–49; Bordes and de Sonneville-Bordes 1970) ethnic or tribal interpretation of lithic variability. Three decades after the fact, it is all too easy to critique both sides. The real measure of the success of the debate is to be seen in the tremendous stimulus it gave to research on both the function of stone tools and their meaning beyond utilitarian function, i.e., style.

This essay takes as its starting point the Binfordian view that there is functional or activity variation between sets of sites, sites, and subsites, and that this variation may be traced at least partially through examination of lithic assemblages and subassemblages. Unlike the earlier Mousterian assays, this exercise focuses more on our ability to distinguish patterned modes of activity based on general lithic frequencies, and much less on specific types and type frequencies. The latter is possible only when there is more or less consensus agreement on the utilitarian function of specific types, as in the latter part of the chapter (table 5.1). Nevertheless, the argument is similar.

Class	Function
1. sickles	harvesting, reaping
2. blade tools, backed pieces	cutting
3. chopper	plant processing
4. arrowheads	hunting
5. tabular scrapers	ritual, fleshworking
6. scrapers, awls	hideworking
7. notches, denticulates, retouched flakes	all-purpose, woodworking
8. borers, burins	chiseling, engraving
9. cores	lithic reduction

TABLE 5.1. General functional classes, based partially on McConaughy (1979).

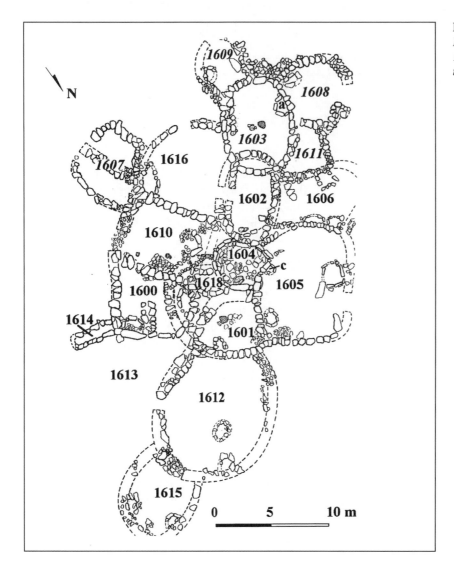

Fig. 5.1. *Plan of Uvda Valley 16.
Italicized loci, 1603, 1607, 1608,
1609, and 1611 are attributed to
the Middle Bronze I.*

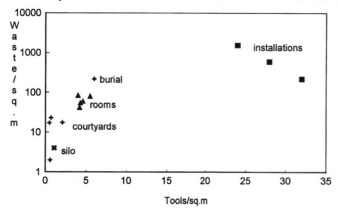

Fig. 5.2. *Scattergram of tool versus waste densities
according to architectural type at Uvda Valley 16.*

Intra-Assemblage Comparisons: Site Structure

The real key to intra-assemblage analysis is finding some reasonable means of dividing the assemblage into meaningful units of analysis. In the absence of nonlithic evidence, as in prehistoric sites, this can be a difficult problem requiring complex spatial clustering algorithms (e.g., Kroll and Price 1991, table 1; Gregg et al. 1991; Rigaud and Simek 1991; also see Gilead et al. 1995 for spatial analysis in this region). The results of these analyses are often hard to interpret (Kroll and Price 1991). However, in the periods under discussion here, architectural features provide natural units of analysis, which in themselves can be typed (room, pen, wall, courtyard, hearth, etc.), providing sets of subassemblages that can be compared. That is, using subassemblages derived from independently defined site loci, use, and discard patterns, and perhaps post-depositional effects, can be examined. In fact, ambiguities in functional interpretation of many architectural features render this process of general importance in understanding the site.

The difficulty in distinguishing between use or activity areas and discard, of course, has been one of the prime criticisms of activity area analysis (e.g., O'Connell 1987). However, both constitute important aspects of behavior. In a real sense, discard itself may constitute and important behavior (Hayden and Cannon 1983; O'Connell et al. 1991), and examination of patterns of discard can provide information perhaps no less important than the preceding "primary" activities. Different activities and different tool types may well result in different patterns of discard, which may in turn be reflected in the archaeological record. Clearly all lithic remains, indeed all archaeology, are the result of discard behaviors. Archaeological activity analyses are predicated on the assumption that tools used in specific tasks were discarded in and around the area of use, and that provenience associations thereby reflect functional associations (e.g., Kent 1987 and references). As a basic premise for activity area research, the assumption is demonstrably false. However, as a working hypothesis designed to be confirmed or rejected, it is useful. Strong patterns of association in specific situations can indeed suggest specific activities. These must be evaluated in site and culture context, and not be rejected out of hand by overzealous purists.

The lithic assemblages from the desert pastoral sites of the third and fourth millennia B.C.E. provide good examples of this approach. The site of Uvda Valley 16, an Early Bronze Age "homestead" with a

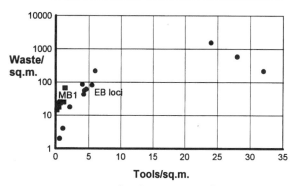

Biqat Uvda 16: EB versus MB1 Lithic Densities

FIG. 5.3. *Scattergram of tool versus waste densities according to period (Early Bronze versus Middle Bronze I) at Uvda Valley 16.*

pastoral component, can serve as a baseline for the more general example. Loci at this site (and indeed at most of these pastoral encampments) can be divided into three basic types: (1) large open pen/courtyard loci, (2) smaller enclosed room loci, and (3) small features (hearths, stone piles, etc.) (fig. 5.1).

Figure 5.2 is a scattergram of waste density versus tool density for each locus on the site, coded by locus type. The discrete clustering of the locus types according to lithic density variables is self-evident. There are several implications to these patterns. The discreteness of the clusters is by itself suggestive of distinct modes of activity and discard. The correspondence between these density modes and architectural types indicates they can be associated with a specific spatial organization of the site. Furthermore, the close correspondence between the waste densities and the tool densities indicates that no clear spatial distinction can be drawn between tool manufacture (waste), use, and discard.

Closer interpretation is more speculative. The low densities of tools and waste (remembering that waste also includes chips and chunks, constituting more than half of the total lithic assemblage) in the "courtyard" or open area loci (pens?), as well as those dating to the Middle Bronze I (and also 1604, a possible silo), seem to reflect a general background lithic scatter, probably more a function of postdepositional dispersion than specific activities.

The tight clustering of the Middle Bronze I loci at the low end of both tool and waste density scales (fig. 5.3; tables 5.2, 5.3) regardless of architectural type suggests either a less intensive occupation or a less intensive lithic exploitation. The former explanation accords better with the architectural remains, ceramics, and other archaeological evidence.

UVDA VALLEY 16

locus	sq.m	type	waste	tools	total	tls/m2	ws/m2
1614	0.5	burial?	109	3	112	6.00	218.00
1605	14.5	ctyd	255	31	286	2.14	17.59
1612	40	ctyd	688	18	706	0.45	17.20
1613–15	10	ctyd	239	7	246	0.70	23.90
1616	10.25	ctyd	20	6	26	0.59	1.95
1603a	0.25	inst	383	6	389	24.00	1532.00
1605c	0.25	inst	147	7	154	248.00	588.00
1618	0.75	inst	163	24	187	32.00	217.33
1603	7	MB1	173	5	178	0.71	24.71
1607	5	MB1	329	7	336	1.40	65.80
1608	5	MB1	117	2	119	0.40	23.40
1618	0.75	inst	163	24	187	32.00	217.33
1603	7	MB1	173	5	178	0.71	24.71
1607	5	MB1	329	7	336	1.40	65.80
1608	5	MB1	117	2	119	0.40	23.40
1609	5.75	MB1	81	1	82	0.17	14.09
1611	2.5	MB1	61	3	64	1.20	24.20
1600	5	rm	304	23	327	4.60	60.80
1601	6	rm	254	25	279	4.17	42.33
1602	3.5	rm	194	15	209	4.29	55.43
1606	3	rm	256	12	268	4.00	85.33
1610	3.75	silo	486	33	519	5.50	81.00
1604	3.75	silo	15	4	19	1.07	4.00

MITNAN

locus	sq.m	type	waste	tools	total	tls/m2	ws/m2
113	1	cairn	30	1	30	1.00	30.00
115	9.8	ctyd	56	8	64	0.82	5.71
319-1	11.5	rm	60	13	73	1.13	5.22
111	4.8	rm	275	9	284	1.88	57.29
320-1	8.5	rm-tum	16	2	18	0.24	1.88
329-1	5.5	rm-tum	62	1	63	0.18	11.27
119	7.5	rm-tum	168	5	173	0.67	22.40
120-1	9	rm-tum	7	3	10	0.33	0.78
120-2	7.5	rm-tum	26	1	27	0.13	3.47

SHIQMIM

id#	sq.m	type	waste	tools	total	tls/m2	ws/m2
1	18	ctyd	276	29	305	15.33	1.61
1	34	ctyd	374	54	428	11.00	1.59
267	5	ctyd	4	1	5	0.80	0.20
264	15	ctyd	136	22	158	9.07	1.47
283	14	ctyd	250	18	268	17.86	1.29
276	10	ctyd	28	8	36	2.80	0.80
22	12.5	ctyd	153	20	165	12.24	1.60
219	2	pit	13	2	15	6.50	1.00
274	3	pit	28	2	30	9.33	0.67
20-floor	3	rm	21	5	26	7.00	1.67
25-floor	9	rm	239	22	261	26.56	2.44
25-ash	9	rm	297	14	311	33.00	1.56
28-ash	20	rm	531	20	551	26.55	1.00
269	2	st.rm	60	2	62	30.00	1.00

HAR HORSHA

locus	sq.m	type	waste	tools	total	tls/m2	ws/m2
86	15	ctyd	98	3	101	0.20	6.53
94	4.7	ctyd	106	7	113	1.49	22.55
98	11.7	ctyd	63	4	67	0.34	5.38
99	3.1	ctyd	19	0	19	0.00	6.13
100	6.3	ctyd	41	3	44	0.48	6.51
101	16.4	ctyd	71	2	73	0.12	4.33
83	11.7	ctyd	84	1	85	0.09	7.18
80	7.5	rm	64	11	75	1.47	8.53
81	10.2	rm	172	1	173	0.10	16.86
82	5.5	rm	107	5	112	0.91	19.45
84	9.4	rm	53	2	55	0.21	5.64
87	8.6	rm	89	2	91	0.23	10.35
88	4.7	rm	95	7	102	1.49	20.21
89	5.5	rm	70	3	73	0.55	12.73
96	3.9	rm	39	7	46	1.79	10.00
85	8.6	rm	101	3	104	0.35	11.74
90/91	7.8	rm	73	3	76	0.38	9.36
92	15.6	rm	153	5	158	0.32	9.81
95	8.6	rm	85	9	94	1.05	9.88
97	2.7	rm	10	0	10	0.00	3.70

Table 5.2. Lithic frequencies and densities of different sites by loci. Note that sq.m is area excavated and not necessarily the total area of the locus.

TOOLS	1600	1	2	3	03a	4	5	05c	6	7	8	9	10	11	12	13	14	15	16	18	misc	Total	%
												LOCI											
borers	1	2	1	0	1	0	4						2			1	1		1	3		17	7.2
scrapers	1	1		2		2	2			4		1	2		4	1						20	8.5
ret.flks	3	4	1	1	1	0	5	1	5	2	1		8	1	1	1	1		1	6		42	17.8
tab. scrpr		4						1							1							6	2.5
not/dent	7	2	7	1	3		8	1	3	1	1		14	1	3	2	1			5	1	61	25.8
sickles	2	2	2		1	1	2						1	1	1				1	4		18	7.6
arch b bld	6	9	3			1	1	3	2				3	1	4			1		2	1	37	15.7
ret.blds	3	1		1			6	1	1				3		3	1			2	3	1	26	11.0
ret.bdlts								1							1							2	0.8
choppers							1															1	0.4
knife																			1			1	0.4
hammer		1					2												1		1	5	2.1
Total	23	25	15	5	6	4	31	7	12	7	2	1	33	3	18	6	3	1	6	24	4	236	100.0

TABLE 5.3. Uvda Valley 16 tool-type frequencies by loci.

LOCUS	80	81	82	83	84	85	86	87	88	89	90	91	92	94	95	96	97	98	99	100	101	sur	Total	%
Waste																								
chunk	6	30	25	12	14	10	11	14	24	7		15	20	7	16	8	3	19	7	6	10		264	
chips	34	68	27	42	12	43	47	33	30	30		27	74	64	41	10	4	17	5	14	31	1	654	
flakes	23	63	44	27	19	42	33	28	36	30		23	44	32	25	18	3	17	7	18	21	3	556	
rimary		10	6	2	6	3	4	9	1	3		4	11	1	2	1		6		2	6		77	
blades	1	1		1		1	2							1	1	2					1	1	12	
bldlets					1		1		2			2	1					2		1			10	
CTE			1		1								1										3	
Cores																								
bld				1																			1	
bldlt						1												1			1		3	
flk	1	1	3		1	1	3	2				2	2	1				1			1		19	
Total	64	173	107	84	53	101	98	89	95	70	0	73	153	106	85	39	10	63	19	41	71	5	1599	
Tools																								
scraper	2			1	1				1				3		1	1					2		12	15.4
hammer	1		2					1	3						1								8	10.3
notch					1		2								2			1		1			7	9
dent	1					3			2	3				3									12	15.4
ret.flk	1		1						1			1	1		1	3				1			10	12.8
borers											1					1		2					4	5.1
ret.blade	2																						2	2.6
tab.scrp	4	1	2				1	1				1	1	4	4	2		1		1			23	29.5
Total	11	1	5	1	2	3	3	2	7	3	1	2	5	7	9	7	0	4	0	3	2	0	78	100.1
Total Lithics	75	174	112	85	55	104	101	91	102	73	1	75	158	113	94	46	10	67	19	44	73	5	1677	

TABLE 5.4. Har Horsha lithic frequencies by loci. Percentages do not include selected surface materials or intrusives.

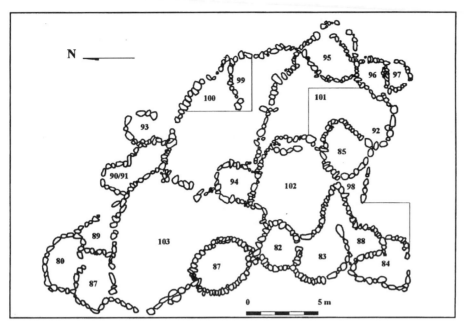

Fig. 5.4. *Har Horsha site plan (after Haiman 1991).*

The room loci, constituting the middle mode, seem to represent general lithic reduction, storage (as least in the presence of used sickle segments), and other activities or discard. In fact, given the expedient mode of manufacture of most of the tools (excluding the tabular scrapers and perhaps the blade tools), the distinction between manufacture, use, repair, discard, and reuse seems difficult. The final mode, seeming to represent intensive use in and around site installations, is deceptive. The small area of these loci, and the relatively low numbers of lithic materials in absolute terms (table 5.2), suggests that single episodes of activity and discard could result in the high lithic densities recorded. Of course, the installations did serve as foci for some activities.

Beyond these generalizations, there is variability in the actual activities carried out in the different rooms, at least insofar as represented by tool type frequencies. Thus for example, table 5.3 shows the widely varying frequencies of the different tool classes in the assemblage. Variation is especially evident in the percentages of notches/denticulates, tabular scrapers, and blade tools. Wide variability in tool type percentages is also present among the small installations. Thus specific activities in the loci seem to have varied in frequency, but perhaps not in kind. Excepting the tabular scrapers, these basic components seem to represent such domestic tasks as plant processing, light woodworking, cutting, storage, agriculture, and, of

course, lithic reduction (cf. McConaughy 1979).

Given these patterns and interpretations, the real test of significance lies in whether similar patterns occur in other sites. Examination of the lithic distribution patterns at Har Horsha (Haiman 1991; Rosen 1991), an Early Bronze Age pastoral encampment in the Central Negev Highlands is a case in point (fig. 5.4). Unlike Uvda Valley 16, there is little evidence for agriculture at Har Horsha, and the site seems to reflect a more mobile system than the former. In terms of lithics, the most notable differences are the much lower lithic densities, the total absence of sickles, the lower proportions of blade tools in general, and the much higher proportions of tabular scrapers (tables 5.2, 5.4). These general differences are indeed probably attributable to the more sedentary agricultural nature of Uvda Valley 16 and to the greater proximity of Har Horsha to the tabular scraper source area in the western Negev.

Although the tight clustering of locus types evident at Uvda Valley 16 is not nearly so evident at Har Horsha (fig. 5.5), the general distributions of rooms and courtyards according to lithic densities are still almost totally mutually exclusive. The only two exceptions, loci 84 and 97, are both peripheral rooms, perhaps functionally different from the others. Furthermore, as at Uvda Valley 16, the room loci show generally higher densities than do the courtyard loci. This suggests that if, on the one hand, intensity of

FIG. 5.5. *Scattergram of tool versus waste densities at Early Bronze Age Har Horsha according to architectural type.*

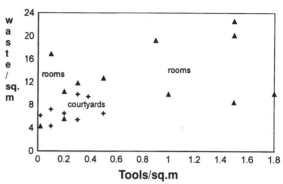

Har Horsha Lithic Densities Versus Architecture

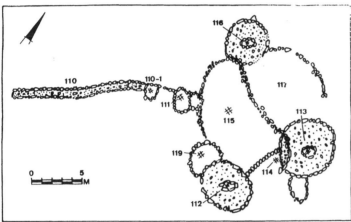

Building 115.

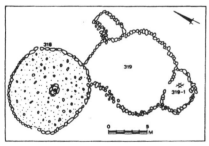

Building 319.

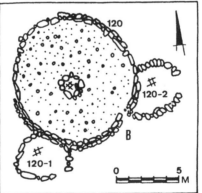

Cairn 120.

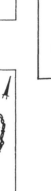

Building 320.

FIG. 5.6. *Plan of Nahal Mitnan (after Haiman 1993).*

	319-1	320-1	329-1	Sur	Total	%	MITNAN 111	113	115	116	119	120-1	120-2	sur	Total	%
Waste																
chunks	5	3	9		17		10		4		21		1	2	38	
chips	12	2	11		25		85	5	11		40		4		145	
flakes	28	7	31		66		140	18	29		76	4	10	5	282	
primary	10	1	6	1	18		25	3	7		22	2	5	1	65	
blades	3	1	3		7		11	2	5		8	1	5	2	34	
CTE			1		1		1								1	
Cores																
blade	1	2			3						1		1		2	
flake	1		1		2		3	2							5	
intrusive														1	1	
Total	60	16	62	1	139		275	30	56	0	168	7	26	11	573	
Tools																
sickles							1								1	3.7
b.blades	2			4	6	13.3			1			1			2	7.4
ret.blade	1				1	6.7	1					1			2	7.4
scrapers	3			2	5	20	2		3				1	1	7	22.2
hammer	1	1		1	3	13.3			1					1	2	3.7
notch			1	1	2	6.7	1							2	3	3.7
denticul	1				1	6.7			1		3			1	5	14.8
ret.flake		1			1	6.7			1					2	3	3.7
borers	1			2	3	6.7					1				1	3.7
tab.scrpe	3			7	10	20	4		1		1	1		5	12	3.7
ax						0		1							1	25.9
intrusives	1			2	3									1	1	
Total	13	2	1	19	35	100.1	9	1	8	0	5	3	1	13	40	99.9
Total	73	18	63	20	174		284	30	64	1	173	10	27	24	213	

TABLE 5.5. Mitnan lithic frequencies by loci. Percentages do not include selected surface materials or intrusives.

activity is of a lesser order than at Uvda Valley 16, the general structure of those activities (including discard) is roughly similar. The absence of a third and highest mode, around small installations, may be a result of lack of grain in analytic units.

Although fig. 5.5 is a scattergram of tool versus waste density, the primary discriminant seems to be waste density, the rooms showing a generally higher level of waste than the courtyards. There is great variability in the tool densities in the rooms. However, in light of the low numbers of actual tools, the differences in tool densities may derive from single episodes of activity or minor differences in discard, rendering more general conclusions difficult.

The third desert example is from Nahal Mitnan, clusters 1 and 3 (Haiman 1993; Rosen 1993b), another Early Bronze Age pastoral encampment from the Central Negev (fig. 5.6). As at Har Horsha, lithic densities are lower than at Uvda Valley 16 (table 5.2),

again probably indicative of a less intensive occupation or less exploitation of chipped stone. This again can probably be attributed to the presence of agricultural exploitation at Uvda Valley 16 and its near absence in the Negev Highlands.

Fig. 5.7 shows that the two rooms excavated on the site show generally higher lithic densities than the single courtyard for which data were available. This, of course, matches the previous examples, although the low number of loci hardly inspires confidence as a reasonable sample of the site. However, an additional locus type here, the room attached to a tumulus or cairn (room-tumuli on the graph), is of key importance in understanding the functional relationships on the site. These loci cluster at the low end of the density scales, even lower than the general background lithic dispersion as reflected in the single courtyard locus (with a single exception). Thus they indeed seem to be functionally distinct from the two other rooms,

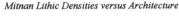
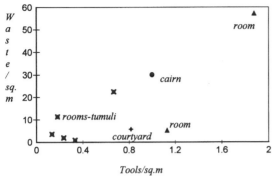

FIG. 5.7. *Scattergram of tool versus waste densities at Early Bronze Age Nahal Mitnan according to architectural type.*

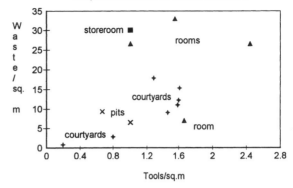

FIG. 5.8. *Scattergam of tool versus waste densities at Chalcolithic Shiqmim according to architectural type.*

especially in tool densities. Their physical association with tumuli is suggestive of cult, and the scarcity of lithic remains would suggest that the domestic tasks usually associated with these tools were not carried out in these loci.

Of course, some of this variability may be deceptive. The cairn, only 1 sq m in area, showed the second highest density in both waste and tools (table 5.5, fig. 5.7). However, the tool was a single polished ax, clearly a grave offering. The waste was almost certainly in secondary fill context, deriving from elsewhere on the site, since the small area of the cairn physically could not have accommodated flint knapping. Regardless, the general functional distinctions seem to hold. Importantly, the distinction between rooms and rooms-attached-to-tumuli could not be established by reference to the architecture alone.

A final example of the relationship between architectural types and lithic densities derives from the Chalcolithic agro-pastoral village site of Shiqmim, in the Beersheva Basin (Levy 1987). The first point to be noted is that, contrary to expectations, the general level of lithic densities (table 5.2, fig. 5.8) of this village site seems more closely to resemble those of the pastoral Negev Highland sites than the agro-pastoral hamlet at Uvda Valley 16. It is difficult to explain this without seeming to engagae in *post hoc* reasoning. However, the very intensity of occupation at Shiqmim, and at other village sites, probably required a fundementally different pattern of discard and refuse disposal than at the pastoral encampments. That is, the vast majority of lithic artifacts recovered from village and urban sites derive from secondary contexts such as pits and fills, and can be of little use in reconstruc-

tion of activity areas or tool kits. If these artifacts had remained in their primary contexts, lithic densities on or near floors would be much higher. The materials analyzed from the desert sites were all inclusive—there were no fills, and only a few surface finds were excluded from these analyses. Those from Shiqmim constitute only a sample of well provenienced materials, and only a fraction of the materials collected.

Beyond this issue of scale and intensity of occupation, as in the previous examples, rooms and courtyards at Shiqmim generally seem to cluster separately, with the rooms showing higher densities than the courtyard loci. Furthermore, the primary determinant again seems to be waste density, tool density showing considerable variation, especially among the room loci. The two pits fall more or less within the courtyard range, probably reflecting the secondary nature of the deposit. The storeroom falls within the general room range.

The appearance of apparently distinct modalities of lithic activity transcending site types in the third and fourth millennia B.C.E. in southern Israel is of some interest and requires further, more general discussion. The lowest density mode, corresponding to courtyards and rooms attached to tumuli, seems to represent two separate processes. The courtyards show generally low lithic densities, but often with relatively high absolute numbers of artifacts. This suggests postdepositional dispersal of originally more compact subassemblages. In fact, the apparently low densities may in some cases be the result of coarse-grained provenience units. If the architectural locus is the primary provenience unit, then subclusters within a courtyard may go unrecorded. The existence of denser patches of lithic

site	n	sickle	%	blade	%	chop	%	arrow	%	tab	%	scr/awl	%	notch	%	borer	%	cores	%	other	%
BU9	736	47	6.4	235	31.9	2	0.3	14	1.9	18	2.4	65	8.8	151	20.5	41	5.6	154	20.9	9	1.2
BU16	283	18	6.4	76	26.9	1	0.4	0	0.0	6	2.1	21	7.4	91	32.2	15	5.3	52	18.4	3	1.1
BU17	101	6	5.9	22	21.8	0	0.0	0	0.0	10	9.9	19	18.8	22	21.8	6	5.9	7	6.9	7	6.9
BU18	341	22	6.5	66	19.4	0	0.0	0	0.0	6	1.8	39	11.4	129	37.8	31	9.1	45	13.2	3	0.9
BU124	75	9	12.0	13	17.3	0	0.0	0	0.0	5	6.7	15	20.0	19	25.3	1	1.3	12	16.0	0	0.0
Horsha	93	0	0.0	3	3.2	0	0.0	0	0.0	23	24.7	12	12.9	29	31.2	3	3.2	23	24.7	0	0.0
Mitnan	45	1	2.2	4	8.9	0	0.0	0	0.0	12	26.7	7	15.6	11	24.4	1	2.2	8	17.8	0	0.0
HQ15	235	0	0.0	3	1.3	0	0.0	0	0.0	25	10.6	52	22.1	95	40.4	26	11.1	34	14.5	0	0.0
Shadud	472	39	8.3	22	4.7	1	0.2	0	0.0	2	0.4	101	21.4	197	41.7	31	6.6	75	15.9	3	0.6
Hesi (EB)	449	72	16.0	17	3.8	12	2.7	0	0.0	5	1.1	51	11.4	159	35.4	33	7.3	98	21.8	2	0.4
Yerah	178	85	47.8	27	15.2	1	0.6	0	0.0	10	5.6	11	6.2	26	14.6	4	2.2	11	6.2	2	1.1
Yiftahel	324	10	3.1	85	26.2	0	0.0	1	0.3	1	0.3	35	10.8	67	20.7	23	7.1	91	28.1	0	0.0
Hartuv	193	35	18.1	15	7.8	1	0.5	0	0.0	3	1.6	19	9.8	56	29.0	19	9.8	37	19.2	8	4.1
Ir David	158	14	8.9	0	0.0	3	1.9	0	0.0	5	3.2	33	20.9	39	24.7	15	9.5	47	29.7	0	0.0
Yarmuth	91	25	27.5	6	6.6	0	0.0	0	0.0	12	13.2	9	9.9	19	20.9	4	4.4	16	17.6	0	0.0
B.e.Dhra	330	32	9.7	44	13.3	7	2.1	0	0.0	12	3.6	79	23.9	70	21.2	51	15.5	35	10.6	0	0.0
Amuq FGH	327	176	53.8	34	10.4	0	0.0	22	6.7	0	0.0	30	9.2	33	10.1	23	7.0	9	2.8	0	0.0
S.Hagolan	94	35	37.2	12	12.8	0	0.0	0	0.0	0	0.0	13	13.8	22	23.4	11	11.7	1	1.1	0	0.0

TABLE 5.6. Functional class frequencies by site.

artifacts around small installations at Uvda Valley 16 is indeed suggestive of this possibility, and certainly prehistoric sites excavated using small scale grid systems show density variation on quite small scales. Thus, the general background lithic scatter in courtyards probably represents the remains of more discrete activities carried out in smaller subareas of the courtyards, but dispersed either postdepositionally or archaeologically.

On the other hand, the even lower lithic densities associated with rooms attached to tumuli are suggestive of true scarcity of activities involving lithic implements. It is difficult to speculate beyond this, and the cultic nature of the tumuli themselves has already been mentioned.

Room loci constitute a middle mode of lithic activity. Lithic reduction seems to have been a common activity conducted inside rooms. Beyond the generally high lithic waste densities found in rooms, the recovery of cores from many rooms also supports this. Activities using tools seem more variable; some rooms show relatively high numbers and densities, others showing lower. The expedient nature of the production and use of most of the tools and the low absolute numbers should be considered here. On one hand, even the removal of a few tools from one locus to another could significantly affect tool densities. On the other hand, expedient production and use would tend to minimize such movement.

The issue of discard is obviously of prime concern. Unfortunately, provenience units are too imprecise to determine whether tools were found clustered in loci, scattered about the sides of rooms, or randomly distributed. There is no evidence that rooms were used as secondary refuse dumps. Notably, the walls of the loci probably prevented greater postdepositional dispersal, preserving the original associations, at least to some degree.

In terms of absolute numbers, it is worth noting that where rooms constitute only 28.5% of the area sampled in the sites discussed, the lithic waste recovered from the rooms totaled 41.1% of the total waste, and the tools 40.3% of the total tools. This pattern of proportionally greater lithic material in the rooms is consistent over all the sites with no exceptions, indicating that rooms were indeed major foci for lithic activities.

The highest density mode, consisting of the small installations at Uvda Valley, and some of the small rooms at other sites, probably represents restricted episodes of lithic activity in limited areas. Our ability to define these episodes seems a function of the vagaries of both preservation of context and archaeological methods.

Finally, reconstruction of specific activities and tool kits, as defined by recurring sets of artifacts as in Binford and Binford's (e.g., 1966) pioneering studies of Middle Paleolithic Mousterian assemblages, is not possible using these data. Although defining areas and episodes of tool use and production can be accomplished since tool types can be aggregated, numbers of individual types in each locus are simply too low to provide reliable or significant correlations that might indicate what specific activities took place where. Furthermore, our ability to actually define tool use is compromised by the expedient nature of the industry.

Inter-Assemblage Comparisons: Site and Region

Inter-assemblage analysis can be conducted on many levels. The simple comparison of type frequencies, when those types have not been explicitly defined and tested, either functionally or otherwise, will result in a confusion that can be virtually impossible to sort out. To this end, the following analyses are based on general functional classes, as defined partially by the microwear analyses cited in Chapter 3. These consist of (1) sickles, (2) blade tools and backed pieces, (3) choppers, (4) arrowheads (including lunates), (5) tabular scrapers, (6) scrapers, awls, (7) notches, denticulates, and retouched flakes, (8) borers and burins, and (9) cores (hammerstones are not included here due to inconsistencies in field recognition, collection, and attribution from assemblage to assemblage). Some types (e.g., celts, microlithic drills) are excluded from the analysis either because are assumed to be intrusive in the analyzed assemblages or because they are absent from the assemblages. Assumed functions, based on for the most part on microwear analyses (Chapter 3), are summarized in table 5.1.

Obviously, some identifications of function are more reliable than others. Thus, clearly cores can be used as a measure of lithic reduction, sickle segments for harvesting, arrowheads for hunting, etc. Categories such as "all-purpose" are difficult. Therefore, type classes that may overlap functionally are placed adjacent to one another in the graphic comparisons so that variation caused by problems in definition and variability of function will less affect the general shape of the graph. Clearly discrete and identifiable functions, such as hunting versus harvesting, are separated, so as to maximize visibility of variation. Data are presented in table 5.6.

Analyses are restricted to the Early Bronze Age, with the inclusion of Middle Bronze 1 Sha'ar Hagolan, since it is for this general period that the most data are available. Examination of inter-assemblage variation across periods is problematic since the general role of lithic technology changes significantly precisely during

these times (Chapter 7; Rosen 1996).

The five Early Bronze Age sites from Uvda Valley for which good data are available present a remarkably uniform picture (fig. 5.9), suggesting a general functional configuration for these sites, dominated by harvesting, other cutting, perhaps some ritual, a range of domestic tasks such as wood and hide working, and lithic reduction. The stability or homogeneity of this configuration is best understood in comparison to other graphs. It is worth noting that these sites were all excavated at the same time in a major salvage project in 1980 by the Israel Department of Antiquities. As a consequence, some effort was made to ensure reasonable collection of the lithic artifacts, such that all seen pieces were collected for all sites and some were sieved (e.g. Avner 1990).

The assemblages from Early Bronze sites in the Central Negev, Har Horsha (Haiman 1991), Nahal Mitnan (Haiman 1993), and Har Qeren 15 (Rosen and Goring-Morris n.d.b) (fig. 5.10) contrast markedly with those of the Uvda Valley in three categories: harvesting (sickles), cutting (retouched blades), and proportion of tabular scrapers. In other functions there seems to be fair similarity. The contrast in number of tabular scrapers is most likely a result of proximity to source materials. In regard to the other contrasts, integrating stylistic and other information concerning the cultural affinities between the Uvda Valley sites and those of the Central Negev, the Uvda Valley assemblages seem to reflect a special functional variant (read agricultural) of the general desert adaptation.

The three Central Negev sites also seem to show configurations similar one to another. Of particular importance here is the assemblage from Har Qeren 15, notable for the presence of tabular scraper manufacture. The general tool assemblage does not indicate great contrast with the other sites from the Central Negev, indicating that although a special activity occurred on the site, it was not dominant. Furthermore, that special activity is not recognizable as such at this level of analysis, except perhaps insofar as there is a reduced number of tabular scrapers, probably since they were being exported.

Northern sites seem to show greater functional variability and are therefore more difficult to characterize. There is especially great variation in proportions of sickles, retouched blades, and cores. Looking at the villages in more detail (fig. 5.11), of the four sites, Yiftahel shows the greatest contrast. In terms of

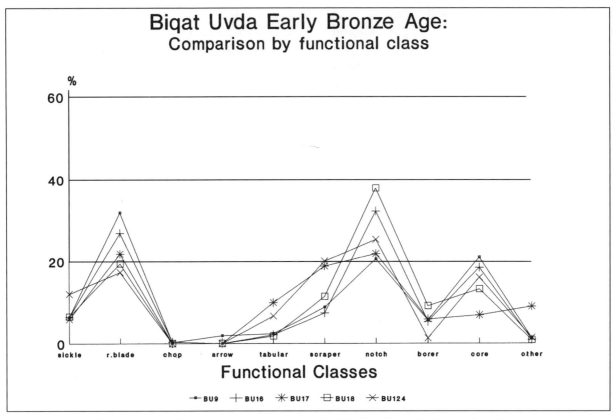

FIG. 5.9. *Functional comparison of Early Bronze Age sites in the Uvda Valley (Biqat Uvda), southern Negev.*

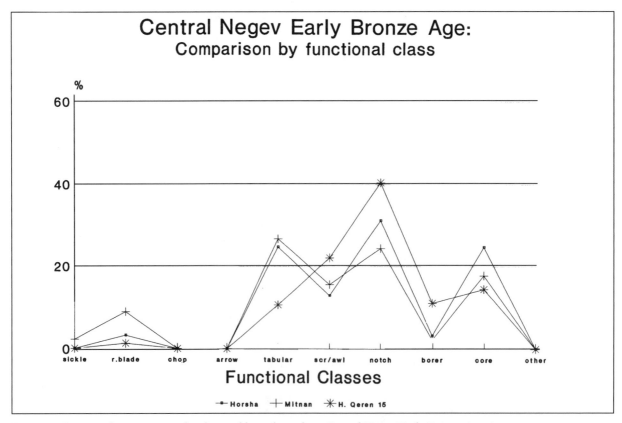

FIG. 5.10. *Functional comparison of tool assemblages from three Central Negev Early Bronze Age sites.*

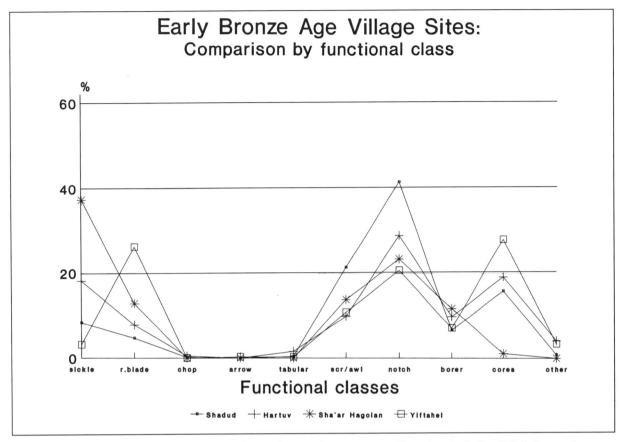

Early Bronze Age Village Sites:
Comparison by functional class

Functional classes

Shadud   Hartuv   Sha'ar Hagolan   Yiftahel

FIG. 5.11. *Functional comparison of tool assemblages from Early Bronze Age village sites, including Middle Bronze I Sha'ar Hagolan.*

general configuration, it seems more closely to resemble the assemblages from Uvda Valley. This is especially evident in the relatively lower proportions of sickles, and the high proportions of retouched blades, and cores (as well as the generally high frequency of tools reflecting domestic activities, as in most sites). One is tempted to interpret this similarity as reflecting like functional arrays, suggesting that pastoralism was a significant component at Yiftahel as at Uvda Valley, and agriculture of lesser importance than at other northern Early Bronze Age villages. Notably, the lower proportion of notches/denticulates at Yiftahel relative to other Early Bronze sites is probably a statistical artifact of the relative rise in blades. Unfortunately, problems of period and culture attribution of materials are acute at Yiftahel (Braun n.d.; Rosen and Grinblatt n.d.). There is some likelihood that much of the assemblage has been severely disturbed and may actually derive from other horizons. This is evident, for example, in the presence of neolithic celts in the Early Bronze Age level (but nevertheless included in

the "other" category for the sake of consistency). Regardless, the lithic assemblages suggest that this is a hypothesis worth examining in detail from other perspectives. The assumption that all Early Bronze Age villages were functionally similar is a null hypothesis worth disproving.

Beyond the obvious anomaly of Yiftahel, variation is evident especially in the sickle and core categories. At Sha'ar Hagolan, the high frequency of sickles may reflect any of several factors. Aside from the possibility that agriculture was practiced more intensely there (i.e., that more people were engaged in agriculture, thereby resulting in a higher proportion of sickle segments), the fact that the site is dated to the Middle Bronze I, postdating the other sites, suggests the possibility that the general role of other lithic implements may be on the decline (see Chapter 7; also Rosen 1996). That is, if other categories are reduced, sickles will rise proportionally. It is also possible that the dense clay soils of this site hindered the recovery of smaller tools, effectively biasing recovery in favor of

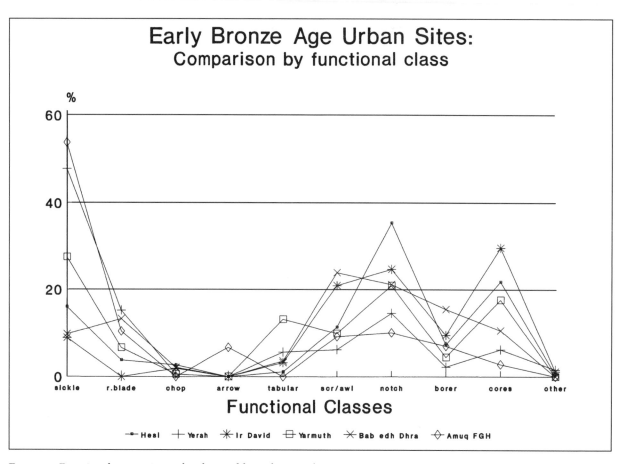

FIG. 5.12. *Functional comparison of tool assemblages from Early Bronze Age city sites.*

larger ones, like sickles. On the other hand, the low frequency of cores at the site may well represent a lesser role for lithic reduction in the area of the site excavated.

Urban sites show an even greater variability (fig. 5.12). While it is tempting to explain the high proportion of sickles at the Syrian city site of Amuq, Layers FGH (Crowfoot Payne 1960), and Beit Yerah as due to selective recovery techniques, the high proportions of waste recovered from Beit Yerah (Rosen n.d.c) belie this, at least at that site. Considering the large silos discovered there, perhaps agriculture was indeed of special importance at this site. The presence of relatively numerous arrowheads at Amuq FGH is probably a consequence of intrusions, but without renewed critical study of the assemblage, and other nearby assemblages, it is impossible to come to a definite conclusion.

In other categories, there is also a seemingly wide range of variation. Some of this may be attributable to the effect of the varying proportions of sickles as indi- cated above, as suggested, for example, by the fact that Ir David and Bab edh Dhra show the highest propor- tions of scraper/awls and notches, and the lowest of sickles, and Beit Yerah and Amuq FGH show the low- est proportions of notches, scrapers/awls, and cores, and the highest of sickles. On the other hand, changes in curve shape, as opposed to mere amplitudinal changes, such as the higher proportion of scraper/awls at Bab edh Dhra relative to other tool classes, indicate that some of the variability is not merely an artifact of the statistics. It may indeed reflect proportion differ- ences in general assemblage functions.

Beyond the functional contrasts between assem- blages, there are even more striking similarities. Lithic assemblages in the both village and urban Early Bronze Age are dominated functionally by the scraper/ awls, notches, and borer classes, i.e., hideworking, small-scale woodworking, boneworking, and general- ized tool uses (cf. McConaughy 1979). These consti- tute what I have classed technologically as the *ad hoc* tool component. If cores, which are almost exclusively expedient flake cores and therefore also representative of the *ad hoc* class, are also included here, then the dominance is even more striking.

Functionally, these classes seem to represent "household" or "domestic" activities. Gero (1991), working in South America, has gone so far as to identify similar phenomena with women's activities, although here there seems to be little evidence indicating gender of manufacturer or user of either the *ad hoc* tools or the functionally and/or technologically specialized ones. Regardless, these are the lithic classes representing the everyday activities of the bulk of the population, and they dominate virtually all Early Bronze Age assemblages, regardless of region or general subsistence pattern. Once specialized production modes are ignored, there is, in fact, remarkable functional similarity between virtually all lithic assemblages recovered from Early Bronze Age sites.

Lessons

The above notes on function are perhaps not especially surprising. That there is variation in agricultural practices between different regions and/or sites, that different architectural loci functioned differently, and that on the lithic assemblage level most Early Bronze Age sites are roughly similar—these are conclusions more or less expected from general knowledge of the period derived from other sources. However, general knowledge is no substitute for the details. The documentation of a specialized agro-pastoral adaptation at Uvda Valley is important, and derives almost exclusively from the lithic analysis, and which could not have been "predicted" from "general knowledge." Patterns of functional variation, such as at Uvda Valley, can indeed be sought in the lithic record, and comparison between Yiftahel and the Uvda Valley sites is one such example. Anomalies, such as the extremely high sickle percentages at Amuq and Beit Yerah, can serve as foci for further investigation.

Furthermore, the integration of material culture studies with provenience data is of special importance here. As with the southern sites, once spatial data can be incorporated into analyses, we may better be able to interpret the structure of Early Bronze Age society, taking our understanding beyond the description of architectural forms and assumptions concerning their function. The potentials are certainly there.

6 A Study of Style

Introduction

The interpretation of stylistic variation has been one of the core issues of archaeology since its inception as an academic discipline. Historically, in American archaeology (e.g., Conkey 1990), shifts in analytic emphasis can be traced, beginning with virtually intuitive approaches to style that stressed archaeological time-space systematics and, in some cases, were virtually devoid of greater cultural meaning. At a later stage, especially evident beginning in the 1960s, stylistic variation was viewed as reflective of a range of social, cultural, and ecological phenomena, and thereby rich in potential for examination of culture process. Most recently, style has been seen as that component of material culture active in the dynamic negotiation of symbols, meaning, and action in the greater social and cultural realm (e.g., Hodder 1990; Shanks and Tilley 1987).

These different approaches vary in applicability and potentials depending on the specific cultural context of the artifactual class in question, the realm of material culture and its physical potentials for encoding cultural information, and the richness of the archaeological background, allowing placement of the style within a larger cultural framework. In a real sense, different approaches to style challenge the archaeologist to address the data in new ways and perhaps generate new data in response to new questions. Conversely, and no less significantly, the data should be used to critically review the theoretical framework.

Chipped stone tools provide an important test case for the general utility of theoretical approaches to stylistic analysis. A theory that cannot accommodate the limited and often problematic stylistic variability residing in lithic assemblages and types will be of limited use to prehistoric (read paleolithic) archaeology.

There are two issues here. First, the question of the very existence of culturally meaningful stylistic variation in chipped stone tools must be addressed. Although we take for granted that prehistoric time-space systematics, based almost exclusively on stylistic analysis of chipped stone assemblages, break the Paleolithic down into units that have/had cultural meaning in some kind of ethnological sense (but see Neeley and Barton 1994 for opposing view), the general scarcity of extra-lithic evidence and the total absence of contemporary written corroboration always seem to leave our constructions open to a smidgen of doubt, with much room for reevaluation. Thus, for example, Bordes' (1972, 146–49; Bordes and de Sonneville-Bordes 1970) interpretation of Middle Paleolithic Mousterian assemblage variation as primarily reflecting cultural traditions, *tribes* in his term, was reinterpreted as functional variation, the differences between different activities and tool kits, by the Binfords (Binford and Binford 1966; S. R. Binford 1968; L. R. Binford 1973). Dibble (1987) has taken the reinterpretation even further, suggesting that even those elements considered to be the most likely candidates for stylistic loading, the different kinds of scrapers, are in fact the result of changes in technological reduction frameworks, stimulated by greater or lesser access to raw materials. That is, he claims that the more intensively retouched scrapers were used more, and sharpened more, essentially due to scarcity. In the absence of extra-lithic material culture, it almost seems as if we only construct and reconstruct, without independent support or corroboration of stylistic and cultural interpretation.

Second, even given the legitimacy of etic constructs of systematics, i.e., that lithic style can indeed be used to construct analytically meaningful archaeological units and subunits, the question of examination of culture process remains. That is, once constructed, do these units have internal cultural meaning, and can that meaning be established from the stone tools? Given more recent ideas concerning the active role of material culture in Culture as a general phenomenon, the question can be extended: can we reasonably construct an active cultural role for style embedded in stone tools?

Because so much of prehistoric archaeology, especially in the Old World, is based on lithic analysis, attempts to address these issues as they relate to Paleolithic groups sometimes verge on the tautological. It is difficult to generate independent lines of evidence to support or refute hypotheses concerning lithic style. On the other hand, examination of the role of lithic style in societies for which there is a richer anthropological or historical background can provide controls on theories of style in lithic analysis. This was clearly the motivation in White's (1967; White et al. 1977) analyses of New Guinea lithic assemblages, where he noted that the categories constructed by native informants bore little relation to those constructed by the archaeologists. Unfortunately, the work is flawed both by the fact that the New Guinea materials are all *ad hoc* and thereby not comparable to the more formal and informal tools of most lithic studies, and in the misapprehension of the difference between etic and emic constructs, and the legitimacy of both (e.g., Hayden 1984).

The analysis of historic and proto-historic lithic assemblages in the Levant is another, perhaps even better, example. The chipped stone tools from early Levantine complex societies can be traced in a cultural trajectory directly back to those of the Paleolithic, suggesting an even stronger rationale to analogies between the two (cf. Ascher 1961; Wylie 1985). Furthermore, the Levantine historical assemblages contain formal tools conceptually similar to those of the Paleolithic, in addition to the *ad hoc* elements. And finally, if we cannot interview informants with respect to the specific roles of chipped stone tools in the ancient Levant, as we can for New Guinea, a rich historical and archaeological record is nonetheless available for analytic control.

Before addressing the data and their applicability to any particular mode of stylistic analysis, it is, of course, necessary to review briefly what style is or, better, what it is thought to be. With respect to archaeological material culture, for descriptive purposes, Sackett's (e.g., 1982, 1990) model, incorporating two analytic axes—adjunctive versus isochrestic style and active versus passive style—is the best general perspective and the only one broad enough to include a wide range of stylistic behaviors.

Essentially, according to Sackett[1] (1982, 1990, and see Chase's [1991] review), style is built into or onto material culture in two ways, adjunctively and isochrestically. Adjunctive style is that deliberately added to an artifact, such as a decorative element. Isochrestic style is the choice between equivalent ways of achieving the same utilitarian end. Thus, in ceramics, the designs painted or incised onto a pot are examples of adjunctive style. Two different shapes for cooking pots, or forks with three or four prongs, are examples of isochrestic style. Sometimes these overlap since it may be difficult to distinguish between utilitarian design elements and adjunctive features. Extreme functionalists can, of course, argue that no types are ever truly equivalent.

Beyond the actual encoding of style onto material culture, style acts on people and in their cultures either passively or actively, or rather on a continuum from passive to active. That is, style by definition encodes cultural information, but the role this information plays in the conduct of culture varies in intensity from virtually nil to very active. Clearly the intensity of this role is dependent on a range of factors, most especially on context. Stylistic elements that act as cultural stimuli in one context need not do so in another.

Notably, style can actively transmit information regardless of the conscious intent of the producer or user. Intent can also be scaled to different levels, from unintentional transmission of background information to deliberate transmission of specific messages, with a range between them.

Finally, the disjunction between producer and user, or transmitter and receiver, should also be noted (cf. Wobst 1977). Style is rarely explicit, often ambiguous, and often subject to idiosyncratic modification. Symbols and styles intended to convey one message may easily be interpreted as another. This is part of the general negotiating process in the evolution of style (cf. Hodder 1990; Shanks and Tilley 1987). Of course, archaeologically, these issues may indeed be difficult to explicate.

Style and Sickle Segments

Within the historic and proto-historic periods in the Levant, the number of standardized types that might be amenable to stylistic analysis is limited. Arrowheads could conceivably provide a good case study since they have been examined for style ethnographically elsewhere (e.g., Wiessner 1983), and typological change and variation within the Levant have been well studied (Gopher 1994). There is no doubt that arrowhead variability encodes stylistic information. However, for all intents and purposes, arrowheads disappear from the Levantine archaeological record with the end of the Neolithic (except in the desert), well before history and the historical contexts requisite for the analytic control sought here.

Tabular scrapers clearly encode style as well, both in their morphological variability and in the incised designs found on the cortices of some of them. Archaeological contexts also support the idea of special roles for these tools. However, as a test case, they are limited because they are relatively short-lived, spanning only two archaeological periods, the Chalcolithic and the Early Bronze Age, only the later falling into the strictly historic period (and notably, the Levantine Early Bronze Age is also preliterate, although writing is known in the neighboring regions, Egypt and Mesopotamia). Furthermore, in most contexts there are relatively few tabular scrapers, limiting the potentials of analysis of variability.

Other types, with the exception of sickle segments, are either rare or *ad hoc*, reducing their value as test cases. Sickle segments, however, provide an excellent case for examining stylistic phenomena for several reasons.

Sickle segments as a class span a long period, covering numerous archaeological periods, beginning in the Epipaleolithic and terminating in the Iron Age. This long span allows examination of a great range of typological variability, long-term perspective on typological and stylistic change, and direct comparison of the place of sickle segments in the prehistoric and historic periods. Most of the analysis is restricted to the later periods in this span since the greater range of archaeological materials associated with the protohistoric and historic periods provides better context for examination of stylistic variation.

In addition to the long life span of the class (table 6.1, figs. 3.3, 3.19), sickle segments are found in a range of geographic areas and environmental zones, crosscutting ethnic and state boundaries and varying forms of agricultural exploitation. Thus, beyond diachronic variability, synchronic variability in sickle assemblages can also be examined.

Sickle segments are found in relative abundance at many sites. This is important in examining style since variability is of the essence in noniconic artifacts. Rare pieces, regardless of how symbolically loaded they may have been, are inherently more difficult to interpret without some key to their meaning. Furthermore, sickle types can be well defined, varying both chronologically and geographically, and providing ample opportunity for evaluating archaeological

	NORTH	SOUTH
Iron Age 1200–800[1] B.C.E.	Large Geometrics	Arched Backed Blades Backed Blades Large Geometrics
Late Bronze 1550–1200 B.C.E.	Large Geometrics	—
Middle Bronze II 1950–1550 B.C.E.	Large Geometrics	—
Middle Bronze I 2200–1950 B.C.E.	Canaanean Sickles	—
Early Bronze 3500–2200 B.C.E.	Canaanean Sickles Simple Blade Sickles Prismatic Bitruncated and Backed Bitruncated (EBI, southern Shephela, Coastal Plain, only)	Arched Backed Blades, Backed Blades
Chalcolithic 4500–3500 B.C.E.	Prismatic, Backed Bitruncated	—
Late Pottery[2] **Neolithic** 5200–4500 B.C.E.	Prismatic Bitruncated Backed Bitruncated	—
Early Pottery Neolithic 5900–5200 B.C.E.	Heavily Denticulated	—
Pre-Pottery Neolithic B 7300–5900 B.C.E.	Prismatic Blades Segments	—
Pre-Pottery Neolithic A 8300–7300 B.C.E.	Beit Tamir Knives Simple Blades	—
Natufian 10,000–8300 B.C.E.	Backed Blades	—

TABLE 6.1. Sequence of sickle types divided by north and south.

1. The Iron Age, as defined in Israel, ends in 586 B.C.E., with the destruction of the Kingdom of Judah. Flint sickle segments seem to go out of use earlier, around the eighth–ninth centuries B.C.E.

2. Although the dates presented for the Chalcolithic and later are either calendric dates or calibrated radiocarbon dates, those for the Neolithic and Natufian are uncalibrated radiocarbon dates. The discrepancy which should appear is masked by extending the Chalcolithic back and the Pottery Neolithic forward.

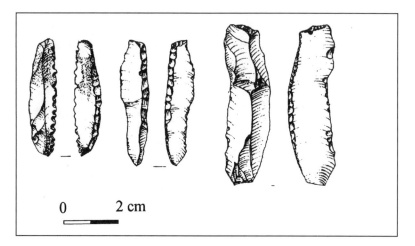

FIG. 6.1. *Natufian sickles from Kebara B (glossy, but gloss not pictured). (Valla 1984, fig. 58)*

0   2 cm

models attempting to explain that variability. Notably, intratype variation can also be examined.

Beyond the historical contexts noted above, functional, technological, and economic frameworks for sickle segments are relatively well understood. The presence of sickle gloss on all pieces attributed to the class assures that all were used for harvesting grasses (e.g., Anderson 1980; Unger-Hamilton 1984, 1989; Witthoft 1967; also Chapter 3). The control of utilitarian function is important since it demonstrates that class variability, either intra- or intertype, is not the result of major changes in use. Of course, it does not rule out changes in modes of use and efficiency within general harvesting functions.

Technological and economic contexts are also well controlled. In most cases, reduction sequences for sickle types are reasonably well understood, and technologies are well defined. In direct relation, the reduction sequence analyses, and the spatial and geographic separation of different stages in the sequence, allow explication of modes of specialist and semispecialist production and distribution (Chapter 4). The distinction between producer and user is of special importance in analyses of style (cf. Wobst 1977).

The Typological Sequence and Geographic Patterns

A minimum of seven distinct types of flint sickles can be defined for the period spanning from ca. 10,000 B.C.E. through the eighth–ninth centuries B.C.E., from the Natufian culture through the middle of the Iron Age. The types are defined according to morphological and technological criteria (e.g., Rosen 1982; Payne 1983; Burian and Friedman 1979; also Chapters 2, 3). In addition to the general types, subtypes

and variants can also be defined. The various types and subtypes fall into distinct chronological and geographical patterns, summarized in table 6.1 (also figs. 3.3, 3.19).

Beginning with the terminal Pleistocene Natufian culture (ca. 10,000–8000 B.C.E.), sickles are small backed blades (fig. 6.1) set into bone hafts in a straight line, essentially forming reaping knives. Blades are rarely retouched on the working edge, although they may show use damage and, of course, gloss. Based on a few complete sickles recovered, gloss patterns, and attempts at reconstruction, it is apparent that little of the actual composite blade projected beyond the haft, i.e., little of the flint part of the tool was actually visible. Notably, the hafts themselves often show elaborate designs and representations (e.g., Garrod and Bate 1937, XIII:1,3), an example of adjunctive style, but not on the lithics themselves.

Notably, the sickles were not the only tools produced from blades and bladelets; rather, a range of microlithic forms and retouched blades were manufactured from the same technology. There is no evidence for specialized or semispecialized manufacture of blades or sickles in the Natufian period, nor for exchange of these pieces or special modes of distribution. However, based on great variability in core:tool ratios, it is unlikely that all sickles were produced on the sites in which they were recovered.

During the Pre-Pottery Neolithic A period, also called the Sultanian culture (ca. eighth millennium B.C.E.), sickles can be divided into two basic types (Payne 1983), those blades showing luster and little further retouch, and backed blades (fig. 6.2). Blades are longer than those of the Natufian period, but show similar edge retouch patterns, mostly use damage and

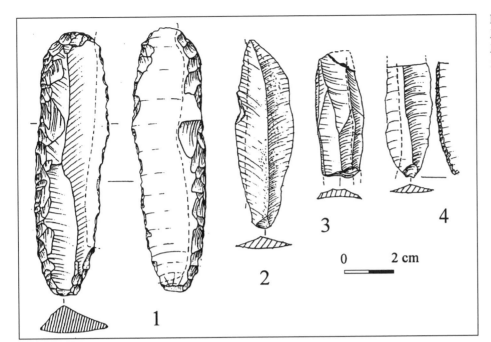

FIG. 6.2. *Pre-Pottery Neolithic A sickles from Nativ Hagdud. (Nadel 1988, 198, figs. 5, 6)*

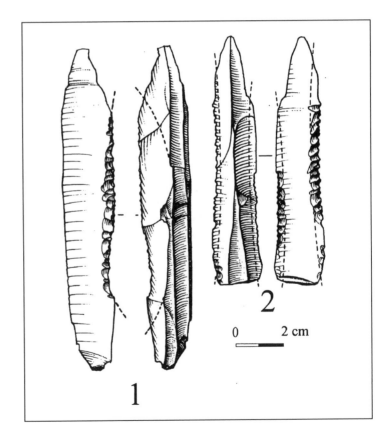

FIG. 6.3. *Pre-Pottery Neolithic B sickles from Munhata. (Gopher 1989, fig. 16)*

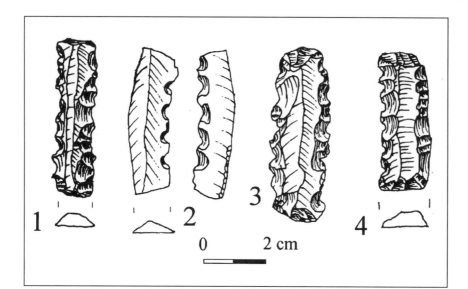

FIG. 6.4. *Early Pottery Neolithic (PNA) sickles from Sha'ar Hagolan (1–3) and Hesi (4).*

occasionally nibbling. Backing retouch is often invasive (Beit Tamir knives). Blades were manufactured on site, with little evidence for specialization in manufacture. Other blade tools are not uncommon. As in the Natufian period, variability in core:tool ratios between sites and areas on sites indicates some exchange or expertise in production.

Pre-Pottery Neolithic B sickles (fig. 6.3), dating to roughly the seventh millennium B.C.E., were manufactured on long prismatic blades, struck from bipolar naviform cores, often heat treated. They were not backed, although they were often truncated. Working edge nibbling is common, and gloss is typical. Hafting was in a straight line, as in the Natufian period, although the longer length of these blades required fewer per composite sickle. Little of the flint blade was actually visible once hafted, as seen by complete sickles recovered and gloss patterns (e.g., Bar-Yosef and Alon 1988, 16–19, pl. V). As the Natufian period, handles were decorated. Great variability in naviform blade core frequencies at different sites suggests the beginnings of specialization or expertise in manufacture of blades during this period (Rosen 1989b). However, sickle blades were not the exclusive products of blade manufacture, and arrowheads, knives, and other retouched blades were also based on this technology.

Sickles in the Early Pottery Neolithic period (ca. sixth millennium B.C.E., fig. 6.4), associated with cultures such as the Yarmukian (e.g., Stekelis 1972, 18–19, pl. 21) and its variants, are characterized by deep and regular pressure flaked denticulation, which may appear on either one or both lateral edges of rela-

tively short, truncated blade segments. Segments vary in the presence/absence of backing, degree of retouch beyond denticulation, and presence/absence of ventral retouch. This variability may fall into chronological or geographic patterns, but data are too scarce and too poorly controlled to examine this. There is some hint that invasive pressure retouch is more common later in the period. Technologically, the sickles are produced from cores similar to those of the Pre-Pottery Neolithic B period and show similar patterns of incipient specialization in manufacture (Rosen 1989b). As in the Pre-Pottery Neolithic B period, arrowheads also continue to be produced from blades struck from these cores. No hafts have been recovered, and gloss patterns are difficult to identify, so hafting technique and shape are impossible to reconstruct.

The Late Pottery Neolithic period (ca. fifth millennium B.C.E.) shows two types of sickles (fig. 6.5). In the Qatifian culture of the northern Negev, sickle were made from bitruncated blade segments (Gilead 1990). The Wadi Raba culture, and its variants, found in central and northern Israel, shows bitruncated backed sickle segments (e.g., Gopher and Orelle 1989). The primary difference between the two types is the dominance of backing on the more northerly sickles. There is, as yet, no good chronological control on the relationships between the cultures. Edge retouch for both varies from serration to nibbling. Gloss typically runs parallel to the blade axis and is found on only a single edge. No complete sickles with hafts have been reported, and patterns of hafting are difficult to directly infer. The short length of the segments and the

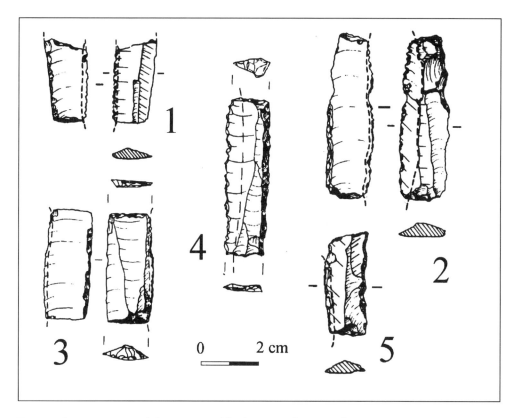

FIG. 6.5. *Late Pottery Neolithic (PNB) sickles from Qatif (3–4) and Y-11 (1–2, 5).*
(Gilead 1990, figs. 4, 6) Note presence of backing on 2–3 and its absence on others.

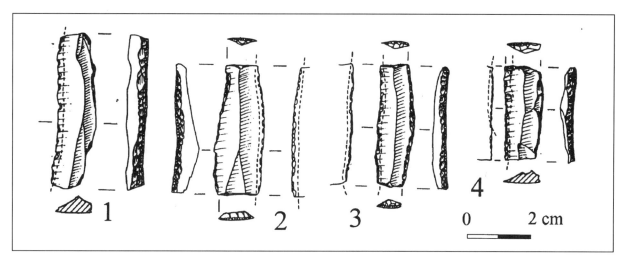

FIG. 6.6. *Chalcolithic sickles from Sataf.*

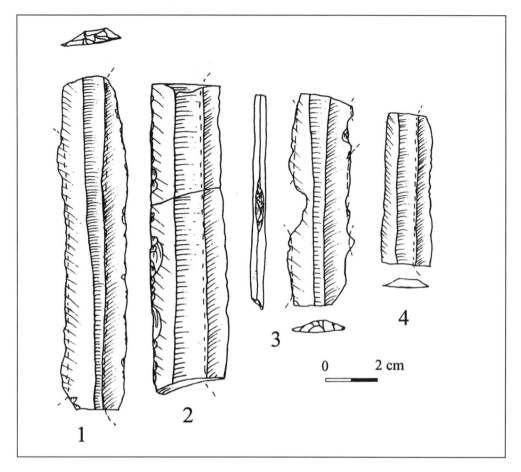

FIG. 6.7. *Canaanean sickles (diagnostic to Early Bronze Age and Middle Bronze I). (Sha'ar Hagolan)*

gloss patterns parallel to the striking axis suggest at least the possibility of curved hafting.

Blade cores for the production of sickles seem to be more rare than in the preceding periods, suggesting increased specialization in manufacture. (That is, more sickles were being produced off-site, or in specialized activity areas, which have not been exposed). Notably, chipped stone arrowheads have dropped out of the material culture repertoire by this period (except in the South), such that for all intents and purposes, sickles are the only significant product of blade technology.

Chalcolithic period (ca. 4500–3600 B.C.E.) sickle segments (fig. 6.6) are similar technologically to those of the Late Pottery Neolithic period, but seem to show less typological variability in the dominance of backed truncated segments and the absence of the unbacked variety (e.g., Gilead et al. 1995). Edge retouch varies from some serrated pieces to nibbling and edge damage. Data are too scarce for geographic or chronological comparison within the Chalcolithic period,

although it is clear that assemblages may differ from site to site in such features as length and width. The use of short, truncated segments with gloss lines parallel to the blade axis suggests a curved haft.

The presence of a workshop site at Gaza Site A, with some 450 blade cores (and an additional 950 bladelet cores) (Roshwalb 1981: 58, 64; Macdonald 1932:10) is an indication of increasing specialization of production (Chapter 4). However, along with the evidence for blade manufacture at Site A, Macdonald (1932, 10, pls. xvii, xxii:2; also Roshwalb 1981, 58, 64) also recovered evidence for secondary production of tabular scrapers and for the manufacture of axes. That is, specialization at Site A is in the manufacture of several lithic types, not only sickle blades.

Canaanean sickle blades (fig. 6.7), appearing in the Early Bronze Age (ca. 3600–2200 B.C.E.), constitute a major typological and technological change from the preceding Chalcolithic and Late Neolithic blade technologies. Blades are longer and wider, and

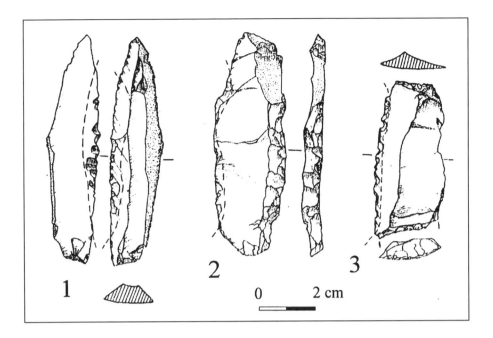

Fig. 6.8. *Sickles from Uvda Valley 16, southern Negev.*

sickles were manufactured either from truncated segments or from complete or near complete blades. Remains of bitumen adhesive on Canaanean sickle segments and blades from Arad (Schick 1978) indicate that they were hafted with little more than the working edge visible beyond the haft. The complete blade sickles were probably hafted straight, as reaping knives, to judge by their length. The segments were most likely hafted in a crescent-shaped handle, judging from both the length of the segments and the parallel-to-striking-axis gloss patterns. Working edge retouch varies from heavy serration through nibbling, occasionally on the ventral face. Approximately 40% of Canaanean sickles show gloss on two edges. Within the Early Bronze Age Canaanean system, there are no clear chronological or geographic patterns, although individual assemblages differ in average metrics.

The trends toward specialization in sickle manufacture culminate in the Canaanean industry. Most sites show a total absence of Canaanean blade cores, and a few show many, such as at Har Charuvim (Meyerhof 1960) and Lahav (Futato 1990). Caches of unretouched blades, clearly derived from the same original core, have been recovered at several sites, such as Motza (Eisenberg 1993), Beit Yerah, Lower Horvat 'Illin (Marder et al. 1995), and Nizzanim (Yekutieli and Gophna 1994) (Chapter 4). These probably were trade packets. Sickles are the only standard products of Canaanean technology, although *ad hoc* use of Canaanean blades occurs.

In addition to Canaanean sickles, several other sickle types occur in the Early Bronze Age. In the Central and southern Negev, the typical sickle segment is backed, either straight or arched (fig. 6.8). Chronological distinctions within the Early Bronze Age of the Negev are still problematic. The technology employed is a simple blade technology, not resembling the sophisticated Canaanean technology farther north. Hafting patterns are difficult to reconstruct, especially for the arched backed blade segments. The generally limited width of the gloss line indicates that most of the sickle was embedded in the haft. Its direction, parallel to the working edge, indicates hafting parallel to the handle. Edge retouch is usually very light. There is little evidence for specialization in the manufacture of these sickles. Blade cores (usually mixed blade/flake cores) and blade waste occur in low quantities are most sites where sickles are found.

Bitruncated and backed bitruncated sickle segments (fig. 6.9), manufactured on short prismatic blades, are found in association with an Egyptian presence in the southern Shephela and Coastal Plain in Early Bronze Age I (late fourth millennium B.C.E.) contexts. At several sites, such as Erani (Rosen 1988a) and Besor Bridge (Gophna and Friedmann 1993; Yeivin 1976), these are found side by side with Canaanean sickles. Unfortunately, it is impossible to reconstruct precise intrasite spatial relations. However, the presence of similar types in contemporary Egypt (Rosen 1988a), numerous Egyptian type ceramics (Brandl

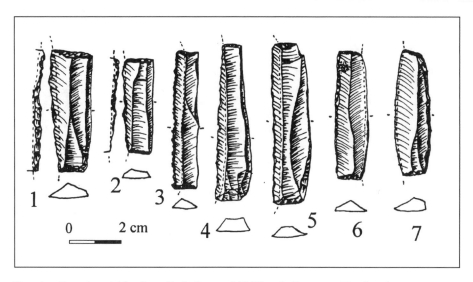

FIG. 6.9. *Egyptian sickles from Early Bronze I Tel Erani. (Rosen 1988a, fig. 6)*

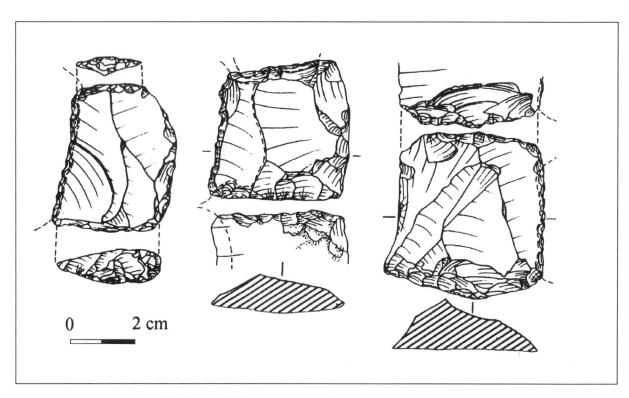

FIG. 6.10. *Large Geometric sickles from Ashdod. (Rosen 1993c, fig. 49)*

1989; Gophna 1990), and other Egyptian artifacts on these sites (e.g., Weinstein 1984) indicates the Egyptian affinities of the type. Notably, there was also a difference in raw material between these Egyptian style sickles and the local Canaanean type (Rosen 1988a). Hafting patterns are again difficult to reconstruct, but as in previous examples, the short length of the segments and parallel-to-blade gloss lines suggest curved handles. Gloss does not penetrate deeply over the blade, indicating that much of it was embedded deeply in the haft. Edge retouch is usually limited. Data are limited with respect to specialization of manufacture, although the absence of cores suggests that blade production was not carried out on all parts of the site(s). Elsewhere I have suggested (Rosen 1988a) that sickles and other Egyptian flint tools at Erani were manufactured by a transplanted Egyptian knapper (or knappers). The limited distribution of the types is notable, probably restricted to the areas of Egyptian influence, and given the general dominance of Canaanean sickles even on sites with Egyptian influence, use of the Egyptian sickles may well have been limited to Egyptians.

The Middle Bronze Age I (Early Bronze Age IV, Intermediate Bronze, etc.), dating to ca. 2200–1950 B.C.E.) shows technological and typological continuity in the use of Canaanean sickles in the Mediterranean zone. Data are limited, but no cores are known from sites thus far investigated, indicating a continuation of the specialized manufacture noted for the Early Bronze Age, this in spite of the collapse of urban society at the end of the Early Bronze Age III. Also notable is the absence of sickle blades in the Negev sites from this period, probably indicative of a major change in subsistence economy.

A major change in technology and typology occurred in the transition from Middle Bronze Age I to Middle Bronze Age II, beginning ca. 1950 B.C.E., corresponding to the reurbanization of the Southern Levant. Canaanean technology disappears with the end of the Middle Bronze Age I, and Large Geometric Sickles (fig. 6.10), based on flake-blade technology, are introduced. These continue in use through the middle of the Iron Age, ca. 800 B.C.E. These sickles are considerably wider than all previous types. They show a range in edge retouch from heavy serration to fresh edges, especially on the nonlustrous blanks. Degree of edge retouch probably corresponds to use-life. Most are backed and bitruncated. Shapes vary considerably, as determined especially by the angle of the truncations. Based on these angles, and rare complete sickles

(Gilead 1973), or sickles recovered *in situ* but lacking the haft (Mozel 1983), Large Geometric composite sickles were undoubtedly crescent shaped. No *clear* patterns can be traced with respect to shape or size of sickles from different assemblages, although there are hints of length reduction with time (Rosen 1982). Variability does occur between sites and between strata at individual sites. The presence of triangular segments in relatively stable proportions (1:4 to 1:6) in most assemblages is probably a result of the specific shape having been used as the end piece of the composite sickle.

Evidence for specialized manufacture derives most especially from Gezer (Rosen 1986), where caches of sickle blanks were uncovered in the courtyard of a putative Iron Age flint knapper. Cores are unknown and may have been discarded at some as yet unidentified quarry site. No other lithic types seem to be associated with this specialization. At Tel Dan, large numbers of sickle blanks were recovered in a general industrial area, suggesting that the specialization in sickle production may have been associated with other manufacturing, most notably, metallurgy. These sickles are ultimately replaced by iron equivalents, probably in the eighth century B.C.E.

In the desert, as at Qadesh Barnea (Cohen 1986, pl. 140:6–7, 10–13) and other Negev sites (Haiman 1986, 93; 1988, fig. 55), a special variant of this type looks similar to the backed and arched backed sickles of the desert Early Bronze Age. However, beyond the existence of the type, and the rarity of typical Large Geometrics, little information is available on reduction, distribution, or economy.

Explaining Variation

The typological and technological variability outlined above cannot be explained by a single factor. Changes in sickle segment form reflect a set of interrelated causes including degree of specialization, relative value, hafting technologies, traditions of manufacture and technology (perhaps reflecting different ethnic groups), availability of and access to raw materials, specificity of exchange networks, and functional efficiency. None of these are sufficient of themselves.

Much of the typological change occurs at the junctures between archaeological periods. Significantly, that periodization has been established almost totally independently of sickle technology and typology, determined by changes in ceramics, architecture, subsistence, political events, and other elements of material culture. Sickles have, at best, played only a minor supporting role in the confirmation of the periodization. That sickle types do correspond to some of these archaeological units is an important statement about the embeddedness of sickle technologies and typologies with the rest of "culture." Furthermore, the lack of correspondence in some cases is no less important. Archaeological periodization has never been an objective process, and the correspondence or lack of correspondence between different traits and periods should provide important insights into the periodization process itself.

GEOGRAPHIC AND REGIONAL VARIATION

Beyond the diachronic variability, there are also clear geographic differences in sickle form and, no less important, geographic continuities. As with the chronological continuities, geographic continuities may act as a control on over-generalization based on interpretation of the differences.

Initial examination here is restricted to the Bronze and Iron Ages, since the historical record and the richer archaeological background provide independent frameworks for interpreting the lithic variability. The models developed thus can hopefully be extended backward to the earlier periods.

Within the Early Bronze Age, the contrasts in sickle types between north and south and the presence of two distinct technologies in the Shephela (southern Coastal Plain and foothills) are reasonably interpreted as resulting from the presence of different lithic traditions, read ethnicity. However, in reality, the variation is not so easily explained. Canaanean technology, extending from the Southern Levant to Turkey, and at least as far east as Iran (e.g., Valla 1978), can hardly be assumed to reflect an "ethnic group." The bitruncated sickles of Tel Erani (Rosen 1988a) most certainly represent an Egyptian presence, but only in the context of contrast with the local Canaanean technology. We are limited in our knowledge of the distribution of the Egyptian type—perhaps it represents a general North African type, or even a pan-African type? The typological contrasts may exist on a plane much higher than that of the local ethnic group, reflecting complexes and areas of much greater extent, which intersect on only a limited scale.

Both Canaanean and Egyptian bitruncated sickles are the products of specialized knapping and distribution. Had the Egyptians not brought a flint knapper (or knappers) with them, trained in the "Egyptian"

tradition of knapping, they most certainly would have adopted local tools for their purposes. Thus, the presence of Egyptian sickles (and other Egyptian tools) represents a perceived need to supply the Egyptian "colony" with its own tools, independently of those of the local Canaanites. The ceramics reflect a similar picture of Egyptian types on local raw materials (Brandl 1989), as do other elements of material culture (cf. Weinstein 1984). Given this, it is more than likely that the Egyptian sickles were used by Egyptian farmers, since Canaanean technology continued in use, presumably by the local population. It is, of course, unfortunate, that detailed provenience information is unavailable for better testing of these ideas, but the disappearance of Egyptian sickles from the material record with the abandonment of the Egyptian colony supports the idea that they were used primarily by Egyptian farmers. The point is that there were Egyptian farmers and that these farmers were tied to a specialized production-distribution network distinct from that of the local inhabitants. Thus, the presence of bitruncated and backed bitruncated sickle blades in the southern Shephela alongside Canaanean sickles in the Early Bronze Age I period reflects far greater complexity than such rubrics as "tradition" or "ethnicity" usually imply.

Unlike the Egyptian sickles, the backed and arched backed sickles of the southern Negev, especially at the Uvda Valley, do not overlap geographically with Canaanean technology (excepting rare trade pieces). A standard interpretation given the material contrasts between north and south in the region during the Early Bronze Age is the existence of two contrasting cultures (e.g., Beit-Arieh 1986), a native desert culture (c.f. Rothenberg and Glass 1992) and a northern Canaanite culture, sometimes intrusive into southern regions. This reconstruction is based both on architectural contrasts between the two "cultures," as well as petrographic analyses of ceramics, indicating movement of pots between north and south (Porat 1989). Thus, the southern sickle types should represent that local desert culture, in apparent ethnic contrast to northern Canaanean technology. However, as in the Egyptian case, such simplistic notions mask greater and far more interesting complexity.

Whereas Canaanean sickles are the products of specialized manufacture, and regional or subregional distribution, sickles in the southern Negev are locally produced, probably by the people who used them, and, if not, nevertheless on site and by people closely associated with the users. That is, the Canaanean exchange network that extended throughout the entire Near East with respect to knowledge and use of the technology (and probably with respect to mode of production/ distribution), did not extend the mere 200 km south of the Beersheva Basin to the southern Negev. Furthermore, this is in spite of ceramic exchange between north and south, well established by petrography (e.g., Amiran et al 1973; Rothenberg and Glass 1992; Porat 1989). Acknowledging that there is material culture contact between semi-autonomous groups north and south verges on the trivial. The important point is that there is a cultural or economic filter in place here, dictating what traits and components of material culture move between or are adopted by the different groups. Comparing this circumstance with the Egyptian example outlined above, no Canaanite knapper moved south with the so-called Aradian or Canaanite colonies (cf. Amiran et al. 1973; Beit-Arieh 1986), even when the inhabitants actively engaged in agriculture, as at Uvda Valley (Avner 1990). What appear to be similar phenomena in the contrasting sickle types in fact reflect fundamentally different levels of cultural connection.

DIACHRONIC CHANGE

The transition from Early Bronze Age III to Middle Bronze Age I in the Southern Levant is marked by the virtually total collapse of urban civilization and a reversion to village and pastoral society and subsistence. Although the causes of this collapse are debated (e.g., Dever 1989; Esse 1989; Richard 1980; A. Rosen 1995) and probably always will be, it is clear that the socioeconomic superstructure comprised of cities, elites, specialized production, long distance trade, and centralized cult broke down during this transition. The Canaanean sickle system apparently did not. There is unbroken technological and typological continuity from the urban to the village system, all the more striking given the specialized nature of the Canaanean sickle production.

That the sickle system crosscuts the periodization scheme may reflect on problems in the periodization, especially in light of controversies over the interpretation of fundamental cultural continuities between the Early Bronze Age III and Middle Bronze Age I (= Early Bronze Age IV, Intermediate Bronze Age, etc., in different terminologies). The pottery too seems to show many continuities (Dever 1970, 1973), although not as strikingly as the sickle assemblage. However, that a

specialized production-distribution system continued through a period of economic breakdown provides important information on that breakdown. The few Canaanean workshop sites thus far discovered are for the most part village sites. Although they seem not to show evidence of Middle Bronze Age I occupation (except perhaps Har Charuvim), the Canaanean system association with villages must obviously continue through the Middle Bronze Age I, in the absence of cities, in light of the continued evidence for specialized production. Thus, if the breakdown in urban economy at the end of Early Bronze Age was not accompanied by a breakdown in village economy, as indeed seems to be the case, Canaanean sickle continuity can be comprehended.

Canaanean sickles are replaced by Large Geometric sickles with the Middle Bronze Age II, a period of major reurbanization in the Southern Levant (e.g., Gerstinblith 1983). Historically, the period seems to be associated with folk migrations, for example, the Amorites (e.g., Kenyon 1980, 119–47), and with the rise of the Old Babylonian Kingdom in Mesopotamia. The sickle replacement process seems to be rapid, and it is tempting to assign the introduction of the new type to the arrival of new people. Indeed there is skeletal evidence for the arrival of new peoples at this time, although the earlier population does not disappear (Smith 1989). Thus, if the introduction of a new type might be associated with a new people, the replacement of Canaanean sickles cannot be assumed to be merely a result of the new people since the "old" people were not replaced. Most likely, the economic shift from countryside to city associated with reurbanization is more the actual agent of change than the fact of introduction.

The continued use of Large Geometric sickles, with no discernible typological variability from Middle Bronze Age II through the middle of the Iron Age, is no less important than the typological discontinuity from Middle Bronze Age I to II. This period of more than a millennium witnessed major social and ethnic change, including periods of Egyptian control, the arrival of the Sea Peoples, most notably the Philistines, and the rise of the Israelite state. That is, although the archaeological and historical record is one of dynamic ethnic and political change, those changes are not reflected in the typological sequence.

In the desert in the Iron Age, the typological contrast between Large Geometrics and backed blade/ arched backed blade sickles is reminiscent of that of the Early Bronze Age. However, the dates and the historical contexts of these desert forts and settlements are disputed. Cohen (1986) claims that they ought to be associated with a Solomonic expansion of the Israelite kingdom in the tenth century B.C.E. Finkelstein (1984) argues that they represent sedentarization of local nomads, claiming a somewhat earlier date as well. Without better contextual background, not to mention better lithic data, it is impossible to further interpret these sickle assemblages.

Finally, some within type variation can be traced, both between sites (Rosen 1982) and within them. The latter is most particularly evident in the sickles collection from Ashdod (Rosen 1993c). The assemblages from Stratum 13 to Stratum 14 at this site show subtle differences in the shape of the sickles, as expressed in length versus width plots. These two strata mark the transition from the earlier Canaanite to the Philistine occupation of the site. Although indeed statistically significant, the differences are not obvious without recourse to measurements and graphs—they do not represent a major paradigm shift in how sickles were produced. Rather, given the specialized nature of manufacture, they seem to reflect the arrival of a new knapper, with a slightly different perception of how sickles should look.

LESSONS

These examples have several morals, the first of which is that there is no one-to-one relationship between ethnicity and sickle type variation. New peoples do not necessarily bring in new types, although they may. Even when they do, those types may or may not be accepted into the greater material culture assemblage. The converse is also true. New types do not necessarily imply new people. It is hard to see a new people arriving throughout the Near East, right upon the transition from Chalcolithic to Early Bronze Age, immediately distributing Canaanean blades (although, obviously some agency of introduction must be postulated). If these lessons seem trivial, they should not, given the simplistic formulations often attendant on material culture change.

More importantly, the introduction, adoption, and replacement of the types described here do not merely constitute a typological phenomenon. In fact, the typological changes reflect the integration of modes of manufacture and distribution into larger economic systems. Canaanean blades were never adopted into the desert Early Bronze Age system because the two systems did not mesh. The specialized commodities of the north had no place nor appeal in the fundamentally domestic economy of the south. Egyptian sickles are present in the Shephela in the Early Bronze Age I because an Egyptian economy seems to have been transplanted from Egypt to Palestine. Canaanean blades were not replaced in the Middle Bronze Age I because the village-level economy maintained its integrity through that period. And finally, the reurbanization of the Middle Bronze Age II was accompanied by a major economic reorganization, apparently including urbanization of specialized production of sickles, this marked by the introduction of Large Geometrics and the disappearance of the village-based Canaanean blades. The typological differences here are almost secondary. The real changes occur on the organizational level. Although the new types must have some agency of introduction or innovation, the key issue is the mechanism of adoption. In a sense, the types ride on structural changes.

THE PREHISTORIC SICKLES

Extending the model to earlier sickle systems cannot be accomplished with the same level of control established for the historical periods. Nevertheless, a case can be made.

Sickle types changed markedly from the Natufian period to the Pre-Pottery Neolithic A, somewhat from the Pre-Pottery Neolithic A to the Pre-Pottery Neolithic B, markedly from the Pre-Pottery Neolithic B to the early Pottery Neolithic, and again markedly from early to late Pottery Neolithic. From the Pottery Neolithic to the Chalcolithic, typological change is barely perceptible, but is again marked from the Chalcolithic to the Early Bronze Age.

The Natufian to Pre-Pottery Neolithic A transition corresponds to major changes in subsistence, settlement systems, mobility patterns, regional exploitation, and social organization. Although the Natufians practiced intensive collection of wild grain, the Pre-Pottery Neolithic A saw the first sowing, effecting the final and conclusive transition to food-producing economies. The introduction of new sickle types may well be tied to exploitation of new flint sources, probably to be associated with new settlement patterns and increasing sedentism. Decreasing mobility may have encouraged incipient expertise and curation behaviors. It is also likely that the Pre-Pottery Neolithic A saw some population influx, perhaps from desert regions. The change in sickle systems thus accords with major economic changes.

The Pre-Pottery Neolithic A to B transition is smoother. Although marked by numerous changes in a range of sociocultural realms, the fundamental base of village society based on agriculture and hunting remained intact through at least the first half of the period. Thus the relative continuity in sickle typology through this transition corresponds to a parallel economic continuity.

Although the introduction of ceramics with the Pottery Neolithic is often seen as a major innovation and primary marker for periodization, in fact the transition from Pre-Pottery Neolithic to Pottery Neolithic is marked by a general collapse of the millennium-long Pre-Pottery Neolithic B system (e.g., Moore 1973; Kohler-Rollefson 1992). This collapse, which may have been environmentally triggered, undoubtedly opened the Levantine Neolithic up to a wide range of innovations. It is instructive to note that whereas sickle types change drastically from Pre-Pottery Neolithic to Pottery Neolithic, arrowhead types continue (at least in the early Pottery Neolithic) with only minor change (e.g., Gopher 1994). The agricultural system intimately associated with village-level organization was affected far more in this collapse than was the hunting system, probably inherently more flexible and resilient.

Similarly, the transition from Early Pottery Neolithic (A) to Late Pottery Neolithic (B) shows major economic innovations, including the rise of a new village system based on secondary products (cf. Sherratt 1983; Gopher and Gophna 1993) and perhaps tied to the Mesopotamian Halaf expansion (Garfinkel 1993). The introduction and adoption of a new sickle type can be tied to the beginning of a new and more complex economic system in the latest Neolithic. The virtual absence of sickle type change from Late Pottery Neolithic to Chalcolithic is paralleled by clear economic continuities between the periods. The introduction of copper metallurgy in the northern Negev in the Chalcolithic is not paralleled in sites farther north, and periodization based so much on a single character is problematic.

Finally, the introduction of Canaanean technology with the Early Bronze Age seems to correspond to ever increasing specialization in manufacture and a shift in raw material exploitation to more restricted sources. The origins of the type itself are difficult to trace, but the period itself clearly saw folk movements, as well as increased trade and foreign contacts.

The Problem with Style

The above review would seem to have little relevance to most of the recent discussions of style in the archaeological literature. The encompassing theme of most of that literature has been that stylistic variation incorporates meaning, usually to producer, user, and/or receiver of messages encoded in the material culture. The problem lies in establishing that meaning for material culture which is noniconic in form. The fundamentally arbitrary nature of the symbols conveying noniconic messages renders that goal impossible in the absence of a larger context providing a key to comprehension of symbols or forms.

The first point is that the variation in sickle blades does fit most definitions of stylistic variation, at least before explanation is attached to the definitions. Specifically, although some attributes of the different types could be ascribed to increasing efficiency in use or production, the variability in types is not fundamentally utilitarian or related to differences in effectiveness or efficiency (cf. Torrence 1989). Thus, for example, Canaanean blades have been suggested to have been more efficiently produced (no backing) and more efficiently used (ability to reverse in haft and double use-life) than their backed Chalcolithic predecessors. However, if efficiency were the overarching principle, it is hard to explain the rise of Large Geometrics, similar to Chalcolithic types in number of production stages and length of use-life. A similar pattern obtains for the Pre-Pottery Neolithic B to Early Pottery Neolithic sickles. Efficiency is not the guiding principle for morphological change.

The cases presented above demonstrate that sickle blades are passive carriers of tradition. They can be associated with specific groups (of varying size scales) and/or periods, and may change with the dynamics of that situation. However, this is only one half of the style debate. The question remains as to whether sickles are components of a material culture actively engaged in the dynamics of cultural negotiation, however that may be construed. Do they transmit messages that are received and acted upon by members of society?

Without informants, the question is ultimately unanswerable, but there are, nevertheless, several points that may have bearing on the issue. As discussed above, virtually all sickle blades are hafted such that attributes distinguishing them typologically one from the other are not visible in the composite tool (backing, truncations, bulb of percussion, angle of truncations, cross section, etc.). The only exception is the deep denticulation found on Early Pottery Neolithic sickles. The stone tools themselves, as distinct from the sickle handles or composite sickles, which are rarely preserved, could not transmit messages between their users because they could not be seen (cf. Wobst 1977).

A related issue is the transmission of messages or other information from producer to user. In post–Early Bronze Age contexts, the evidence suggests that sickles were manufactured as composite tools by specialists and that the user received a complete composite sickle, with segment characteristics obscured inside the haft. Thus, again, no information could be transmitted to users based on sickle segments types since they were not visible.

On the other hand, in the Early Bronze Age, caches of unworked blades suggest that the users modified the specialist-produced blades into sickles. Thus, the farmers must have been aware of the attributes of the blades they were acquiring. However, in the absence of other options for most of the Early Bronze Age over most of the Levant, it is not clear what messages might be conveyed in a uniform type, unless one assumes a repressive centralized control that brooked no alternatives to Canaanean sickle production, a scenario rather difficult to envision. One must ask here whether conformity in general always conveys a message. Put differently, with a more obvious carrier of style, if everyone in the world wore the same style hat, and there were no alternatives, it is difficult to see what message could be conveyed in the specific style of hat worn. There is no contra. The messages needed to run a society would obviously be conveyed on other carriers.

With respect to the Canaanean-Egyptian bitruncated sickle dichotomy, the contrasting types may well have functioned to perpetuate the distinction between economic networks, and hence between communities. It is precisely such specific historical circumstances where lithic artifacts might indeed become active carriers of cultural messages. However, even here, given the near invisibility of the pieces once hafted, the power of the symbols, the ability of the sickles to transmit the messages, could not have been very great.

However, it is important to emphasize that this is only conceivable in a situation where a specialist distributes blades to users who can distinguish between his type and others. In an unspecialized situation, there is no producer-user linkage, since the producer is the user, and therefore no comparable information exchange or transmission system. Obviously, in the unspecialized case, segment attributes are still obscured by hafts so that there can be no transmission between users either.

The final mode of information transmission to be considered is that between master and apprentice. Clearly attributes are taught, transmitted, and recognized, and may incorporate meaning. However, the significance of these meanings must be questioned in light of the absence of further receivers, and it is difficult to trace any variation that might be construed as negotiating. The Early Bronze Age Canaanean-Egyptian dichotomy might represent resistance to a new type, but in the context of all the types reviewed, it is more likely that the transmission of Canaanean technology from master to apprentice represents innate conservatism in lithic production, rather than intentional resistance to Egyptian domination.

Conclusions

The above examination has ramifications for the analysis of style beyond the confines of Levantine sickle segments. Archaeological artifacts are often fragments of complete objects which, like the sickles above, may incorporate stylistic attributes that are in fact invisible in a greater context. Wiessner's (1983) analysis of !Kung arrowheads is a case in point. Although information solicited from informants suggested to her that the arrowheads played an active role in group identity and cultural dynamics, when in actual use, the arrowheads were usually stored head down in quivers. Furthermore, the small size of these points (even the larger ones) renders them near invisible anyway from any but the closest distance and therefore ineffective as conveyors of social messages, although they are clearly reflective of social patterns. In short, reconstruction and evaluation of the physical contexts of artifacts in their cultural context are necessary prerequisites to stylistic interpretation (cf. Wobst 1977).

The sickle types discussed here, and indeed it would seem many if not most lithic types, appear to change on typological cusps, in discontinuous steps. This is a conceptually different form of stylistic change from the continuous variation of constant cultural negotiation. This difference in scale is of fundamental importance in the analysis of style. Confusion over different scales of variation results in inappropriate causes being assigned to explanation of variability.

Thus types that span centuries or millennia cannot be comparable processually to types that vary seasonally, yearly, or even by decade (cf. Rick 1996). Similarly, with respect to areal scale, types that span continents cannot be structurally equivalent to those that span small-scale regions or, for that matter, single knapper idiosyncratic variation (assuming, of course, chronological controls assuring contemporaneity).

Furthermore, the presence/absence of contemporary types providing contradistinction or alternative modes of expression must be considered in the interpretation of a typological system. Thus, large scale types, i.e., those that extend over great areas or long time spans, seem unlikely candidates for significant negotiating roles in material culture systems when operating singly, without alternative counter types. That is, it is difficult to conceive of stable types either actively promoting a dominant culture or class, or acting in opposition to such if there is not evidence of opposition in the form of typological or stylistic alternatives.

On the other hand, the cusps of typological change may well incorporate those same short-term effects described for continuous variation and negotiation. However, apprehension and explanation of these transitions must incorporate the structure of production and distribution—who is producing, transmitting, and receiving typological or stylistic messages, and in what contexts.

NOTES

1. Sackett's model is inclusive enough to incorporate most other approaches, such as Wiessner's (1983, 1984) distinction between emblemic and assertive styles, emic versus etic perspectives (e.g., Hayden 1984), Dunnell's random stylistic drift (1978), and the idea of style as a dynamic negotiating component within culture (e.g., Hodder 1990; Shanks and Tilley 1987). Sackett's (1982, 1990) demonstration that function and style are not opposed, but rather complementary components of any system is of especial importance, assuming functional equivalence can be demonstrated. That, of course, has been the crux of much of the discussion with respect to lithic assemblages. Finally, even given Sackett's model, the real challenge is to apply it substantively and to examine the content of style in a culture and its cultural role with respect to that content.

7 The End of the Stone Age

Technology and Periodization

Archaeologists have long been dividing time by reference to technological change. From Thomsen's (Daniel 1975, 38–53) earliest stone, bronze, and iron ages, the tendency to measure social development in terms of the invention and/or introduction of new technologies has been a dominant theme in archaeological periodization, especially in the Old World.

Although the pragmatic success of the method is indisputable, the drawbacks inherent in the equation of social with technological change have accumulated to the point where the terms themselves lack virtually all technological content they may have once had. Thus, there is no bronze in the Early Bronze Age, and iron occurs before the onset of the Iron Age. Furthermore, even given the recognition of the archaeological (as opposed to technological) meaning of such terms as Stone Age and Iron Age, they have nevertheless often proven a stumbling block when archaeologists attempt to detail the actual history of technologies and technological change. The mere recognition of the continuation of "older" technologies into a "new" era, defined by a new technology, has often proven difficult. The linear nature of the techno-terminological framework combines with hindsight and our own sense of which technology ultimately becomes important in our own time to produce a false perception of ever improving technologies, in an orderly sequence of the better replacing the worse or the more efficient replacing the less. Under such a scheme, the adoption of new technologies needs little explanation since it is a natural outcome of inherent tendencies in human nature. We need only explain the discovery or invention, and natural advantages will be perceived, and the new will replace the old. Thus, once having entered a new technological era, there can be little achieved in the analysis of a decaying, soon to be replaced technology.

In light of the foregoing chapters, the fallacies inherent in this approach would hopefully be apparent. There is great value in the analysis of "decaying"

technologies since from the perspective of the people using them they remain integral to their lives and lifeways, and thus integral to the archaeological record. However, beyond this, the basic logic of linear sequential change must be questioned. If, on the one hand, the assumption that flint was replaced *en toto* in one fell swoop by bronze and iron was rejected relatively early in the history of research, the fact of ultimate replacement, even if it took a long time, is indisputable. The real questions are how did this process occur, and why?

A key issue in this regard is the complexity of both the lithic assemblages and their putative metallic replacements. Although it is perhaps natural to think of lithic technology as a single unified system, earlier chapters have demonstrated the discreteness or near discreteness of different lithic subsystems in terms of production, distribution, function, and discard. Given these subsystems, each in essence a discrete technology, across-the-board replacement in a single event seems indeed unlikely.

Our perceptions, or misperceptions, of metallurgy are similar. Early Chalcolithic copper metallurgy was not a monolithic technology, but shows two distinct modes of manufacture and distribution, associated with different products and functions (e.g., Shalev and Northover 1987; Rosen 1993a; Ilan and Sebbane 1989; Levy and Shalev 1989). Copper continues to be exploited alongside bronze in the Middle Bronze (II) and Late Bronze Ages, and both continue into the Iron Age, even after iron becomes commonplace. Iron, in fact, is first introduced in the Bronze Age (Waldbaum 1978). Raw materials, manufacturing processes, and, initially, end products are distinct for each type of metallurgy. As with lithics, terminological simplicity conceals technological complexity.

The Decline of Flint: A Data Description

The decreasing role of lithic technology in ancient production can be examined from two perspectives. Most simply, within stratified sites a general quantitative decline in lithic artifacts recovered can be traced, probably reflecting the decreasing role of lithic production through time. More importantly, increasing typological restriction can be traced in later lithic assemblages, no doubt reflecting the decreasing uses to which chipped stone tools were put as they were displaced by metal equivalents, or for other reasons (e.g., Rosen 1996).

QUANTITY

It is difficult to define lithic decline quantitatively for two primary reasons. First, excavation of tell sites rarely allows estimation of proportional exposure per stratum. That is, the only way to quantitatively compare general lithic frequencies is to establish some means of comparing how much of each stratum or period was excavated and then to calibrate the lithic frequencies accordingly. Furthermore, differences in length of stratum occupation, population density, areal functions, use-life, discard patterns, and the like are difficult to account for at best. The second problem involves intersite comparison. Differences in the nature of occupations (e.g., population densities, site functions), postdepositional processes, and most especially archaeological collection methods result in assemblages that are simply not comparable in absolute terms.

In an earlier paper (Rosen 1996), lithics per basket were used to calibrate amount of excavation per stratum, as first suggested by Gilead (1995, 107). Recognizing the limitations of the method, it is still reasonable to assume that on the *average*, in a single excavation, the volume of baskets (the lowest level unit of excavation in Levantine historic digs) will remain roughly constant from stratum to stratum. Regardless, in the absence of any other method, this is preferred to doing nothing.

Quantitative intersite comparison cannot be calibrated in this way. Even if baskets could somehow be made to conform to some abstract standard, the specifics of site histories and project methods render each case a special one. However, trends and patterns based on individual sites can be compared for similarities instead.

Figs. 7.1–7.5 (table 7.1) show the quantitative decline of debitage and tools per unit of excavation (either baskets or by proportion exposed at Ir David) at several sites. In order to attempt to equalize between periods with different degrees of on-site/off-site manufacture, debitage includes only flakes, blades, and

IR DAVID

	Chalco/EB	MBII	LB-Iron
Tools	142	109	95
Flakes	740	409	215
Blades	49	29	5
Bladelets	11	4	7
Total debitage	800	442	227
% excavation	7.5	20.5	72
tools/unit	1893	532	132
waste/unit	10667	2156	315

SATAF (Restricted to nonmixed baskets)

	Chalcolithic	Early Bronze
Tools	50	7
Flakes	112	30
Blades	30	2
Bladelets	30	10
Total debitage	172	42
baskets	40	35
	(20 sieved)	(22 sieved)
debitage/basket	4.3	1.2
tools/basket	1.25	0.2

QASIS

	PPNB	EB	MBII	LB	Iron
Tools	12	243	62	43	33
Flakes	18	436	83	14	13
Blades	3	44	15	7	10
Bladelets	9	22	4	0	0
Sickle Flakes	0	5	2	11	2
Total debitage	30	545	116	33	30
baskets	5	349	77	38	34
debitage/basket	6.0	1.56	1.51	1.15	1.13
tools basket	2.4	0.7	0.81	1.13	0.97

YIFTAHEL

	Str. II (EB)	Str. III + IV (PPNB)
Tools	233	657
Flakes	985	3479
Blades	298	767
Bladelets	52	187
Total debitage	1235	4433
baskets	47	100
debitage/basket	26.3	44.3
tools/basket	5.0	6.6

BATASHI

	MBII	LB	Iron I	Iron II
Tools	18	61	33	32
Waste	137	120	35	78
baskets	23	101	40	70
waste/basket	6.0	1.2	0.9	1.1
tools/basket	0.8	0.6	0.8	0.5

TABLE 7.1. Quantitative decline of tools and debitage by site. At Yiftahel the tool totals do not include retouched flakes due to the difficulty of distinguishing between postdepositional damage and intentional retouch. Numbers from Yiftahel used here are from unpublished research by the author on excavations conducted by E. Braun. The counts from Sataf are restricted to nonfill loci. The waste from Batashi includes nondebitage categories such as chunks and chips, as well as more standard categories.

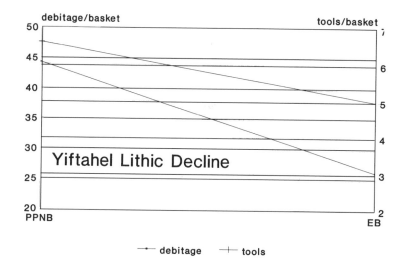

FIG. 7.1. *Quantitative lithic decline at Yiftahel. The lower line relates to debitage/basket, at the left axis, and the upper to tools/basket, at the right axis.*

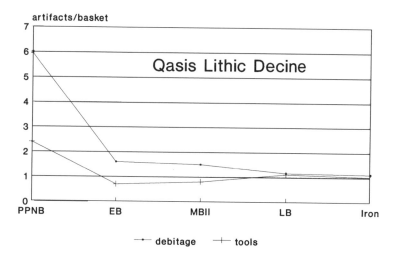

FIG. 7.2. *Quantitative lithic decline at Qasis. The upper line relates to debitage/basket and the lower to tools/basket. Both relate to the left axis.*

bladelets (excepting Batashi for technical reasons). Thus, cores, core trimming elements, and primary flakes have not been included since specialized technologies, such as Canaanean blade production, often show off-site discard of these elements, but import of the unretouched blades and bladelets. This will clearly not account for all the quantitative differences resulting from on-site/off-site production variation, but will at least dampen some of it. Debris has also been excluded from the analysis since it is too readily affected by both postdeposition processes (e.g., burning) and selective recovery and/or sieving of materials (e.g., loss of chips).

Examination of the figures shows several features of importance. First, the materials from both Yiftahel and Qasis (figs. 7.1, 7.2) show that the greatest decline occurs from the Neolithic to the Chalcolithic and Early Bronze Age. Although perhaps seemingly trivial,

in fact this decline precedes not only the introduction of iron, but the introduction of bronze as well, since only copper (and a copper-antimony-arsenic alloy) was used in the Chalcolithic and Early Bronze Age. That is, the major decline in lithic production and use occurs well before the introduction of the harder metals (bronze and iron) most appropriate for replacing flint as a raw material.

Beyond this initial decrease, all the graphs show a steady decrease in lithic production, as represented by the debitage curves. It is difficult to isolate specific patterns. Although the Ir David (fig. 7.3) materials suggest a major decline in production from Early to Middle Bronze Age. This is confounded by the Qasis materials, showing only a slight gradient between these two periods. A similar picture obtains at Batashi (fig. 7.4), showing a major decline in waste products from the Middle to Late Bronze Age, whereas at Qasis

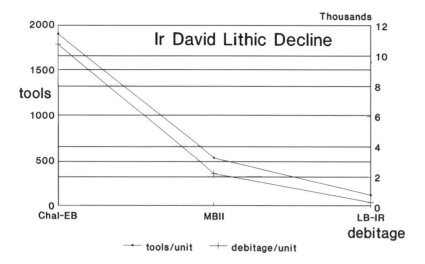

FIG. 7.3. *Quantitative lithic decline at Ir David. Quantification is by proportional representation per unit of excavation area, as provided by the excavators. The upper line and left axis relate to tools/ unit of excavation area, and the lower line and right axis to debitage/unit of excavation area.*

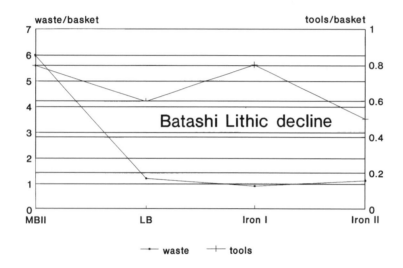

FIG. 7.4. *Quantitative lithic decline at Batashi. The lower line and left axis relate to waste/basket. The upper line and right axis relate to tools/basket. The apparent rise is deceptive and is less than one-half tool per basket, clearly a problem of scale.*

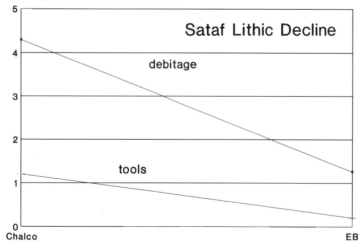

FIG. 7.5. *Quantitative lithic decline at Sataf. Both debitage and tools relate to the left axis.*

and Ir David, slopes are more gentle. Of course, the limited sample from the Batashi Middle Bronze II makes reliance on these figures even more problematic than otherwise. On the other hand, both Qasis and Batashi show more or less constant low-level production in the Late Bronze and Iron Age, as does Ir David. Thus, although the initial date of the low-level of lithic production is unclear, all sites achieve it by the Late Bronze Age, if not earlier.

Tool decreases are more variable. At Yiftahel, Sataf (fig. 7.5), and Ir David, the tool graphs closely parallel the debitage graphs, but at Qasis and Batashi, there is some greater variation. The primary problem may indeed be one of sampling. First, the numbers are simply lower and more subject to sampling problems. Also, since baskets without lithic artifacts were not incorporated into the analysis, the greater number of empty baskets in the later periods actually results in an overestimate in artifacts per basket in these periods. That is, downward slopes ought probably to be even steeper than appear on the graphs.

TYPOLOGY

Figs. 7.6–7.10 (table 7.2) present the basic typological decline from the PPNB through the Iron Age. Specific features and qualifications are important to note.

Arrowheads seem to disappear from the northern assemblages (the only ones examined here) at the transition from the Early to Late Pottery Neolithic (PNA–PNB). This is significant because this disappearance precedes any introduction of metal in this region. That is, a major component of the lithic production system disappears without any reference to metal replacements and is probably best attributed to some final decline in the importance of hunting in Neolithic economies and the completion of the hunting-to-herding transition. It is probably no coincidence that the decline seems also to coincide with what has been termed "the secondary products revolution" (cf. Sherratt 1983), the complex of technologies allowing intensive exploitation of animals and plants. Thus, for example, an abundance of spindle whorls were found at the Late Neolithic site of Nahal Zehora (Gopher and Gophna 1993), and in the Chalcolithic there is clear evidence for dairying in the form of ceramic churns (e.g., Amiran 1969, 33–34). The continued presence of arrowheads in desert regions is, of course, indicative of the continued importance of hunting, either for subsistence or perhaps for social status. The

Period	Burins	Arrowheads	Sickles	Axes	Other
PPNB (n=7 assemblages)					
avg. %	18.4	16.5	23.7	5.4	36.0
s.d.	±12.5	±9.1	±13.7	±4.5	±15.1
PN1 (n=2 assemblages)					
avg. %	16.7	4.2	8.1	5.0	66.1
s.d.	±18.5	±1.5	±8.1	±2.3	±14.1
PN2 (n=3 assemblages)					
avg. %	9.9	0	7.5	6.7	75.9
s.d.	±7.1	±0	±1.4	±4.0	±8.2
Chalco (n=5 assemblages)					
avg. %	0.1	0.2	11.6	3.3	84.8
s.d.	±0.2	±0.5	±9.8	±2.1	±10.4
EB/MB I (n=10 assemblages)					
avg.%	1.1	0.1	23.7	0.9	74.1
s.d.	±1.5	±0.3	±15.5	±1.5	±14.7
MB-LB (n=8 assemblages)					
avg. %	0	0	55.2	0.7	44.1
s.d.	±0	±0	±21.6	±1.3	±20.7
IRON (n=5 assemblages)					
avg %	0	0	49.8	0	50.2
s.d.	±0	±0	±16.9	±0	±16.9

TABLE 7.2. Summary of typological decline of tool types by period.

use of chipped stone points for war is well known from Egypt during later times, certainly during the Old Kingdom (e.g., Emery 1961, 113; Clark et al. 1974), and their absence in the Early Bronze Age Levant seems perhaps anomalous given the presence of fortifications and other indications of warfare. Apparently wood points sufficed. Notably, the presence of a few rare arrowheads at some Chalcolithic and Early Bronze Age sites is most likely a result of stratigraphic intrusions or perhaps scavenging/curation. For the sake of methodological consistency, the numbers are presented as generated. Regardless, the decline of chipped stone arrowheads must also imply a general quantitative decline in lithic production, well before the earliest smelting of metals.

Burins (fig. 7.7) disappear from the lithic repertoire with the end of the Neolithic. Although occasional examples occur in later periods, they are almost always single spall removals on natural surfaces or breaks, and are most likely chance occurrences and

Arrowheads

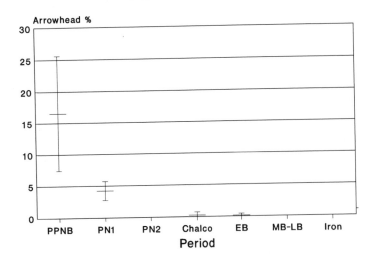

FIG. 7.6. *Quantitative decline of arrowheads by period. For precise data, see table 7.2.*

Burins

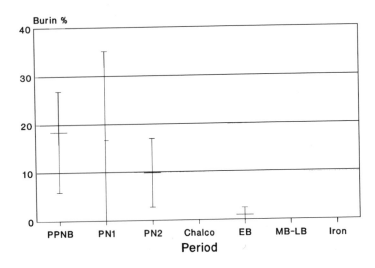

FIG. 7.7. *Quantitative decline of burins by period. For precise data, see table 7.2.*

Axes

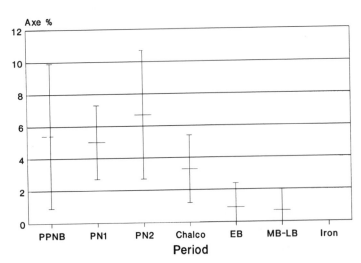

FIG. 7.8. *Quantitative decline of celts by period. For precise data, see table 7.2.*

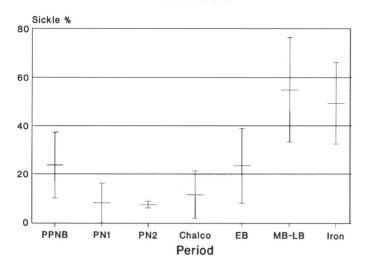

Sickles

Sickle %

FIG. 7.9. *Quantitative decline of sickles by period. For precise data, see table 7.2*

not deliberately conceived tools. Although the transition from Neolithic to Chalcolithic coincides with the earliest metallurgy, it is hard to see in the earliest copper tools any obvious replacements for burins. Burins are usually interpreted as engraving and boneworking tools. Although conceivably copper awls could be used for such purposes, this seems unlikely in view of the softness of the pure copper points. The development of the flint borer class seems a more likely explanation for the decline of burins. In short, as with arrowheads, there appears to be little relationship between the decline of burins and the rise of metallurgy.

Celts (fig. 7.8) disappear with the end of the Chalcolithic period and the beginning of the Early Bronze Age. Although the graphs suggest the possibility of continued use of celts into the Bronze Age, in fact, virtually no celts have been recovered from single period occupations (i.e., with no earlier occupations) dating to the Early Bronze Age, as at Hartuv and En Shadud. The early date of these two sites within the Early Bronze Age suggests that the celts disappeared rapidly with the onset of the new period. The same is true for the Negev Early Bronze Age sites (except for votive axes; see Chapter 3). The significant point here is that both copper and chipped stone celts are found in the Chalcolithic, in a temporal overlap probably spanning on the order of six hundred–eight hundred years. Although it is difficult to evaluate how many copper celts were actually in circulation and use during the Chalcolithic, to judge from the archaeological

remains, stone celts far outnumbered copper ones. Regardless, there was clearly no immediate replacement of the stone tools upon introduction of metal equivalents. In fact, equivalence can only be assumed since at this juncture, the function of these implements can only be assumed. That is, although likely that both copper and flint celts were used for felling trees, simply based on morphology and analogy with ethnographically known tools, flint celts may well have been used for digging and hoeing as well (e.g., Gazit 1986), adding another dimension to the equation.

In contrast to the previous types, sickles (fig. 7.9) show a pattern of consistent increase from the Pottery Neolithic. Beyond the obvious fact that they continue in use throughout the periods under discussion (well recognized by earlier scholars [e.g., Neuville 1930, 1934–35; Curwen 1930, 1935; Waechter 1958; Crowfoot 1935, 1937]), the rise in frequency also requires explanation. Basically, sickles dominate the later period assemblages due to the increasing restriction of other types in the repertoire. That is, as other types drop out, any types remaining will automatically increase proportionally.

The specific percentages, and apparent minor decline in sickle proportion from Middle/Late Bronze to Iron Age, are also worth comment. First, if analysis of Middle/Late Bronze and Iron Age assemblages is restricted to those with no underlying Early Bronze Age strata, then the average sickle percentage rises to 76.1% for the Iron Age (Batashi) and 74.5% for the Middle/Late Bronze Age (Batashi, Wawiyat, Deir el

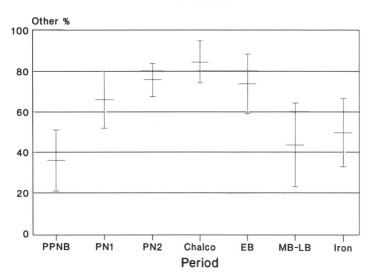

Other

Other %

FIG. 7.10. *Quantitative decline of other tools by period. For precise data, see table 7.2.*

Balah).[1] Early Bronze Age assemblages can contribute high proportions of nondiagnostic *ad hoc* tools that cannot be objectively separated from the in situ assemblages (but see Chapter 2 and Rosen and Grinblatt n.d. for a technique of statistical manipulation). Thus, the sickle frequencies for these periods are most likely even higher than depicted in the graphs (and the *ad hoc*, or "other" tools correspondingly lower). Given this, and the lack of any statistically significant difference between the sickle percentages from the MB-LB and Iron Age assemblages, the apparent decline in sickle proportions probably does not reflect a true decline in sickle use or production.

Flint sickles seem to disappear in Israel sometime in the middle of the Iron Age, perhaps in the ninth–eighth centuries B.C.E. Detailed stratigraphic information, combined with lithic data, is available only from Tell Batashi (table 7.1). Although basket frequencies were not available for this analysis, the decline in number of sickles from Stratum IV to III is of importance since both Stratum II and Stratum III were, in fact, opened more extensively than the lower strata (A. Mazar, pers. comm.). Thus, Stratum IV (eighth–ninth century B.C.E.) probably represents the final period of common flint sickle use.[2] This is centuries after the introduction of iron technology (and, obviously, millennia after the introduction of copper and bronze). As with other types, the introduction of a metal technology, or technologies, does not correspond directly to the demise of a lithic equivalent.

Finally, Other Tools (including the dominant *ad hoc* class and a range of rare types, like tabular scrapers, microdrills, etc.) either follow a pattern different from that of linear disappearance or increase. Instead, they rise proportionally during the Late Neolithic to a peak in the Chalcolithic and Early Bronze Ages and then decline in the post–Early Bronze Age. As indicated earlier, this decline is probably underestimated due to the effects of stratigraphic intrusions. The minor and statistically nonsignificant rise in the Iron Age may be safely ignored, as per sickles above. As discussed in Chapter 4, the rise of this *ad hoc* class is probably a complement to the rise of specialized manufacture. Furthermore, expedient tools, easily discarded, will by their nature be amplified quantitatively in the archaeological record. That is, where a valued tool might be reused numerous times leaving only a single tool or a few tools reflecting a particular function, expedient tools will be discarded after each use, or at least fairly often, leaving a greater number of tools reflecting the functions in which they were involved (cf. Shott 1989). The decline over a period of some two millennia probably reflects the slow replacement of these expedient tools by metal equivalents, but is by no means an obvious process.

Within this general group, two formal tool types, tabular scrapers and microlithic drills, require discussion since they do not fall into the *ad hoc* class. As reviewed in Chapter 3, tabular scrapers appear for the first time in the Late Pottery Neolithic, perhaps a development from bifacial tabular knives. They constitute a diagnostic type for both the Chalcolithic and the Early Bronze Ages, but do not appear to show a typical battleship curve frequency pattern (cf. Deetz 1967, 26–37; Clarke 1978, 217–36; also Gopher 1994) of rise, peak, and decline in popularity. Frequency at different sites seems more related to distance from source area (Rosen 1983b, 1989a), and the disappearance of the type occurs with the end of Early Bronze Age civilization. Middle Bronze I assemblages do not appear to incorporate these tools. No obvious metal replacements for tabular scrapers have been recovered, regardless of whether one considers them ritual knives, scrapers, or shearing knives.

Microlithic drills, as opposed to borers and awls, can be considered a rare type in the sense that they do not occur at all at most sites. On the other hand, in those assemblages in which they do occur, they occur in very large numbers (e.g., Burian and Friedman 1987). It is therefore difficult to be sure of any earliest or latest occurrences since such determinations are dependent on chance finds. Thus, for example, prior to the recent discovery of an assemblage of microlithic drills at the Early Bronze II Camel Site in the middle of the Negev, the type was assumed to occur exclusively in the Late Neolithic/Chalcolithic (Rosen 1995).

Contrary to earlier assumptions regarding the replacement of microlithic drills by copper awls (Rosen 1984a) with the end of the Chalcolithic, the discovery at the Camel Site indicates that, as with celts, there was considerable overlap between copper awls and flint drills. Furthermore, the copper awls found in the Levant during the Chalcolithic and Early Bronze Ages, and for that matter at the Camel Site, do not resemble the hollow copper drills known from late contexts, for example, Late Bronze Age (New Kingdom) Egypt (Stocks 1989). That is, while flint drills do drop out of the lithic repertoire, presumably sometime during the Early Bronze Age or at its close, we have no evidence for metal replacements until much later in the archaeological record.

Metal and Flint

The above description should suffice to demonstrate that the displacement of lithic technology by metallurgy was a long and complex process. Better comprehension of that process requires examination of the interrelationships between the technologies in terms of utilitarian function, economic structure, and social roles.

COPPER

The earliest use of metal, copper, in the Near East occurs in various preceramic Neolithic sites in Anatolia, where native copper was cold-worked into beads and other small objects (e.g., Heskel 1983). The significance of this early metalworking does not lie in the early date of production, nor in the beads manufactured, but rather in the lack of development of this early exploitation of copper into metallurgy proper. The social complexity prerequisite to specialized and semispecialized metallurgical production had not yet developed, and the metallurgy alone was not sufficient stimulus to the development of such systems (Heskel 1983). Given the earliest appearance of smelting several millennia later, in the Chalcolithic (with the apparent exception of Catal Huyuk [see Heskel 1983 for discussion]), it is likely that this extremely low level of copper exploitation continued through the Neolithic. The question of specifically how the change from cold-working to smelting, and a proper metallurgical system, occurred is one of speculation. However, the socioeconomic contexts of that change are of far greater importance than the specific instance of first smelting. It is only in special contexts that copper smelting could be recognized as something that could indeed be exploited. Thus from preceramic Neolithic Anatolia to the Chalcolithic Negev, copper may well have been smelted on numerous occasions, but the potentials of those first experiments were not realizable in the earlier contexts.

Of course, "socioeconomic contexts" is a nebulous term, reminiscent of Braidwood's (1967, 89) "culture was ready for it" explanation of the origins of agriculture, and caricatured, perhaps unjustly, by Binford (L. R. Binford 1968). Three specific issues are of especial importance. First, examination of Chalcolithic copper assemblages shows that the vast majority are cult or ritual related. Even discounting the Nahal Mishmar horde (Bar-Adon 1980)—and it is not clear that we should in fact do so—the copper implements recovered from domestic sites are still dominated by "scepters" and "maceheads." The symbolic or ritual nature of the scepters is difficult to dispute, and certainly no reasonable utilitarian interpretation has been put forward for these. In spite of a few opinions to the contrary (e.g., Moorey 1988), maceheads show little evidence for use as weapons, and their contextual associations, especially with other symbolically loaded copper implements, do suggest cult. Axes and awls, both present as well, are far less common than these other tools. Thus, the first primary uses in this region for smelted copper (and copper alloys) appear to be cultic.

Second, this industry is concentrated in the desert and on its fringes (Ilan and Sebbane 1989). Given the closer proximity to raw material resources, and the probable existence of native copper, found on the surface and simply collected and cold-worked, this perhaps should be of little surprise. However, there is little evidence for Ghassulian-Beersheva penetration into the regions where raw materials procurement must have occurred, and, furthermore, there is little evidence for copper penetration beyond the Ghassul-Beersheva axis into the Mediterranean heartland. The northern Negev Chalcolithic seems have been very much at the receiving end of a copper industry, and I have suggested elsewhere (Rosen 1993a; also Gilead 1992) that this industry was part of a desert or pastoral nomadic adaptation. It is not unusual for innovations to occur in the periphery. This, at least, would explain the scarcity of copper objects at sites even only marginally north of the Beersheva Basin, if these sites were outside the pastoral round. That is, if primary copper production had been controlled by the Ghassul-Beersheva folk, one would expect greater diffusion north since (1) the primary focus in the Beersheva Basin is closer to the Mediterranean zone, and (2) production could be easily intensified to meet the demands of a northern market in contact with Ghassul-Beersheva. On the other hand, if production were controlled by a desert population, then intensification might have been constrained both by the nature of the pastoral nomadic adaptation and by its more limited populations. Thus, the limited supplies available might not have been adequately large to pass through the immediate supply zone.

Finally, the fundamental social and economic differences between the Chalcolithic and the Pre-Pottery Neolithic are also prerequisites to the rise of metallurgy. Thus, the ever increasing integration between the desert systems and the heartland, based at least in part on the rise of pastoral nomadic societies, cannot but have played a role in the origins of copper exploitation. This, in turn, must be related to the ability to exploit secondary products (Sherratt 1983, Rosen 1988c), such as dairy products as well as transport (e.g., Ovadia 1992). Beyond this, although there has been some dispute over the degree of "complexity" inherent in Chalcolithic systems (see Levy 1986 and references, and Gilead 1988 and references), such

features as site size, economic specialization, regional differentiation, presence of unquestionable Chalcolithic temples (cf. Ussishkin 1980), and elaborate distribution networks covering a range of materials and goods all suggest a system that could (1) support the specialization or semispecialization requisite for metallurgical production; (2) provide a market for its goods, i.e., wealth enough to "purchase" the goods; (3) provide access to raw materials; and (4) allow the integration of those goods economically and socially.

In this context it is significant that Garfinkel (1992; and earlier Kaplan 1958) has recently suggested that the latest phases of the Neolithic, i.e., the Wadi Raba culture and its variants (e.g., the Qatifian in the northern Negev), should perhaps best be considered an early Chalcolithic,[3] without the metals. That is, the fundamental socioeconomic components seem to have been in place before the first smelting.

Returning to the original point, given this background, it is no wonder that in the initial stages of metallurgy there was no displacement of flint. The two technologies were so widely disparate that there were virtually no points of overlap or intersection where replacement could be conceived. Lithic industries in the Neolithic and Chalcolithic periods constituted an economic, social, and technological array fundamentally independent of metallurgy. The people producing and trading copper objects were different from those engaged in lithic production, the only exception perhaps being tabular scrapers, also deriving from the desert. Even given the evidence for some on-site copper production at Chalcolithic villages, the chipped stone tools produced on-site, the *ad hoc* elements, were hardly likely to be replaced by imports at this stage of economic development. The metal was still too rare, and specialization not yet invasive enough in the organization of society. The flint tools produced by specialists and semispecialists were part of a long-established economic system with its own inertia. The replacement process is obviously not at all obvious.

COPPER AND FLINT

Whereas the late Neolithic and Chalcolithic periods do not show any apparent replacement of flint tools by metal, in spite of a decline in lithic production caused by other factors, the Early Bronze Age does. It is somewhat paradoxical that the sophisticated alloys and lost wax casting used during the Chalcolithic fell out of use during the Early Bronze Age (e.g., Ilan and Sebbane 1989; Hanbury Tenison 1986, 151–59), when quantitatively, copper use seems to have expanded significantly. This is at least partially related to a shift in production from the cultic to the utilitarian. Thus, dozens of copper axes were recovered from Early Bronze Age Arad, along with an even greater number of awls (Ilan and Sebbane 1989). It seems clear enough that copper axes replaced flint celts in this period, and that somehow this replacement is related to the change in production focus. However, this change is not self-evident and also requires explanation.

First, the transition from Chalcolithic to Early Bronze Age is indeed a cultural transition. Aside from features such as site abandonment, architectural changes, ceramic typological changes, and generally increased socioeconomic complexity, there also appear to be changes in symbolic aspects of society and religious organization, in spite of underlying continuities. These changes may well have effected a decline in demand for the cultic objects associated with Chalcolithic ritual.

No less important, a major cultural florescence is evident in the Early Bronze Age in the pastoral periphery (e.g., Rothenberg and Glass 1992; Beit-Arieh 1986; Rosen 1988c), i.e., the Negev, Sinai, and southern Jordan. The reasons for this growth are beyond the scope of this essay, but at least some of these pastoralists were involved in the metal trade (e.g., Amiran et al. 1973; Beit-Arieh 1986; Rothenberg and Glass 1992; Rosen 1988c), and in a larger way than in the preceding Chalcolithic (e.g., Hauptmann and Weisberger 1987). The industry expands even more in the later subperiods of the Early Bronze Age. In conjunction, numerous authors (e.g., Kempinski 1989; Ilan and Sebbane 1989; Amiran et al. 1973; Beit-Arieh 1986) have remarked on the apparently increasing control exerted by Arad on the copper trade. This "control" should perhaps be best read as "organization." Early Bronze Age Arad seems to have provided a central market for copper and other goods, a market that did not exist in the Chalcolithic.

These are the necessary conditions, providing access and opportunity for the initial stage of metal-flint replacement, but they are not sufficient in and of themselves to explain the disappearance of flint celts. For this we need to return to the tools themselves.

In the absence of experimental work, it is difficult to determine relative utilitarian efficiency of copper versus flint axes. This is even more so in light of the problems establishing the specific functions of these tools. Meyer and Mathieu (n.d.) have shown that for trees less than 10 cm thick, there is little difference in the effectiveness of steel, bronze, or stone axes, but for thicker trees, the metal axes require significantly fewer strokes for felling. On the other hand, copper is far softer than bronze and undoubtedly much less effective a material. Furthermore, Sharp (1952) indicated that for aboriginal purposes in Australia, there was little difference in utility between steel and stone axes (also see Coles 1973, 20–21; and see Carneiro 1979 for effectiveness of stone axes for tree felling). Given this background, it is hard to imagine utilitarian efficiency as the prime stimulus to the replacement of flint celts.

No experimental work has been conducted on the relative manufacturing efficiency of the two technologies either. However, here it is possible to speculate with some confidence. Copper axes were manufactured using pure, unalloyed copper (e.g., Key 1980; Potaszkin and Bar-Avi 1980; Shalev and Northover 1987), in simple, single mold casts. The essence of this method is that once raw materials are available, and the capital investment in furnaces and other equipment (e.g., crucibles, hammerstones, etc.) has been made, axes can be produced almost *en masse*. The actual casting into molds is relatively easy.

Flint axes cannot be mass-produced. Each must be individually chipped and ground, the latter an especially time-consuming process (e.g. Dickson 1981, 41; also Hayden 1977 for the difficulties of maintenance). Although ethnographic study of ax manufacture (e.g., Gould 1980, 154–55) suggests that this production may be well embedded in daily activities, it is not difficult to see production efficiency as one important stimulus to the replacement process.

Beyond the simple measure of production efficiency, the issue of relative value can also be addressed or at least speculated on. Flint celts were produced from within the Chalcolithic (and probably Late Neolithic) village system by semispecialists engaged in exchange relations. There was probably a balance in the relative value of the exchange goods established by a range of factors over the long span of these relations.

Copper was produced external to the system, at least in part. The general disruptions at the end of the Chalcolithic, certainly affecting trade as well as other aspects of the society, along with the growth of the pastoral periphery, may well have "caused" copper production to take on greater importance to these pastoralists, and the "celt market" may have been especially prone to takeover.

The relative rapidity of the flint celt decline seems remarkable. To date, all Chalcolithic sites have numerous flint celts, whereas the earliest Early Bronze Age sites show either absence of flint celts (e.g., Hartuv) or single isolated occurrences (e.g., Shadud) which may well be intrusions or curations.[4] This is not merely a typological or technological change, but constitutes the replacement of one entire production-distribution system by another totally different one and over an archaeologically short span of time. Analogy may be drawn with the introduction of European steel axes to aboriginal Australians, which effected a major disruption of what had been a finely balanced exchange system (e.g. Sharp 1952). Steel axes were "cheap" to the Europeans and thus rapidly displaced the locally produced and traded stone axes, whose value, as measured in conch shells, declined rapidly.

Similarly, it is conceivable that copper goods were, in fact, relatively accessible once the primary production-distribution system of the Early Bronze Age was in place. Copper axes may not have been "cheap," but given the above background, they may well have been "cheaper" than their flint counterparts.

Early Bronze Age lithic systems, as described earlier, are comprised of three primary components: *ad hoc* tools, tabular scrapers, and Canaanean sickles. Given that copper axes seem to have replaced flint celts with the onset of this period, a natural question is, why not the rest?

Whereas both copper and flint axes were the products of semispecialized or specialized production, *ad hoc* tools were produced expediently by the user. Besides such obvious problems as the generation of the large quantities of copper and the difficulties of intensification of production to meet the demands of replacement of the *ad hoc* tools, the displacement of this most basic domestic level of production requires a new economic order, not merely a new technology. The specialized must replace the homemade.

In this light, it is informative to note that the well-collected assemblages from contemporary Mesopotamia (e.g., Pope and Pollock 1995) show relatively few *ad hoc* elements. The differences in complexity of economic organization between the Southern Levant and Mesopotamia require little discussion. It is possible that this greater specialization and differentiation in Mesopotamia saw an earlier decline of *ad hoc* tools, or its general economic framework, the domestic or household economy. Of course, a relative scarcity of flint in Mesopotamia may also play a role.

BRONZE AND FLINT

The decline of *ad hoc* tools is difficult to define chronologically, as noted earlier. It clearly occurs sometime post–Early Bronze Age and presumably before the Iron Age. It may be linked tentatively to two factors, the reurbanization of the Middle Bronze II and the rise of bronze technology proper.

The resurgence of cities in the Middle Bronze II has been tied to major changes in socioeconomic organization and the rise of a truly international trade system (e.g., Mazar 1968; Gerstenblith 1983). These enhanced trade systems also increased access to metals, most notably, tin sources, necessary for the copper-tin alloy, which is bronze. Thus, while difficult to demonstrate given the state of the data, the decline of *ad hoc* tools may well be a function of increasing economic specialization and increased availability of metal.

Furthermore, it should be noted that bronze is significantly harder than copper and therefore appropriate to a greater range of tasks. Although bronze technology was undoubtedly developed as a replacement technology for pure copper, and not for chipped stone, once the technology was in place, other potentials could be achieved as well. It can be no accident that so many of the earlier bronze artifacts are axes, perhaps battle axes. These certainly played little role in the decline of lithic technology. The key point is the initial establishment of specialist metallurgical production, for whatever specific functions, which later expanded beyond those functions.

Tabular scrapers disappear at the end of the Early Bronze Age, but spanned the Chalcolithic–Early Bronze Age transition. Two reasons can be suggested for their continued use in the Early Bronze Age. First, accepting their cultic status as primary, at least in the Mediterranean zone, then their symbolic meaning is not subject to quite the same economic forces as other tools. Their importance and value cannot be measured simply by reference to efficiency in performing certain functions, so that replacement stimulated by "more efficient" tools is unlikely as an explanation. The symbols themselves must be replaced in a different kind of transformation, as indeed must have occurred with the demise of Early Bronze Age civilization. Of course, there is a ritual transformation from Chalcolithic to Early Bronze Age, but where the copper cultic objects did not survive this transition, the tabular scrapers did. Explanation of this survival requires more detail than the archaeological record can as yet provide.

Second, tabular scrapers seem to be attached, at least in part, to a desert-heartland trade system (Rosen 1993a). It is likely that the same people who engaged in the metal trade were also engaged in the tabular scraper trade. Replacement could well have been literally counterproductive.

Finally, flint sickles continue in use through the entire Bronze Age, and well into the Iron Age. Here too one needs to ask, why?

Unlike celts, for which comparative experimental work between flint and copper tools has not been conducted, Steensberg (1943, 11–26; also Coles 1973, 34–39) demonstrated long ago that the flint sickle is, in fact, superior to copper and more or less the equal of bronze. Unlike flint celts, which require relatively time-consuming edge grinding for tool completion, given requisite expertise in flint knapping, blades are relatively quickly manufactured. The high-quality flint used for sickles, while not literally at hand in all situations, is certainly more accessible than copper or, for that matter, bronze. And the production-distribution system is already a specialized one. That is, the relatively greater economic efficiency of specialized production has no role to play here since both systems, the lithic and the metallurgical, were specialized.

It is worth noting that sickles are used by farmers or, more precisely, harvesters. If metals began to penetrate southern Levantine Bronze Age markets from the upper end of the wealth spectrum, farmers might well be among the later groups to benefit from the new technology.

IRON AND FLINT

Of course, flint sickles do ultimately disappear, replaced not by bronze but by iron. As has been the theme of this chapter, this replacement is not as obvious as seems.

There is little doubt that iron sickles are truly more efficient reaping tools than those of flint (e.g., Steensberg 1943, 11–26). Nevertheless, flint sickles continue in use at least until the ninth century B.C.E., and perhaps into the eighth, three hundred–four hundred years into the Iron Age. Conceivably this lag is simply the length of time needed for iron technology to penetrate the "lower" classes. Certainly one can trace increasing use of iron through the Iron Age, so that it only seems to achieve a quantitative peak, at least archaeologically, by the ninth century B.C.E. (Waldbaum 1978, 41–42, 57). It is possible to see the stubborn continuation of flint sickles as merely a func-

tion of a long adoption process for iron. But this would miss two significant points.

First, iron technology was developed as a replacement for bronze, after the breakdown of international trade, with the consequent disruption of copper and tin supplies at the end of the Late Bronze Age (e.g., Muhly 1980). The rise of iron technology itself should thus be seen as a response to specific sociopolitical conditions and not to some inevitable technological progression spurred on by the need for ever greater "efficiency." For us, the point is, of course, that the introduction of iron was totally unrelated to lithic technologies. Iron was not intended to replace flint. That it does so later is again the result of a technology filling out unforeseen potentials, a kind of ancient Teflon effect, Teflon being one of the most well known and often proffered by-products of the NASA space program.

Second, Near Eastern iron[5] smelting resulted in a bloom, a spongy mass of metal that had to hammered into shape, with repeated reheating. Casting was not possible. That is, each object had to be individually fashioned, and "mass production," as was possible using cast bronze, or for that matter flint blade knapping, was not feasible.

Combining these two points, iron was introduced as an emergency replacement for bronze, a result of a scarcity in that metal. It must initially have been available only on a restricted basis because of an absence of general techno-economic frameworks (i.e., equipment, requisite skills, and market distribution networks) and the difficulties of production in quantity. Notably, ores themselves are not rare. Ironsmithing, significantly different from bronzeworking, needed to become established and to develop as a profession. Only after it had developed to a reasonable level of proficiency, with a large number of agents, could it fully replace bronze. And only after fully replacing bronze could it expand into other functions as well. This seems to have occurred only in the middle of the Iron Age (Waldbaum 1978).[6] Thus, the replacement of flint sickles occurred as a result of the convergence of a series of social, economic, and technological trends and events, and with this replacement we have little further archaeological evidence for chipped flint technologies in the Levant.

Even then, it is clear that the use of chipped stone did not end. Threshing teeth of basalt and flint were manufactured into the twentieth century (e.g., Bordaz 1965, 1969; Avitsur 1976, 30–31). Strike-a-lights from flint were a necessity until the wide availability of matches (cf. Runnels 1994). Gunflints were also used. However, these are truly the last poor vestiges of earlier lithic industries. Archaeologically they are all but absent.

In the End

Western perceptions of history, especially those guided by conceptions of progress and even culture-evolutionary paradigms, tend to view change as more or less linear. This is dictated, at least in part, both by the apparent linearity of time and by the fact that knowledge accumulates, lending it what appears to be directionality. However, appearances are deceiving.

Technological changes are rarely either linear or optimizing. What appears as directed and logical change in simplistic hindsight is rarely so in reality. The seemingly obvious replacement of lithic technology by metallurgy was neither obviously logical nor a foregone conclusion. The fact that New World societies knew the use of sophisticated metallurgical techniques, as in the manufacture of copper bells and other objects in late prehistoric times (e.g., Morley et al. 1983, 442–47), but rarely exploited these materials beyond the symbolic level, has nothing to do with intellectual capabilities nor sociocultural evolution. Rather, the concatenation of unrelated historical stimuli, which in the Near East brought about metallurgical development over the course of three thousand years, simply did not occur in a way as to result in the transfer of metallurgy from bell production to other realms of exploitation. The point has undoubtedly been belabored enough.

The Stone Age ended, not with the rise of metallurgy ca. 4000 B.C.E., as the period names imply, but slowly over the course of three millennia (cf. Ford et al. 1984 for Britain). Although we tend to think of stone as inelastic and ultimately limited in its potentials, chipped stone technologies proved amenable to a wide range of tasks, and indeed a wide range of social and economic frameworks. New technologies arise and old ones decline in complex interaction, and although we often think of technologies as "advanced" or "primitive," in reality they are often simply available or unavailable, known or unknown, realized or unrealized. The decline of lithic technology was marked not with a bang, but with a whimper.

NOTES

1. This average does not include MB layers from Batashi due to insufficient sample size—only eighteen tools.

2. The claims for extensive use of chipped stone tools during the succeeding Persian Period at Tell Hesi (Bennett et al. 1989; Hammond 1977) are problematic. In both studies, so-called Persian assemblages derive from severely disturbed Persian strata and contain numerous unrecognized intrusions from earlier periods. Furthermore, no flint artifacts distinctly and exclusively attributable to the Persian Period have been identified, and *all* chipped stone artifacts recovered can easily be attributed to the Iron Age or earlier periods found on the site.

3. Levy (1983) has contrasted Chalcolithic and Late Neolithic adaptations in the northern Negev, claiming the rise of chiefdom societies only in the Chalcolithic. Without entering the debate over the evolution of complexity in these periods, the Wadi Raba sites in northern Israel currently being excavated by Gopher (e.g., Gopher and Orelle 1989; Gopher and Gophna 1993) seem not to be fundamentally different from the southern Chalcolithic sites in terms of such features as site size, architectural complexity, economic organization, etc. They are lacking metal.

4. The Yiftahel flint celts recovered from Early Bronze Stratum II are probably all Neolithic. The problem of stratigraphic intrusion here is insoluble.

5. Most of the "iron" recovered from Levantine contexts seems, in fact, to have been crude steel, the carbon absorbed as a by-product of the use of charcoal for heating the furnaces. This, too, is significant since pure iron probably would have been too brittle for most of the uses to which bronze was put.

6. The biblical account of an apparent Philistine monopoly on iron technology well into the Iron Age (e.g., Boling 1975, 94) is perhaps a reflection of the difficulties in the spread of the new technology, as much as an account of deliberate control.

References

Adams, R. M. 1966. *The Evolution of Urban Society.* Chicago: Aldine.

———. 1975. An Ancient Uruk Threshing Sledge or Harrow? *Sumer* 31:17–20.

Aharoni, Y. 1973. Remarks on the Israeli Method of Excavation. *Eretz Israel* 11:48–53.

———. 1979. *Land of the Bible.* Philadelphia: Westminster Press.

Ahler, S. A. 1989. Mass Analysis of Flaking Debris: Studying the Forest Rather Than the Tree. In *Alternative Approaches to Lithic Analysis,* ed. D. O. Henry and G. H. Odell, 85–118. Archaeological Papers of the American Anthropological Association 1. Washington, D.C.

Albright, W. F. 1936–37. *The Excavation of Tell Beit Mirsim.* Annual of the American Schools of Oriental Research 17.

Algaze, G. 1989. The Uruk Expansion. *Current Anthropology* 30:571–608.

Allen, C. J. 1969. *The Broadman Bible Commentary.* Vol. 4. Nashville: Broadman Press.

Amiran, D., et al., ed. 1985. *Atlas of Israel.* Tel Aviv: Survey of Israel.

Amiran, R. 1969. *Ancient Pottery of the Holy Land.* Jerusalem: Massada Press.

Amiran, R., I. Beit-Arieh, and J. Glass. 1973. The Interrelationship between Arad and Sites in the Southern Sinai in the Early Bronze II. *Israel Exploration Journal* 23:33–38.

Ammerman, A. J., and W. Andrefsky, Jr. 1982. Reduction Sequences and the Exchange of Obsidian in Neolithic Cantabria. In *Contexts for Prehistoric Exchange,* ed. J. E. Ericson and T. K. Earle, 149–72. New York: Academic Press.

Anderson, P. C. 1980. A Testimony of Prehistoric Tasks: Diagnostic Residues on Stone Tool Working Edges. *World Archaeology* 2:181–94.

Anderson, P. C., and M. L. Inizan. 1994. Utilisation du tribulum au début du IIIe millénaire: des lames "canaanéenes" lustrées à Kutan (Ninivé V) dans la region de Mosoul, Iraq. *Paléorient* 20/2:85–103.

Andrefsky, W., Jr. 1994. Raw Material Availability and the Organization of Technology. *American Antiquity* 59:21–34.

Ascher, R. 1961. Analogy in Archaeological Interpretation. *Southwest Journal of Anthropology* 17:317–25.

Ataman, K. 1992. Threshing Sledges and Archaeology. In *Préhistoire de l'agriculture: nouvelles approches expérimentales et ethnographiques,* ed. P. C. Anderson, 305–19. Paris: Monographies de Centre de Recherches Archéologiques 6. Paris: Centre National de la Recherche Scientifique.

Avitsur, S. 1976. *Man and His Work* [in Hebrew]. Jerusalem: Carta and the Israel Exploration Society.

Avner, U. 1990. Ancient Agricultural Settlement and Religion in the Uvda Valley, Southern Israel. *Biblical Archaeologist* 53:125–41.

Baird, D. 1987. A Preliminary Analysis of the Chipped Stone from the 1985 Excavations at Tell esh-Shuneh North. *Annual of the Department of Antiquities of Jordan* 31: 461–80.

Bar-Adon, P. 1980. *The Cave of the Treasure.* Jerusalem: Israel Exploration Society.

———. 1989. Mizpe Shalem. In *Excavations in the Judean Desert,* P. Bar-Adon. *Atiqot* 9:50–60.

Bar-Yosef, O. 1981. The Epi-Paleolithic Complexes in the Southern Levant. In *Préhistoire du Levant,* ed. J. Cauvin and P. Sanlaville, 389–408. Colloques Internationaux du Centre National de la Recherche Scientifique 598. Paris.

———. 1987. Late Pleistocene Adaptations in the Levant. In *The Pleistocene Old World: Regional Perspectives,* ed. O. Soffer, 219–36. New York: Plenum Press.

Bar-Yosef, O., and D. Alon. 1988. *Nahal Hemar Cave.* Atiqot 18 (English series). Jerusalem: Israel Antiquities Authority.

Bar-Yosef, O., and A. Belfer-Cohen. 1989. The Origins of Sedentism and Farming Communities in the Levant. *Journal of World Prehistory* 3:447–98.

Bar-Yosef, O., A. Belfer, A. Goren, and P. Smith. 1977. The Nawamis near Ein Hudera. *Israel Exploration Journal* 27:65–88.

Bar-Yosef, O., A. Belfer-Cohen, A. Goren, I. Herskovitz, H. Mienis, B. Sass, and O. Ilan. 1986. Nawamis and Habitation Sites Near Gebel Gunna, Southern Sinai. *Israel Exploration Journal* 27:65–88.

Bar-Yosef, O., F. Burian, and E. Friedman. 1971. Transversal Arrowheads from the Coastal Plain [in Hebrew; English summary]. *Mitekufat Haeven* 10:22–24.

Bar-Yosef, O., and J. L. Phillips. 1977. *Prehistoric Investigations in Gebel Mughara, Northern Sinai.* Qedem 7, Monographs of the Institute of Archaeology. Jerusalem: Hebrew University.

Bar-Yosef, O., and B. Vandermeersch. 1972. The Stratigraphic and Cultural Problems of the Passage from the Middle to the Upper Paleolithic in Palestinian Caves. In *Origins of Homo Sapiens,* ed. F. Bordes, 221–26. Paris: UNESCO.

Baumgartel, E. 1960. *The Cultures of Prehistoric Egypt.* London: Oxford Press.

Beck, C., and G. T. Jones. 1989. Bias and Archaeological Classification. *American Antiquity* 54:244–62.

Beit-Arieh, I., 1986. Two Cultures in South Sinai in the Third Millennium B.C. *Bulletin of the American Schools of Oriental Research* 263:27–54.

Beit-Arieh, I. and R. Gophna. 1976. Early Bronze II Sites in Wadi el-Qudeirat (Kadesh Barnea). *Tel Aviv* 3:142–50.

Bennett, W. J., Jr., J. B. Sollberger, and A. F. Gettys. 1989. Flint Tools. In *Tell el Hesi: The Persian Period (Stratum V),* W. J. Bennett, Jr., and J. A. Blakely, 231–56. Winona Lake, Ind: Eisenbrauns.

Ben-Tor, A. 1975. Two Burial Caves of the Proto-Urban Period at Azor. *Qedem* 1: 1–54.

———, ed. 1992. *The Archaeology of Ancient Israel.* New Haven: Yale Univ. Press and Open Univ. of Israel.

Betts, A.V.G. 1989. The Solubba: Non-Pastoral Nomads in Arabia. *Bulletin of the American Schools of Oriental Research* 274:61–70.

———. 1991. The Chipped Stone Assemblage. In *Excavations at Jawa 1972–1986: Stratigraphy, Pottery, and Other Finds,* ed. A. V. G. Betts, 140–53. Excavations and Exploration in the Hashemite Kingdom of Jordan. Edinburgh: Edinburgh Univ. Press.

———. 1992a. The Chipped Stone Assemblage. In *Excavations at Tell Um Hammad 1982–1984: The Early Assemblages (EBI–II),* ed. A.V.G. Betts, 122–31. Excavations and Explorations in the Hashemite Kingdom of Jordan. Edinburgh: Edinburgh Univ. Press.

———. 1992b. Teel el-Hibr: A Rockshelter Occupation of the Fourth Millennium B.C. in the Jordanian Badiya. *Bulletin of the American Schools of Oriental Research* 287:5–23.

Binford, L. R. 1968. Post-Pleistocene Adaptations. In *New Perspectives in Archaeology,* ed. S. R. Binford and L. R. Binford, 313–42. Chicago: Aldine.

———. 1972. *An Archaeological Perspective.* New York: Seminar Press.

———. 1973. Interassemblage Variability in the Mousterian and the "Functional Argument." In *The Explanation of Culture Change: Models in Prehistory,* ed. C. Renfrew, 227–54. London: Duckworth.

Binford, L. R., and S. R. Binford. 1966. A Preliminary Analysis of Functional Variability in the Mousterian of Levallois Facies. *American Anthropologist* 68 (2); pt. 2:238–95.

Binford, S. R. 1968. Variability and Change in the Near Eastern Mousterian of Levallois Facies. In *New Perspectives in Archaeology,* ed. S. R. Binford and L. R. Binford, 49–60. Chicago: Aldine.

Bliss, F. J. 1898. *A Mound of Many Cities.* London: Murray.

Boling, R. G. 1975. *Anchor Bible: Judges.* Garden City, N.J.: Doubleday.

Bordaz, J. 1965. The Threshing Sledge—Ancient Turkish Grain Separating Method Still Proves Efficient. *Natural History* 74 (4): 216–29.

———. 1969. Flint Flaking in Turkey. *Natural History* 78 (2):73–79.

Bordes, F. 1961. *Typologie du Paléolithique ancien et moyen.* Publications de l'Institut de Préhistoire de l'Université de Bordeaux Memoire No. 1. Bordeaux.

———. 1972. *A Tale of Two Caves.* New York: Harper and Row.

Bordes, F., and D. de Sonneville-Bordes. 1970. The Significance of Variability in Paleolithic Assemblages. *World Archaeology* 2:61–73.

Braidwood, R. J. 1967. *Prehistoric Men.* 7th ed. Glenview, Ill.: Scott, Foresman.

Brandl, B. 1989. Observations on the Early Bronze Age Strata of Tel Erani. In *L'urbanisation de la Palestine à l'âge du Bronze ancien,* ed. P. de. Miroschedji, 41–52. British Archaeological Reports International Series 527. Oxford.

Braun, E. n.d. *Excavations at Yiftahel.* In press.

Brezillon, M. N. 1968. *La dénomination des objets de pierre taillée. VIe Supplément à Gallia Préhistoire.* Paris: Centre National de la Recherche Scientifique.

Burian, F., and E. Friedman. 1979. A Typology of Arrowheads and Sickle Blades and Its Chronological Implications [in Hebrew; English summary]. *Mitekufat Haeven* 16:1–16.

———. 1985. Flint Borers: Methods of Production and Use. *Mitekufat Haeven* 18:63–66.

———. 1987. Chalcolithic Borer Industry at Site 103—Nahal Nitzana. *Mitekufat Haeven* 20:160–72.

Buttrick, G. A. 1952. *The Interpreter's Bible.* Nashville: Abingdon Press.

Butzer, K. W. 1982. *Archaeology as Human Ecology.* Cambridge: Cambridge Univ. Press.

Cahen, D., L. H. Keeley, and F. L. Van Noten. 1979. Stone Tools, Tool Kits, and Human Behavior in Prehistory. *Current Anthropology* 20:661–84.

Caneva, I. 1993. From Chalcolithic to Early Bronze III at Artslantepe: A Lithic Perspective. In *Between Rivers and Over Mountains,* ed. M. Frangipane et al., 2–15. Rome: Univ. of Rome.

Carneiro, R. 1979. Tree Felling with the Stone Ax: An Experiment Carried out Among the Yanomamo Indians of Southern Venezuela. In *Ethnoarchaeology,* ed. C. Kramer, 21–58. New York: Columbia Univ. Press.

Cauvin, J. 1968. *Fouilles de Byblos IV: les outillages néolithiques de Byblos et du litoral libanais.* Paris: Maisonneuve.

Cauvin, M. C. 1973. Problèmes d'emmanchement des faucilles du Proche-Orient: Les documents de Tell Assouda (Djezireh, Syrie). *Paléorient* 1:101–6.

———. 1974. Flèches à encoches de Syrie: Essai de classification et d'interpretation culturelle. *Paléorient* 2:311–22.

———, ed. 1983a. *Traces d'utilisation sur les outils Néolithiques du Proche Orient.* Lyon: GIS-Maison de l'Orient.

———. 1983b. Les faucilles préhistoriques du Proche-Orient: données morphologiques et fonctionelles. *Paléorient* 9:63–79.

Champion, T. 1982. Fortification, Farming, and Subsistence. In *Ranking, Resources, and Exchange,* ed. C. Renfrew and S. Shennan, 61–66. Cambridge: Cambridge Univ. Press.

Chapman, R. 1982. Autonomy, Ranking, and Resources in Iberian Prehistory. In *Ranking, Resources, and Exchange,* ed. C. Renfrew and S. Shennan, 46–51. Cambridge: Cambridge Univ. Press.

Chase, P. G. 1991. Symbols and Paleolithic Archaeology: Standardization and the Imposition of Arbitrary Form. *Journal of Anthropological Archaeology* 10:193–213.

Childe, V. G. 1951a. *Man Makes Himself.* New York: Mentor Books.

———. 1951b. *Social Evolution.* New York: Schuman Press.

Clark, G. A. 1989. Romancing the Stones: Biases, Style and Lithics at La Riera. In *Alternative Approaches to Lithic Analysis,* ed. D. O. Henry and G. H. Odell, 27–50. Archaeological Papers of the American Anthropological Association 1. Washington, D.C.

Clark, J. D. 1975–77. Interpretation of Prehistoric Technology from Ancient Egypt and Other Sources, Part 2: Prehistoric Arrow Forms in Africa as Shown by Surviving Examples of Traditional Arrows from Ancient Egypt and Other Sources. *Paléorient* 3:127–50.

Clark, J. D., J. L. Phillips, and P. Staley. 1974. Interpretations of Prehistoric Technology from Ancient Egypt and Other Sources. *Paléorient* 2:323–88.

Clarke, D. L. 1978. *Analytical Archeology.* New York: Columbia Univ. Press.

Coe, M. D. 1992. *Breaking the Maya Code.* New York: Thames and Hudson.

Cohen, R. 1986. *The Settlement of the Central Negev in the Light of Archaeology and Literary Sources during the 4th–1st Millennia.* Ph.D. diss., Hebrew Univ., Jerusalem.

Coles, J. 1973. *Archaeology by Experiment.* New York: Scribner's.

———. 1979. An Experiment with Stone Axes. In *Stone Axe Studies,* ed. T. McKclough and W. A. Cummins, 106–7. Council for British Archaeological Research Report 23. London.

Conkey, M. 1990. Experimenting with Style in Archaeology: Some Historical and Theoretical Issues. In *Uses of Style in Archaeology,* ed. M. Conkey and C. Hastorf, 5–17. Cambridge: Cambridge Univ. Press.

Coqueugniot, E. 1991. Outillage de pierre taillée au Bronze Recent, Ras Shamra 1978–1988. *Ras-Shamra-Ougarit VI: Arts et Industries de la Pierre,* ed. M. Yon, 127–204. Paris: Éditions Recherche sur les Civilisations.

———. 1993. Un atelier specialisé dans le Palais de Mari. *Mari, Annales de Recherches Interdisciplinaires* 7:205–50.

Crabtree, D. E. 1967. Notes on Experiments in Flintknapping: 4. Tools Used for Making Flaked Stone Artifacts. *Tebiwa* 10:60–73.

Crowfoot, J. 1935. Notes on the Flint Implements from Jericho 1935. *Liverpool Annals of Archaeology and Anthropology* 22:174–84.

———. 1937. Notes on the Flint Implements of Jericho 1936. *Liverpool Annals of Archaeology and Anthropology* 24:35–52.

———. 1948a. Some Flint Implements from Affula. *Journal of the Palestine Oriental Society* 21:72–79.

———. 1948b. Flint Implements and Three Limestone Tools. In *Megiddo II.,* G. Loud, 141–44. Chicago: Univ. of Chicago Press.

Crowfoot Payne, J. 1960. Flint Implements from Tell al Judaidah. In *Excavations in the Plain of Antioch.* R. L. Braidwood and L. Braidwood, 525–29. Chicago: Univ. of Chicago Press.

Curwen, E. C. 1930. Prehistoric Flint Sickles. *Antiquity* 4:179–86.

———. 1935. Agriculture and the Flint Sickle in Palestine. *Antiquity* 9:61–66.

Daniel, G. 1975. *A Hundred and Fifty Years of Archaeology.* London: Duckworth.

Deetz, J. 1967. *Invitation to Archaeology.* Garden City, N.Y.: Natural History Press.

Dever, W. G. 1970. The Middle Bronze Period in Syria and Palestine. In *Near Eastern Archaeology in the Twentieth Century: Essays in Honor of Nelson Glueck,* ed. J. A. Sanders, 132–63. New York: Doubleday.

———. 1973. The EBIV/MBI Horizon in Transjordan and Southern Palestine. *Bulletin of the American Schools of Oriental Research* 210:37–63.

———. 1982. Retrospects and Prospects in Biblical and Syro-Palestinian Archaeology. *Biblical Archaeologist* 45:103–8.

———. 1989. The Collapse of the Early Bronze Age in Palestine—Toward a Systemic Analysis. In *L'urbanisation de la Palestine à l'âge du Bronze ancien,* ed. P. de Miroschedji, 225–46. British Archaeological Reports International Series 527. Oxford.

Dever, W. G., and H. D. Lance, ed. 1978. *A Manual of Field Excavation.* New York: Hebrew Union College.

Dever, W. G., H. D. Lance, and G. E. Wright. 1970. *Gezer I.* Jerusalem: Hebrew Union College.

Dibble, H. L. 1987. The Interpretation of Middle Paleolithic Scraper Morphology. *American Antiquity* 52:109–17.

Dickson, F. P. 1981. *Australian Stone Hatchets.* Sydney: Academic Press.

Dollfus, G., Z. Kafafi, J. Rewerski, N. Vaillant, E. Coqueugniot, J. Desse, and R Neef. 1988. Abu Hamid, an Early Fourth Millennium Site in the Jordan Valley: Preliminary Results. In *The Prehistory of Jordan: The State of Research in 1986* (ii), ed. A. Garrard and H. G. Gebel, 567–601. British Archaeological Reports International Series A396. Oxford.

Dunnell, R. C. 1978. Style and Function: A Fundamental Dichotomy. *American Antiquity* 43:192–202.

———. 1986. Methodological Issues in Americanist Artifact Classification. *Advances in Archaeological Method and Theory* 9:149–208.

Earle, T. 1977. A Reappraisal of Redistribution: Complex Hawaiian Chiefdoms. In *Exchange Systems in Prehistory,* ed. T. Earle and J. Ericson, 213–32. New York: Academic Press.

Edens, C. 1995. Hacinebi Lithic Analysis 1995. Manuscript.

Eisenberg, E. 1993. A Settlement from the Beginning of the Early Bronze Age I at Moza. *Atiqot* 22:41–48.

Elliott, C. 1977. The Religious Beliefs of the Ghassulians c. 4000–3100 B.C. *Palestine Exploration Quarterly* 109:3–25.

Emery, W. B. 1961. *Archaic Egypt.* London: Penguin Books.

Epstein, C., and T. Noy. 1988. Observations Concerning Perforated Tools from Chalcolithic Palestine. *Paléorient* 14:133–44.

Esse, D. L. 1989. Secondary State Formation and Collapse in Early Bronze Age Palestine. In *L'urbanisation de la Palestine à l'âge du Bronze ancien,* ed. P. de Miroschedji, 81–96. British Archaeological Reports International Series 527. Oxford.

Evans, R. K. 1978. Early Craft Specialization: An Example from the Balkan Chalcolithic. In *Social Archaeology, Beyond Dating and Subsistence,* ed. C. L. Redman et al., 113–130. New York: Academic Press.

Farrand, W. R. 1971. Late Quaternary Paleoclimates of the Eastern Mediterranean Area. In *Late Cenozoic Glacial Ages,* ed. K. Turekian, 529–64. New Haven: Yale Univ. Press.

Feinbrun-Dothan, N. 1978. *Flora Palaestina.* Vol. 3. Jerusalem: Israel Academy of Sciences.

Finkelstein, I. 1984. The Iron Age "Fortresses" of the Negev Highlands: Sedentarization of the Nomads. *Tel Aviv* 11:189–209.

Ford, S., R. Bradly, J. Hawkes, and P. Fisher. 1984. Flint Working in the Metal Age. *Oxford Journal of Archaeology* 3:157–74.

Forrest, W. G. 1963. Introduction to *Herodotus: History of the Greek and Persian War,* ed. W. G. Forrest, trans. G. Rawlinson. New York: Twayne Publishers.

Forshey, H. 1987. Tell Halif/Lahav 1986 Season. *Newsletter of the American Schools of Oriental Research* 38 (3):2–4.

Freeman, L. G. 1978. The Analysis of Some Occupation Floor Distributions from Earlier and Middle Paleolithic Sites in Spain. In *Views of the Past,* ed. L. G. Freeman, 57–116. Paris: Mouton.

Fry, R. E. 1980. Models of Exchange for Major Shape Classes of Lowland Maya Pottery. In *Models and Methods in Regional Exchange,* ed. R. E. Fry, 3–18. Society for American Archaeology Papers 1. Washington, D.C.

Futato, E. 1990. Analysis of Early Bronze Age Lithics from Tell Halif. *Bulletin of the American Schools of Oriental Research Supplement* 26:21–23.

Garfinkel, Y. 1993. The Material Culture in the Central Jordan Valley in the Pottery Neolithic and Early Chalcolithic Periods. Ph.D. diss. Jerusalem: Hebrew Univ.

Garrod, D.A.E. 1934. Notes on the Flint Implements. In *Notes on the Chalcolithic and Early Bronze Age Pottery of Megiddo,* R. M. Engberg and L. Shipton, 78–91. Chicago: Univ. of Chicago Press.

Garrod, D.A.E., and D.M.A. Bate. 1937. *The Stone Age of Mount Carmel.* Vol 1. Oxford: Clarendon Press.

Garstang, J. 1932. Jericho: City and Necropolis. *Liverpool Annals of Archaeology and Anthropology* 19:3–22. (And following years for later reports.)

Gazit, D. 1986. Polish on Flint Axes: The Result of Mining? [in Hebrew]. *Michmanim* 3:37–39.

Gero, J. 1991. Genderlithics: Women's Roles in Stone Tool Production. In *Engendering Archaeology: Women and Prehistory,* ed. J. M. Gero and M. W. Conkey, 163–94. Oxford: Blackwells.

Gerstinblith, P. 1983. *The Levant at the Beginning of the Middle Bronze Age.* American Schools of Oriental Research Dissertation Series 5. Winona Lake, Ind.: Eisenbrauns.

Gilead, D. 1973. Flint Industry of the Bronze Age from Har Yeruham and Tell Nagila. In *Excavations and Studies* [in Hebrew; English summary], ed. Y. Aharoni, 133–43. Tel Aviv: Tel Aviv Univ.

Gilead, I. 1984. The Microendscraper: A New Tool Type of the Chalcolithic Period. *Tel Aviv* 11:3–10.

———. 1988. The Chalcolithic Period in the Levant. *Journal of World Prehistory* 2:397–443.

———. 1989. Grar: A Chalcolithic Site in the Northern Negev, Israel. *Journal of Field Archaeology* 16:377–94.

———. 1990. The Neolithic-Chalcolithic Transition and the Qatifian of the Northern Negev and Sinai. *Levant* 27:47–63.

———. 1992. Farmers and Herders in Southern Israel during the Chalcolithic Period. In *Pastoralism in the Levant*, ed. O. Bar-Yosef and A. M. Khazanov, 29–42. Madison: Prehistory Press.

———. 1995. *Grar: A Chalcolithic Site in the Northern Negev*. Beersheva VII, Studies by the Department of Bible and Ancient Near East. Beersheva: Ben-Gurion Univ.

Gilead, I., and Y. Goren. 1986. Stations of the Chalcolithic Period in Nahal Sekher, Northern Negev. *Paléorient* 12:83–90.

Gilead, I., D. Hershman, and O. Marder. 1995. The Flint Assemblages from Grar. In *Grar, A Chalcolithic Site in the Northern Negev*, I. Gilead, 223–80. Beer-Sheva VII. Beersheva: Ben-Gurion Univ. Press.

Glock, A. E. 1985. Tradition and Change in Two Archaeologies. *American Antiquity* 50:464–77.

Goodfriend, G. A. 1990. Rainfall in the Negev Desert during the Middle Holocene based on 13C of Organic Matter in Land Snail Shells. *Quaternary Research* 34:186–97.

Gopher, A. 1989. *The Flint Assemblages of Munhata (Israel)*. Les Cahiers du Centre de Recherche Français de Jerusalem 4. Paris: Association Paléorient.

———. 1994. *Arrowheads of the Neolithic Levant*. American Schools of Oriental Research Dissertation Series 10. Winona Lake, Ind: Eisenbrauns.

Gopher, A., and R. Gophna. 1993. Cultures of the Eighth and Seventh Millennia B.P. in the Southern Levant: A Review for the 1990s. *Journal of World Prehistory* 7:297–353.

Gopher, A., and E. Orelle. 1989. The Flint Industry of Nahal Zehora I, a Wadi Raba Site in the Menashe Hills. *Bulletin of the American Schools of Oriental Research* 276:67–76.

Gophna, R. 1990. The Egyptian Pottery of 'En Besor. *Tel Aviv* 17:144–62.

Gophna, R., and E. Friedmann. 1993. The Flint Implements from Tel 'En Besor. *Tel Aviv* 20:147–63.

Goren, N. 1990. *Quneitra: A Mousterian Site on the Golan Heights*. Qedem 31, Monographs of the Institute of Archaeology. Jerusalem: Hebrew Univ.

Goring-Morris, A. N. 1987. *At the Edge: Terminal Pleistocene Hunter-Gatherers in the Negev and Sinai*. British Archaeological Reports International Series 361. Oxford.

Goring-Morris, A. N., and A. Gopher. 1983. Nahal Issaron: A Neolithic Settlement in the Southern Negev. *Israel Exploration Journal* 33:149–62.

Goring-Morris, A. N., A. Gopher, and S. A. Rosen. 1994. The Tuwailan Cortical Knife Industry of the Negev, Israel. In *Neolithic Chipped Stone Industries of the Fertile Crescent: Studies in Early Near Eastern Production, Subsistence, and Environment I*, ed. H. G. Gebel and S. K. Kozlowski, 511–24. Berlin: ex Oriente.

Goring-Morris, A. N., and S. A. Rosen. 1986. *Final Report to TAHAL on the Results of the Prehistoric Conducted by the Archaeological Survey of Israel and Other Projects Within 25 Km of the Site*. Haifa: Israel Electric Corp.

Gould, R. A. 1980. *Living Archaeology*. Cambridge: Cambridge Univ. Press.

Greenhut, Z. 1989. Flint Tools. In *Excavations in the Judean Desert*, P. Bar-Adon. *Atiqot* 9:60–77.

Gregg, S. A., K. W. Kintigh, and R. Whallon. 1991. Linking Ethnoarchaeological Interpretation and Archaeological Data: The Sensitivity of Spatial Analytic Methods to Postdepositional Disturbance. In *The Interpretation of Archaeological Spatial Patterning*, ed. E. M. Kroll and T. D. Price, 149–96. New York: Plenum Press.

Guy, P.L.O., and R. M. Engberg. 1938. *Megiddo Tombs*. Chicago: Univ. of Chicago Press.

Haiman, M. 1986. *Archaeological Survey of Israel Map of Har Hamran Southwest (198) 10–00*. Jerusalem: Israel Antiquities Authority.

———. 1988. The Iron Age Sites of the Negev Highlands. Master's thesis, Hebrew Univ., Jerusalem.

———. 1991. A Site of the Early Bronze Age at the Foot of Har Horsha [in Hebrew; English abstract]. *Atiqot* 20:1*–20*.

———. 1992. Sedentism and Pastoralism in the Negev Highlands in the Early Bronze Age: Results of the Western Negev Highlands Emergency Survey. In *Pastoralism in the Levant: Archaeological Materials in Anthropological Perspective*, ed. O. Bar-Yosef. and A. M. Khazanov, 93–105. Madison: Prehistory Press.

———. 1993. An Early Bronze Age Cairn Field at Nahal Mitnan. *Atiqot* 22:49–61.

W. M. Hammond. 1977. *The Raw and the Chipped: An Analysis of Correlations between Raw Materials and Tools of a Lithic Industry from Tell el Hesi, Israel*. Ann Arbor: University Microfilms.

Hanbury-Tenison, J. W. 1986. *The Late Chalcolithic to Early Bronze I Transition in Palestine and Transjordan.* British Archaeological Reports International Series 311. Oxford.

Harris, E. C. 1989. *Principles of Archaeological Stratigraphy.* London: Academic Press.

Hauptmann, A., and G. Weisberger. 1987. Archaeometallurgy and Mining—Archaeological Investigations in the Area of Feinan, Wadi 'Arabah (Jordan). *Annual of the Department of Antiquities of Jordan* 31:419–37.

Hayden, B. 1977. Sticks and Stones and Ground Edge Axes: The Upper Paleolithic in South East Asia? In *Sunda and Sahul,* ed. J. Allen, J. Golson, and R. Jones, 73–110. London: Academic Press.

———, ed. 1979. *Lithic Use-Wear Analysis.* New York: Academic Press.

———. 1984. Are Emic Types Relevant to Archaeology? *Ethnohistory* 31:79–92.

Hayden, B., and A. Cannon. 1983. Where the Garbage Goes: Refuse Disposal in the Maya Highlands. *Journal of Anthropological Archaeology* 2:117–63.

Helms, S. W. 1987. Tell Um Hammad and the EBI/Late Chalcolithic Landscape. *Levant* 19:49–82.

Henry, D. O. 1995. *Prehistoric Cultural Ecology and Evolution.* New York: Plenum Press.

Henry, D. O., and P. Turnbull. 1985. Archaeological and Faunal Evidence from Natufian and Timnian Sites in Southern Jordan with Notes on Pollen Evidence. *Bulletin of the American Schools of Oriental Research* 257:45–64.

Hennessy, J. B. 1967. *The Foreign Relations of Palestine During the Early Bronze Age.* London: Quaritch.

Heskel, D. 1983. A Model for the Adoption of Metallurgy in the Ancient Middle East. *Current Anthropology* 24:362–66.

Hesse, B. 1986. Animal Use at Tel Miqne-Ekron in the Bronze and Iron Age. *Bulletin of the American Schools of Oriental Research* 264:17–28.

Hietala, H. J. 1983a. Boker Tachtit: Spatial Distributions. In *Prehistory and Paleoenvironments in the Central Negev, Israel,* ed. A. E. Marks, 191–216. Dallas: Southern Methodist Univ. Press.

———. 1983b. Boker Tachtit: Intra-Level and Inter-Level Spatial Analysis. In *Prehistory and Paleoenvironments in the Central Negev, Israel,* ed. A. E. Marks, 217–82. Dallas: Southern Methodist Univ. Press.

———. 1983c. Appendix B. Boker Tachtit: Summary of Technological Data. In *Prehistory and Paleoenvironments in the Central Negev, Israel,* ed. A. E. Marks. 343–49. Dallas: Southern Methodist Univ. Press.

Hill, J. N., and R. K. Evans. 1972. A Model for Classification and Typology. In *Models in Archaeology,* ed. D. L. Clarke, 231–73. London: Methuen.

Hodder, I. 1990. Style As Historical Quality. In *The Uses of Style in Archaeology,* ed. M. Conkey and C. Hastorf, 44–51. Cambridge: Cambridge Univ. Press.

Holmes, D. L. 1989. *The Predynastic Lithic Industries of Upper Egypt.* British Archaeological Reports International Series 469. Oxford.

Hours, F. 1974. Rémarques sur l'utilisation des liste-types pour l'étude du Paléolithique Superieur et de l'Epipaléolithique du Levant. *Paléorient* 2:3–18.

———. 1979. L'industrie lithique de Saida-Dakerman. *Berytus* 27:57–76.

Ilan, O., and M. Sebbane. 1989. Copper Metallurgy, Trade, and the Urbanization of Southern Canaan in the Chalcolithic and Early Bronze Age. In *L'urbanisation de la Palestine à l'âge du Bronze ancien,* ed. P. de Miroschedji, 139–62. British Archaeological Reports International Series 527. Oxford.

Isaac, G. Ll. 1977. *Olorgesailie.* Chicago: Univ. of Chicago Press.

Issar, A. S., Y. Govrin, M. A. Geyh, E. Wakshal, and M. Wolf. 1992. Climate Changes during the Upper Holocene in Israel. *Israel Journal of Earth Science* 40:219–23.

Jacobs, P. 1984. Canaanean Blades as a Typological Tool for Archaeological Dating. Paper Presented at Southwest Meeting of the American Schools of Oriental Research, 17 March.

Jelinek, A. J. 1982. The Tabun Cave and Paleolithic Man in the Levant. *Science* 216:545–47.

Johnson, J. 1996. Lithic Analysis and Questions of Cultural Complexity: the Maya. In *Stone Tools: Theoretical Insights into Human Prehistory,* ed. G. Odell, 159–80. New York: Plenum Press.

Kaplan, J. 1958. Excavations at Wadi Rabah. *Israel Exploration Journal* 8:149–60.

Kaufman, D. 1986. A Proposed Method for Distinguishing between Blades and Bladelets. *Lithic Technology* 15:34–40.

———. 1987. Interassemblage Variability of Metric Attributes from Lithic Assemblages of the Late Upper Paleolithic of Israel. *Mitekufat Haeven* 20:37–49.

Keeley, L. H. 1980. *Experimental Determination of Stone Tool Uses.* Chicago: Univ. of Chicago Press.

———. 1982. Hafting and Retooling: Effects on the Archaeological Record. *American Antiquity* 47:798–809.

———. 1983. Microscopic Examination of Adzes. In *Excavations at Jericho V,* K. M. Kenyon and T.A.P. Holland, 759. Oxford: British School of Archaeology in Jerusalem.

Kelterborn, P. 1984. Towards Replicating Egyptian Predynastic Flint Knives. *Journal of Archaeological Science* 11:433–53.

Kempinsky, A. 1989. Urbanization and Metallurgy in Southern Canaan. In *L'urbanisation de la Palestine à l'âge du Bronze ancien*, ed. P. de. Miroschedji, 163–68. British Archaeological Reports International Series 527: Oxford.

Kent, A., ed. 1987. *Method and Theory for Activity Area Research. An Ethnoarchaeological Approach*. New York: Columbia Univ. Press.

Kenyon, K. 1957. *Beginning in Archaeology*. New York: Praeger.

———. 1980. *Archaeology in the Holy Land*. Rev. ed. New York: Benn Norton.

Key, C. A. 1980. The Trace Element Composition of Copper and Copper Ally Artifacts of the Nahal Mishmar Hoard. In *The Cave of the Treasure*, P. Bar-Adon, 238–43. Jerusalem: Israel Exploration Society.

Kohler-Rollefson, I. 1992. A Model for the Development of Nomadic Pastoralism on the Transjordanian Plateau. In *Pastoralism in the Levant: Archaeological Materials in Anthropological Perspective*, ed. O. Bar-Yosef and A. M. Khazanov, 11–18. Monographs in World Archaeology 10. Madison: Prehistory Press.

Kozloff, B. 1972–73. A Brief Note on the Lithic Industries of Sinai. *Museum Ha'aretz Yearbook* 15/16:35–49.

Kroll, E. M., and T. D. Price. 1991. Postscript: The End of Spatial Analysis. In *The Interpretation of Archaeological Spatial Patterning*, ed. E. M. Kroll and T. D. Price, 301–6. New York: Plenum Press.

Lance, H. D. 1978. The Field Recording System. In *A Manual of Field Excavation*, ed. W. G. Dever and H. D. Lance, 73–106. New York: Hebrew Union College.

Leakey, M. D. 1971. *Olduvai Gorge III*. Cambridge: Cambridge Univ. Press.

Lee, J. R. 1973. *Chalcolithic Ghassul: New Aspects and Master Typology*. Ph.D. diss., Hebrew Univ., Jerusalem.

Levy, T. E. 1983. The Emergence of Specialized Pastoralism in the Southern Levant. *World Archaeology* 15:15–36.

———. 1986. The Chalcolithic Period. *Biblical Archaeologist* 49:82–108.

———, ed. 1987. *Shiqmim I: Studies Concerning Chalcolithic Societies in the Northern Negev Desert, Israel (1982–1984)*. British Archaeological Reports International Series 356. Oxford.

———. 1992. Transhumance, Subsistence, and Social Evolution in the Northern Negev Desert. In *Pastoralism in the Levant: Archaeological Materials in Anthropological Perspective*, ed. O. Bar-Yosef and A. M. Khazanov, 65–82. Monographs in World Archaeology 10. Madison: Prehistory Press.

———. 1995. The Late Neolithic-Early Chalcolithic Transition—New Views from the Northern Negev. Paper Presented at 60th Annual Meeting of the Society for American Archaeology, Minneapolis.

Levy, T. E., and S. A. Rosen. 1987. The Chipped Stone Industry at Shiqmim: Typological Considerations. *Shiqmim I: Studies Concerning Chalcolithic Societies in the Northern Negev Desert, Israel (1982–1984)*. British Archaeological Reports International Series 356. Oxford.

Levy, T. E., and S. Shalev. 1989. Prehistoric Metalworking in the Southern Levant: Archaeometallurgical and Social Perspectives. *World Archaeology* 20:352–72.

Luedtke, B. E. 1992. *An Archaeologist's Guide to Chert and Flint*. Archaeological Research Tools 7. Los Angeles: Institute of Archaeology, University of California.

Macalister, R.A.S. 1912. *The Excavation of Gezer*. Vol 2. London: John Murray.

Macdonald, E. 1932. *Beth Peleth II*. London: Bernard Quantch.

Magaritz, M., and G. A. Goodfriend. 1987. Movement of the Desert Boundary in the Levant from Latest Pleistocene to Early Holocene. In *Abrupt Climatic Change*, ed. W. H. Berger and L. D. Labeyrie, 173–83. Dordecht: Reidel.

Mahan, G. S. 1940. The Stone Industry of the Campaign of 1936. In *Teleilat Ghassul II*, R. Koeppel, 89–114. Rome: Pontifical Biblical Institute.

Mallon, A., R. Koeppel, and R. Neuville. 1934. *Teleilat Ghassul I, 1929–1932*. Rome: Pontifical Biblical Institute.

Mallory, J. K. 1986. "Workshops" and "Specialized Production" in the Production of Maya Chert Tools: A Response to Shafer and Hester. *American Antiquity* 51:152–58.

Marder, O., E. Braun, and I Milevski. 1995. The Flint Assemblage of Lower Horvat 'Illin: Some Technical and Economic Considerations. *Atiqot* 27:63-93.

Marks, A. E. 1976. Glossary. In *Prehistory and Paleoenvironments in the Central Negev, Israel*, ed. A. E. Marks, 371–83. Dallas: Southern Methodist Univ. Press.

———. 1992. Typological Variability in the Levantine Middle Paleolithic. In *The Middle Paleolithic: Adaptation, Behavior, and Variability*, ed. H. Dibble and P. Mellars, 127–42. Philadelphia: University Museum Press.

Marks, A. E., and D. Kaufman. 1983. Boker Tachtit: The Artifacts. In *Prehistory and Paleoenvironments in the Central Negev, Israel*, ed. A. E. Marks, 69–126. Dallas: Southern Methodist Univ. Press.

Marks, A. E., and P. Volman. 1983. Changing Core Reduction Strategies: A Technological Shift from the Middle to the Upper Paleolithic in the Southern Levant. In *The Mousterian Legacy: Human Biocultural Change in the Upper Pleistocene*, ed. E. Trinkhaus, 13–34. British Archaeological Reports International Series 164. Oxford.

Mazar, A. 1990. *The Archaeology of the Land of the Bible*. New York: Doubleday.

Mazar, B. 1968. The Middle Bronze Age in Palestine. *Israel Exploration Journal* 18:1–22.

McConaughy, M. 1979. *Formal and Functional Analysis of Chipped Stone Tools from Bab edh Dhra*. Ann Arbor: University Microfilms.

———. 1980a. F. Chipped Stone Tools [from Bab edh Dhra]. *Bulletin of the American Schools of Oriental Research* 240:53–58.

———. 1980b. Early Bronze Age Chipped Stone Tools from Bab Edh Dhra and Numeira and Their Implications Concerning Regional Development in the Levant. Paper presented at Annual Meetings of the American Schools of Oriental Research, Dallas.

Meeks, N. D., G. de G. Sieveking, and M. S. Tite. 1982. Gloss and Use-Wear Traces on Flint Sickles and Similar Phenomena. *Journal of Archaeological Science* 9:317–40.

Meyer, D. A., and J. R. Mathieu. n.d. Experimental Archaeology with Stone, Bronze, and Steel Axes. *Journal of Field Archaeology*. In press.

Meyerhof, Ezra. 1960. Flint Cores at Har Haharuvim [in Hebrew]. *Mitekufat Haeven* 1:23–26.

Miller, R. 1985. *Flint Knapping and Arrowhead Manufacture at Tell Hadidi, Syria*. Milwaukee: Milwaukee Public Museum.

Milstein, S. 1981. The Flint Implements (from Sheikh 'Awad). *Tel Aviv* 8:119–25.

Milstein, S., and A. Ronen. 1985. Flint Implements. In *A Chalcolithic Building at Fasa'el*, Y. Porath. *Atiqot* 7:11–13.

Moholy-Nagy, H., F. Asaro, and F. H. Stross. 1984. Tikal Obsidian: Sources and Typology. *American Antiquity* 49:104–17.

Moore, A. M. 1973. The Late Neolithic in Palestine. *Levant* 5:36–68.

Moorey, P.R.S. 1988. The Chalcolithic Hoard from Nahal Mishmar, Israel, in Context. *World Archaeology* 20:171–89.

Morley, S. G., G. W. Brainerd, and R. J. Sharer. 1983. *The Ancient Maya*. Stanford: Stanford Univ. Press.

Morris, C. 1978. The Archaeological Study of Andean Exchange Systems. In *Social Archaeology, Beyond Subsistence and Dating*, ed. C. L. Redman et al., 315–28. New York: Academic Press.

Morrow, T. A. 1996. Lithic Refitting and Archaeological Site Formation Processes: A Case from the Twin Ditch Site, Greene County, Illinois. In *Theory and Behavior from Stone Tools*, ed. G. Odell, 345–76. New York: Plenum Press.

Mortensen, P. 1970. A Preliminary Study of the Chipped Stone Industry from Beidha. *Acta Archaeologica* 41:1–54.

Mozel, I. 1983. A Reconstructed Sickle from Lachish. *Tel Aviv* 10:182–85.

Muheisen, M. Sh., H. G. Gebel, C. Hanss, and R. Neef. 1988. 'Ain Rahub: A New Final Natufian and Yarmoukian Site near Irbid. In *The Prehistory of Jordan: The State of Research 1986*, ed. A. N. Garrard and H. G. Gebel, 472–502. British Archaeological Reports International Series 396. Oxford.

Muhly, J. 1980. The Bronze Age Setting. In *The Coming of the Age of Iron*. ed. T. A. Wertime and J. D. Muhly, 25–68. New Haven: Yale Univ. Press.

Murray, G. W. 1935. *Sons of Ishmael*. London: Routledge.

Nadel, D. 1988. The Lithic Assemblage from Netiv Hagdud (Jordan Valley). Master's thesis, Hebrew Univ., Jerusalem.

Nasrallah, R.P.J. 1936. Le gisement ghassoulien de Tell es-Soma. *Journal of the Palestine Oriental Society* 16:293–315.

———. 1948. Une station ghassoulien du Hauran. *Revue Biblique* 55:81–103.

Neeley, M. P., and C. M. Barton. 1994. A New Approach to Interpreting Late Pleistocene Microlith Industries in Southwest Asia. *Antiquity* 68:275–88.

Neuville, R. 1930. Notes de préhistoire Palestinienne. *Journal of the Palestine Oriental Society* 10:193–221.

———. 1934a. Le préhistoire de Palestine. *Revue Biblique* 43:237–59.

———. 1934b. Objets en silex. In *Teleilat Ghassul I*, ed. A. Mallon, R. Koeppel, and R. Neuville, 219–44. Rome: Pontifical Biblical Institute.

———. 1934–35. Les débuts de l'agriculture et la faucille préhistorique en Palestine. *Bulletin of the Jewish Palestine Exploration Society* 3:17–42.

Noy, T., and R. Cohen. 1974. Nahal Boker: An Early Pre-Pottery Neolithic B Site [in Hebrew]. *Mitekufat Haeven* 12:15–25, 78–79.

Oakley, K. 1975. *Man the Tool Maker*. London: British Museum.

O'Connell, J. 1987. Alyawara Site Structure and Its Archaeological Implications. *American Antiquity* 52:74–108.

O'Connell, J. F., K. Hawkes, and N. B. Jones. 1991. Distribution of Refuse-Producing Activities at Hadza Residential Base Camps: Implications for Analyses of Archaeological Site Structures. In *The Interpretation of Archaeological Spatial Patterning*, ed. E. M. Kroll and T. D. Price, 61–76. New York: Plenum Press.

Odell, G. H. 1988. Addressing Prehistoric Hunting Practices Through Stone Tool Analysis. *American Anthropologist* 90:335–56.

———. 1989. Fitting Analytical Techniques to Prehistoric Problems with Lithic Data. In *Alternative Approaches to Lithic Analysis*, ed. D. O. Henry and G. H. Odell, 159–82. Archaeological Papers of the American Anthropological Association 1. Washington, D.C.

Odell, G. H., and F. Odell-Vereecken. 1980. Verifying the Reliability of Lithic Use-Wear Assessments by Blind Tests: The Low-Power Approach. *Journal of Field Archaeology* 7:87–120.

Olami, Y. 1970. Methode d'étude de la typologie des haches, tranchets, ciseaux, etc. dans le Néolithique et le Chalcolithique. *Actes de VIIe Congres de UISPP.* Prague: Academie des Sciences.

Oren, E., and I. Gilead. 1981. Chalcolithic Sites in Northeastern Sinai. *Tel Aviv* 8:25–44.

Orni, E., and E. Efrat. 1971. *Geography of Israel.* Jerusalem: Israel Univ. Press.

Otte, M., J. Pelegrin, and F. Collin. 1990. Towards an Integrated Approach: The Use of Canaanean Blades. In *The Interpretative Possibilities of Microwear Studies,* Proceedings of the International Conference on Lithic Use-Wear Analysis, Societas Archaeologica Upsaliensas, *Aun* 14:135–45.

Ovadia, E. 1992. The Domestication of the Ass and Pack Transport by Animals: A Case of Technological Change. In *Pastoralism in the Levant: Archaeological Materials in Anthropological Perspectives,* ed. O. Bar-Yosef and A. M. Khazanov, 19–28. Monographs in World Archaeology 10. Madison: Prehistory Press.

Parry, W. J. 1987. *Chipped Stone Tools in Formative Oaxaca, Mexico.* Memoirs of the Museum of Anthropology 20. Ann Arbor: Univ. of Michigan.

Parry, W. J., and R. L. Kelly. 1987. Expedient Core Technology and Sedentism. In *The Organization of Core Technology,* ed. J. K. Johnson and C. A. Morrow, 285–304. Boulder: Westview Press.

Payne, J. C. 1978. A Hoard of Flint Knives from the Negev. In *Archaeology in the Levant: Essays for Kathleen Kenyon,* ed. P.R.S. Moorey and P. Parr, 19–21. Warminster, England.

———. 1980. An Early Dynastic III Flint Industry from Abu Salabikh. *Iraq* 42:105–19.

———. 1983. The Flint Implements of Jericho. In *Jericho IV,* ed. K. M. Kenyon and T. A. Holland, 622–758. London: British School of Archaeology in Jerusalem.

Pelegrin, J., and M. Otte. 1991. Einige Bemerkungen zur Praparations- und Ausbeuttechnik der Kernsteine aus Raum 29. *Hassek Huyuk. Naturwissenschaftliche Untersuchungen und Lithiische Industrie,* ed. Behm-Blancke, 219–24. Tubingen: Istanbuler Forschungen.

Perlman, I., and J. Yellin 1980. The Provenance of Obsidian from Neolithic Sites in Israel. *Israel Exploration Journal* 30:83–88.

Perrot, J. 1955. Excavations at Tell Abu Matar, near Beersheva. *Israel Exploration Journal* 5:17–40, 73–84, 167–89.

———. 1961. Gat-Govrin. *Israel Exploration Journal* 11:76.

Perrot, J., N. Zori, and R. Reich. 1967. Neve Ur, un nouvel aspect du ghassoulien. *Israel Exploration Journal* 17:201–32.

Petrie, W.M.F. 1891. *Tell el Hesy.* London: Committee for the Palestine Exploration Fund.

———. 1902. *Abydos I.* London: Egypt Exploration Fund.

———. 1904. *Tarkhan II.* London: Egypt Exploration Fund.

———. 1917. *Tools and Weapons.* London: British School of Archaeology in Egypt.

Piperno, M. 1973. Microdrilling at Shahri-Sokhta; the Making and Use of Lithic Drill-heads. In *South Asia Archaeology,* ed. N. Hammond, 119–29. Park Ridge, N.J.: Noyes Press.

Pope, M., and S. Pollock. 1995. Trade, Tools, and Tasks: A Study of Uruk Chipped Stone Industries. *Research in Economic Anthropology* 16:227–65.

Porat, N. 1989. Petrography of Pottery from Southern Israel and Sinai. In *L'urbanisation de la Palestine à l'âge du Bronze ancien,* ed. P. de Miroschedji, 169–88. British Archaeological Reports International Series 527. Oxford.

Potaszkin, R., and K. Bar-Avi. 1980. A Material Investigation of the Metal Objects from the Nahal Mishmar Treasure. In *The Cave of the Treasure.* P. Bar-Adon, 235–37. Jerusalem: Israel Exploration Society.

Redman, C. L. 1978. *The Rise of Civilization.* San Francisco: Freeman.

Reisner, G. A. 1908. *The Early Dynastic Cemeteries of Naga ed-Der.* Leipzig: J. C. Hinrichs.

Renfrew, C. 1982. Socio-economic Change in Ranked Societies. In *Ranking, Resource, and Exchange,* ed. C. Renfrew and S. Shennan, 1–8. Cambridge: Cambridge Univ. Press.

———. 1984. The Anatomy of Innovation. In *Approaches to Social Archaeology,* C. Renfrew, 390–418. Edinburgh: Univ. of Edinburgh.

Richard, S. 1980. Toward a Consensus of Opinion on the end of the Early Bronze Age in Palestine-Transjordan. *Bulletin of the American Schools of Oriental Research* 237:5–34.

Rick, J. 1996. Projectile Points, Style, and Social Process in the Preceramic of Central Peru. In *Stone Tools: Theoretical Insights into Human Prehistory,* ed. G. Odell, 245–78. New York: Plenum Press.

Rigaud, J.-P., and J. F. Simek. 1991. Interpreting Spatial Patterns at Grotte XV: A Multiple Method Approach. In *The Interpretation of Archaeological Spatial Patterning,* ed. E. M. Kroll and T. D. Price, 199–220. New York: Plenum Press.

Rizkana, I., and J. Seeher. 1985. The Chipped Stones at Maadi: Preliminary Reassessment of a Predynastic Industry and its Long Distance Relations. *Mitteilungen des Deutschen Archäologischen Instituts, Abt. Kairo* 41:235–36.

Rolland, N., and H. L. Dibble. 1990. A New Synthesis of Middle Paleolithic Variability. *American Antiquity* 55:480–99.

Ronen, A. 1970. Flint Implements from South Sinai: Preliminary Report. *Palestine Exploration Quarterly* 102:30–41.

Rosen, A. M. 1986a. Environmental Change and Settlement at Tel Lachish. *Bulletin of the American Schools of Oriental Research* 263:55–60.

———. 1986b. *Cities of Clay: The Geoarchaeology of Tells.* Chicago: Univ. of Chicago Press.

———. 1989. Environmental Change at the End of the Early Bronze Age in Palestine. In *L'urbanisation de la Palestine à l'âge du Bronze ancien,* ed. P. de Miroschedji, 247–55. British Archaeological Reports International Series 527. Oxford.

———. 1995. The Social Response to Environmental Change in Early Bronze Age Canaan. *Journal of Anthropological Archaeology* 14:26–44.

Rosen, S. A. 1982. Flint Sickle Blades of the Late Protohistoric and Early Periods in Israel. *Tel Aviv* 9:139–45.

———. 1983a. The Canaanean Blade and the Early Bronze Age. *Israel Exploration Journal* 33:15–29.

———. 1983b. The Tabular Scraper Trade: A Model for Material Culture Dispersion. *Bulletin of the American Schools of Oriental Research* 249:79–86.

———. 1983c. The Microlithic Lunate: An Old-New Tool Type from the Negev, Israel. *Paléorient* 9:81–83.

———. 1983d. *Lithics in the Bronze and Iron Ages in the Levant.* Ph.D. diss., Univ. of Chicago.

———. 1984a. The Adoption of Metallurgy in the Levant: a Lithic Perspective. *Current Anthropology* 25:504–5.

———. 1984b. Kvish Harif: Preliminary Investigation at a Late Neolithic Site in the Central Negev. *Paléorient* 10:11–121.

———. 1985. The En Shadud Lithics. In *En Shadud, Salvage Excavations at a Farming Community in the Jezreel Valley, Israel,* ed. E. Braun, 153–67. British Archaeological Reports International Series 249. Oxford.

———. 1986. The Gezer Flint Caches 1970–71. In *Gezer IV,* ed. W. G. Dever, 259–63. Jerusalem: Nelson Glueck School of Biblical Archaeology.

———. 1987. The Potentials of Lithic Analysis in the Chalcolithic of the Northern Negev. In *Shiqmim I,* ed. T. E. Levy, 295–312. British Archaeological Reports International Series 356. Oxford.

———. 1988a. A Preliminary Note on the Egyptian Component of the Chipped Stone Assemblage from Tel 'Erani. *Israel Exploration Journal* 38:105–16.

———. 1988b. Notes on the Flint Implements from Tel Yarmuth, 1980–1982. In *Yarmouth I,* ed. P. de Miroschedji, 135–42. Paris: Éditions Recherche sur les Civilisations.

———. 1988c. Notes on the Origins of Pastoral Nomadism: A Case Study from the Negev and Sinai. *Current Anthropology* 29:498–506.

———. 1989a. The Analysis of Early Bronze Age Chipped Stone Industries: A Summary Statement. In *L'urbanisation de la Palestine à l'âge du Bronze ancien,* ed. P. de Miroschedji, 199–222. British Archaeological Reports International Series 527. Oxford.

———. 1989b. The Origins of Craft Specialization: Lithic Perspectives. In *People and Culture in Change,* ed. I. Hershkovitz, 107–114. British Archaeological Reports International Series 508 (i). Oxford.

———. 1991. The Lithic Assemblage from the EB Site at Har Horsha. *Atiqot* 20:169–76.

———. 1993a. Metals, Rocks, Specialization, and the Beginning of Urbanism in the Northern Negev. In *Biblical Archaeology Today 1990: Pre-Congress Symposium Supplement—Population, Production, and Power,* ed. A. Biran and J. Aviram, 41–56. Jerusalem: Israel Exploration Society.

———. 1993b. Lithic Assemblages from Nahal Mitnan. *Atiqot* 22:62–69.

———. 1993c. A Note on the Flint Assemblage (from Ashdod Area G). *Atiqot* 23:117–21.

———. 1995. Microlithic Drills from the Camel Site, Mitzpe Ramon. *Journal of the Israel Prehistoric Society* 26:148–58.

———. 1996. The Decline and Fall of Flint. In *Stone Tools: Theoretical Insights into Human Prehistory,* ed. G. Odell, 129–58. New York: Plenum Press.

———. n.d.a The Lithic Assemblage from Biqat Uvda 16. *Atiqot* in press.

———. n.d.b The Lithic Assemblage from Hartuv. *Bulletin of the American Schools of Oriental Research,* in press.

———. n.d.c The Lithic Assemblage from Sataf. Unpublished report.

———. n.d.d The Lithic Assemblages from Ir David. *Qedem,* in press.

———. n.d.e Notes on the Chipped Stone Tools from the Excavations at Bert Yerah. *Atiqot* in press.

Rosen, S. A., and I. Eldar. 1993. Horvat Beter Revisited: The 1982 Salvage Excavations. *Atiqot* 22:13–27.

Rosen, S. A., and A. N. Goring-Morris. n.d.a. The Deir el Balah Lithics. In *Deir el Balah,* by T. Dothan. Jerusalem: Qedem, Institute of Archaeology, Hebrew Univ. In press.

———. n.d.b. Har Qeren XV. In *Prehistoric Investigations Around the Haluza Dunes,* A. N. Goring-Morris, Jerusalem: Israel Antiquities Authority. In press.

Rosen, S. A., and M. Grinblatt. n.d. The Lithic Assemblages from Yiftahel. In *Excavations at Yiftahel,* E. Braun. In press.

Roshwalb, A. F. 1981. Protohistory in the Wadi Ghazzeh: A Typological and Technological Study Based on the Macdonald Excavations. Ph.D. diss., Univ. of London.

Rothenberg, B., and J. Glass. 1992. The Beginnings and Development of Early Metallurgy and the Settlement and Chronology of the Western Arabah from the Chalcolithic Period to the Early Bronze IV. *Levant* 24:141–57.

Rowan, Y. 1990. *A Chalcolithic Chipped Stone Assemblage from the Northern Negev Desert: Phase II (1987–1989) Investigations at Shiqmim.* Master's thesis, Univ. of Texas at Austin.

Rowan, Y., and T. E. Levy. 1991. Use Wear Analysis of a Chalcolithic Scraper Assemblage from Shiqmim. *Journal of the Israel Prehistoric Society (Mitekufat Haeven)* 24:112–32.

———. 1994. Proto-Canaanean Blades of the Chalcolithic Period. *Levant* 26:167–74.

Runnels, C. 1985. Lithic Studies: Some Theoretical Considerations. *Lithic Technology* 14:100–6.

———. 1994. Tinderflints and Firemaking in the Historical Period. *Lithic Technology* 19 (1):7–16.

Sackett, J. R. 1966. Quantitative Analysis of Upper Paleolithic Stone Tools. *American Anthropologist* 68 (2), pt. 2:356–92.

———. 1968. Method and Theory of Upper Paleolithic Archaeology in Southwestern France. In *New Perspectives in Archeology,* ed. L. R. Binford and S. R. Binford, 61–84. Chicago: Aldine.

———. 1982. Approaches to Style in Lithic Archaeology. *Journal of Anthropological Archaeology* 1:59–112.

———. 1990 Style and Ethnicity in Archaeology: The Case for Isochrestism. In *The Uses of Style in Archaeology,* ed. M. Conkey and C. Hastorf, 32–43. Cambridge: Cambridge Univ. Press.

Sahlins, M. 1972. *Stone Age Economics.* Chicago: Aldine.

Saidel, B. A. 1995. Pastoralism in the Early Bronze Age: The View from Har Nafha 396. Paper presented at 60th Annual Meeting of the Society for American Archaeology, Minneapolis.

Schele, L., and D. Friedel. 1990. *A Forest of Kings.* New York: William Morrow.

Schick, T. 1978. Flint Implements. In *Early Arad,* R. Amiran et al., 58–63. Jerusalem: Israel Exploration Society.

Schiffer, M. B. 1976. *Behavioral Archeology.* New York: Academic Press.

———. 1987. *Formation Processes of the Archaeological Record.* Albuquerque: Univ. of New Mexico Press.

Schmidt, K. 1992a. Tell Ibrahim Awad: Preliminary Report on the Lithic Industries. In *The Nile Delta in Transition: 4th–3rd Millennium B.C.,* ed. E.C.M. van den Brink, 75–96. Jerusalem: Israel Exploration Society.

———. 1992b. Tell el-Fara'in/Buto and El-Tell el-Iswid (South): the Lithic Industries from the Chalcolithic to the Early Old Kingdom. In *The Nile Delta in Transition: 4th–3rd Millennium B.C.,* ed. E.C.M. van den Brink, 31–41. Jerusalem: Israel Exploration Society.

Seger, J. D., et al. 1990. The Bronze Age Settlements at Tell Halif: Phase II Excavations 1983–87. *Bulletin of the American Schools of Oriental Research Supplement* 26:1–32.

Sellet, F. 1993. Chaîne d'Operatoire: The Concept and its Applications. *Lithic Technology* 18:106–12.

Semenov, S. A. 1976. *Prehistoric Technology.* New York: Barnes and Noble.

Service, E. R. 1962. *Primitive Social Organization.* New York: Random House.

Shafer, H. J., and T. R. Hester. 1983. Ancient Maya Chert Workshops in Northern Belize, Central America. *American Antiquity* 48:519–43.

Shalev, S., and P. Northover. 1987. Chalcolithic Metalworking from Shiqmim. In *Shiqmim I,* ed. T. E. Levy, 356–71. British Archaeological Reports International Series 356. Oxford.

Shanks, M., and C. Tilley. 1987. Style and Ideology. In *Reconstructing Archaeology,* ed. M. Shanks and C. Tilley, 137–55. Cambridge: Cambridge Univ. Press.

Sharp, L. 1952. Steel Axes for Stone Age Australians. *Human Organization* 11:17–22.

Shea, J. J. 1987. On Accuracy and Relevance in Lithic Use-Wear Studies. *Lithic Technology* 16:44–50.

Shennan, S. 1982. Exchange and Ranking: The Role of Amber in the Earlier Bronze Age of Europe. In *Ranking, Resource, and Exchange,* ed. C. Renfrew and S. Shennan, 33–45. Cambridge: Cambridge Univ. Press.

Sherratt, A. 1983. The Secondary Exploitation of Animals in the Old World. *World Archaeology* 15:90–104.

Shott, M. 1989. On Tool-Class Use Lives and the Formation of Archaeological Assemblages. *American Antiquity* 54:9–30.

Silberman, N. A. 1982. *Digging for God and Country.* New York: Knopf.

Smith, P. 1989. The Skeletal Biology and Paleopathology of Early Bronze Populations in the Levant. In *L'urbanisation de la Palestine à l'âge du Bronze ancien,* ed. P. de Miroschedji, 297–316. British Archaeological Reports International Series 527. Oxford.

de Sonneville-Bordes, D., and J. Perrot. 1954–56. Lexique typologique du Paléolithique Superieur. *Bulletin de la Société Préhistorique Française* 51:327–35, 52:76–79, 53:408–12, 547–59.

Speth, J. D. 1972. Mechanical Basis of Percussion Flaking. *American Antiquity* 37:34–60.

Spurrel, F.C.J. 1898. Analysis of Flint Implements. In *A Mound of Many Cities*, F. Bliss, 190–95. London: Palestine Exploration Fund.

Stager, L. E. 1992. The Periodization of Palestine from Neolithic through Early Bronze Times. In *Chronologies in Old World Archaeology*, ed. R. Ehrich, 22–60. Chicago: Univ. of Chicago Press.

Steensberg, A. 1943. *Ancient Harvesting Implements.* Copenhagen: Nationalmuseets skrifter.

Stekelis, M. 1972. *The Yarmukian Culture of the Neolithic Period.* Jerusalem: Magnes Press.

Stevens, E. T. 1870. *Flint Chips.* London: Bell and Daldy.

Stocks, D. A. 1989. Ancient Factory Mass-Production Techniques: Indications of Large Scale Stone Bead Manufacture during the Egyptian New Kingdom Period. *Antiquity* 63:526–31.

Sullivan, A. P., III, and K. C. Rozen. 1985. Debitage Analysis and Archaeological Interpretation. *American Antiquity* 50:755–79.

Swauger, J. L. 1968. Bethel Flints from the Early Canaanite High Place and the Middle Bronze I Temple Above It. In *The Excavation of Bethel (1934–1960)*, James Kelso, 93–95. Annual of the American Schools of Oriental Research 39. Philadelphia.

Tixier, J. 1963. *Typologie de l'Epipaléolithique Maghreb.* Centre de Recherche Anthropologiques Préhistoriques et Ethnographiques d'Alger, Memoir 2. Paris: Arts et Metiers.

Tixier, J., M.-L. Inizan, and H. Roche. 1980. *Préhistoire de la Pierre Taille 1. Terminologie et Technologie.* Valbonne: Cercle de Recherche et d'Étude Préhistorique.

Torrence, R. 1986. *Production and Exchange of Stone Tools.* Cambridge: Cambridge Univ. Press.

———. 1989. Tools as Optimal Solution. In *Time, Energy and Stone Tools,* ed. R. Torrence, 1–6. Cambridge: Cambridge Univ. Press.

Tosi, M. 1984. The Notion of Craft Specialization and Its Representation in the Archaeological Record of Early States in the Turanian Basin. In *Marxist Perspectives in Archaeology*, ed. M. Spriggs, 22–52. Cambridge: Cambridge Univ. Press.

Unger-Hamilton, R. 1984. The Formation of Use-Wear Polish on Flint: Beyond the "Deposit Versus Abrasion" Controversy. *Journal of Archaeological Science* 11:91–98.

———. 1989. The Epi-Paleolithic Southern Levant and the Origins of Cultivation. *Current Anthropology* 30:88–103.

———. 1991. Microwear Analysis of Scrapers and "Sickle Blades." In *Excavations at Jawa 1972–1986: Stratigraphy, Pottery, and Other Finds,* vol. 1, ed. A.V.G. Betts, 149–53. Excavations and Explorations in the Hashemite Kingdom of Jordan I. Edinburgh: Univ. of Edinburgh Press.

Ussishkin, D. 1980. The Ghassulian Shrine at En-gedi. *Tel Aviv* 7:1–44.

Valla, F. 1978. Essai de typologie des objets de silex lustre de Susiane. *Paléorient* 4:325–34.

———. 1984. Les Industries de silex de Mallaha (Eynan) et du Natoufien dans le Levant. Memoire et travaux du Centre de Recherche Français de Jerusalem 3. Paris: Association Paléorient.

Villa, P. 1982. Conjoinable Pieces and Site Formation Processes. *American Antiquity* 47:276–90.

Volman, P. 1983. Boker Tachtit: Core Reconstructions. In *Prehistory and Paleoenvironments in the Central Negev, Israel*, vol. 3, ed. A. E. Marks, 127–90. Dallas: Southern Methodist Univ. Press.

Waechter, J. 1958. Flint Implements. In *Lachish IV,* O. Tufnell, 325–27. London: Oxford Press.

Waldbaum, J. 1978. *From Bronze to Iron.* Studies in Mediterranean Archaeology 54. Gotberg: Paul Astroms.

Walker, A. 1978. Principles of Excavation. In *A Manual of Field Excavation,* ed. W. G. Dever and H. D. Lance, 1–22. New York: Hebrew Union College.

Warburton, M. 1980. The Stone Tools from Tell Halif, Israel: A Technological Perspective. Master's thesis, Washington State Univ., Pullman.

Weinstein, J. 1984. The Significance of Tel Areini for Egyptian Palestinian Relations at the Beginning of the Bronze Age. *Bulletin of the American Schools of Oriental Research* 256:61–69.

Whallon, R. 1978. Threshing Sledge Flints: A Distinctive Pattern of Wear. *Paléorient* 4:319–24.

Whallon, R., and J. W. Brown, eds. 1982. *Essays on Archaeological Typology.* Evanston: Center for American Archaeology Press.

White, J. P. 1967. Ethnoarchaeology in New Guinea: Two Examples. *Mankind* 6:409–14.

White, J. P., N. Modjeska, and I. Hipuya. 1977. Group Definitions and Mental Templates: An Ethnographic Experiment. In *Stone Tools as Cultural Markers,* ed. R.V.S. Wright, 380–90. Canberra: Australian Institute of Aboriginal Studies.

Wiessner, P. 1983. Style and Social Information in Kalahari San Projectile Points. *American Antiquity* 49:253–76.

———. 1984. Reconsidering the Behavioral Basis for Style: a Case Study Among the Kalahari San. *Journal of Anthropological Archaeology* 3:190–234.

Willoughby, P. 1985. Spheroids and Battered Stones in the African Early Stone Age. *World Archeology* 17:44–60.

Witthoft, J. 1967. Glazed Polish on Flint Tools. *American Antiquity* 32:383–89.

Wobst, M. 1977. Stylistic Behavior and Information Exchange. In *Papers for the Director: Research Essays in Honor of James B. Griffin,* ed. C. Cleland, 317–42. Papers of the Museum of Anthropology 61. Ann Arbor: University of Michigan.

Woolley, L. 1954. *Digging Up the Past.* London: Ernest Benn.

Wylie, A. 1985. The Reaction Against Analogy. *Advances in Archaeological Method and Theory* 8:63–111.

Yeivin, E. 1959. Flint Tools from Horvat Beter. *Atiqot* 2:40–44.

———. 1976. Notes on the Flint Implements from 'En Besor. *Atiqot* 11:10–12.

Yekutieli, Y., and R. Gophna. 1994. Excavations at an Early Bronze Age Site near Nizzanim. *Tel Aviv* 21:162–85.

Yerkes, R. 1983. Microwear, Microdrills, and Mississippian Craft Specialization. *American Antiquity* 48:499–518.

Yogev, O. 1983. A Fifth Millennium Sanctuary in the 'Uvda Valley [in Hebrew]. *Qadmoniot* 16 (4):118–22.

Zaccagnini, C. 1983. Patterns of Mobility Among Ancient Near Eastern Craftsmen. *Journal of Near Eastern Studies* 42:245–64.

Zeitlin, R. 1982. Toward a More Comprehensive Model of Interregional Commodity Distribution: Political Variables and Prehistoric Obsidian Procurement in Mesoamerica. *American Antiquity* 47:260–75.

Zohary, M. 1956. Vegetation. *Atlas of Israel,* Sec. 4. Jerusalem: Bialik Institute and the Ministry of Labor.

Index